4.25

Helen C. Stanbery.
1320. C Chicago Ave
Evanston, Ill

THE COURSE OF MY LIFE

RUDOLF STEINER

THE COURSE OF
MY LIFE

Revised translation by the authorized translator
Olin D. Wannamaker

1951

ANTHROPOSOPHIC PRESS

NEW YORK

Printed in the United States of America

The Original Work, Mein Lebensgang

The autobiography of which this volume is a revised translation appeared originally in serial form, as contributed weekly by Rudolf Steiner to *Das Goetheanum*, organ of the *Allgemeine Anthroposophische Gesellschaft* (General Anthroposophical Society), Dornach, Switzerland. Serial publication began on December 8, 1923. From the latter part of September 1924, the author was ill, confined most of the time to a bed in his studio, but writing much besides the latter part of the autobiography during the following months up to his death, on March 30, 1925. The final instalment in the account of the course of his life, written very near its end, appeared six days later, on April 5. That instalment was identical with the final chapter in the book form of publication, which appeared in its first edition in 1925. He had arrived only at the year 1907 in the story.

First Translation

The original edition of this authorized translation was published in 1928, under the title *The Story of My Life,* by Anthroposophical Publishing Company, London, and Anthroposophic Press, New York.

An Expression of Thanks

To Lisa D. Monges thanks are warmly expressed for criticisms and suggestions of the utmost value in the course of this difficult task in translation.

The Translator

TRANSLATION OF LETTER

Schlachtensee, September 22, 1903

Dear Fräulein M . . .

There was no time left yesterday for what I should have liked to
say to you: that your last letter was deeply gratifying to me. You will
not misunderstand me: it was not because of your kind and good
words to me, but on account of the whole way in which you relate
yourself to our cause. For a long time I have known that you love
the truth; it has been a joy and satisfaction to me that we have found
one another in this love for truth, and your recent letter confirms
and strengthens this feeling. I can only say to you that this love for
truth has always been my guide. I have been much misunderstood,
and shall no doubt be much misunderstood in the future also. That
lies in the very nature of my path. Every imaginable rôle has been
ascribed to me—not least, that of a fanatic in one direction or
another. Fanaticism, of all things, is one trait of which I know that
I am free. For it is the true tempter into illusion, and it has always
been my principle to remain aloof from all illusion.

You write that I make the Spirit manifest in my life. In *one*
respect, I assure you, I strive to do so: I shall never speak of anything
spiritual that I do not know by the most direct spiritual *experience*.
This principle is my guiding star, and it has enabled me to rise above
all illusions. I can see through them. And I can truly say that for
me the spiritual is absolutely real—not a whit less real than the table
at which I am now writing. Whoever would be willing to look into
all that I have said and done would find consistency where, because
of not looking at the whole, he finds only contradictions. I can but
say to you that the same kind of experience which has taught me the
truth in science has also taught me the "mystical fact" in Chris-

vii

tianity. Moreover, those who know me well know that I have not unduly *changed* in my life. One thing I can say to you: I do not force myself, I exert constraint upon nothing within me, when I relate truths of the spiritual life just as I relate the realities of the sense world. We shall, no doubt, speak further some time of these things.

Your devoted
Rudolf Steiner

Schlachtensee bei Berlin
Seestrasse 40

Contents

CONTENTS

THE COURSE OF MY LIFE

THE COURSE OF MY LIFE

I

Into the public discussions of the Anthroposophy to which I devote myself, there have been injected for some time past statements and judgments about the course that my life has taken. From what has been said in this regard, conclusions have been drawn as to the origin of what is looked upon as deviations in the course of my spiritual development. In view of this fact, friends have expressed the opinion that it might be well if I myself should write something about the course of my life.

This does not accord, I must confess, with my own inclinations. For it has always been my endeavor so to order what I had to say and what I thought I ought to do according as the matter itself might demand, and not from personal considerations. To be sure, it has always been my conviction that in many provinces of life the personal element gives to human action a coloring of the utmost value; only, it seems to me that this personal element should be manifest in the way in which one speaks and acts, and not through conscious attention to one's personality. Whatever may come about as a result of this attention is something a man has to settle with himself.

And so it has been possible for me to resolve upon the following narration only because it is my duty to set in a true light, by means of an objective written statement, many a false judgment regarding the consistency between my life and that which I have fostered, and because those who through friendly interest have urged this upon me seem to me justified in view of such false judgments.

1

The home of my parents was in Lower Austria. My father was born in Geras, a very small place in the Lower Austrian forest region; my mother at Horn, a city of the same district.

My father passed his childhood and youth in the most intimate association with the seminary of the Premonstratensian Order at Geras. He always looked back with great affection upon this time in his life. He liked to tell how he served in the college, and how the monks instructed him. Later on he was a gamekeeper in the service of Count Hoyos. This family had a place at Horn. It was there that my father became acquainted with my mother. Then he gave up the occupation of gamekeeper and became a telegrapher on the South Austrian Railway. He was assigned at first to a little station in southern Styria. Then he was transferred to Kraljevec, on the border between Hungary and Croatia. It was during this period that he married my mother. Her maiden name was Blie. She was descended from an old family of Horn. I was born at Kraljevec on February 27, 1861. Thus it happened that the place of my birth was far removed from that part of the world from which my family came.

My mother, and my father as well, were true children of the glorious South Austrian forest country, north of the Danube. It is a region into which the railway was late in coming. Even to this day it has left Geras untouched. My parents loved the life they had lived in their native region. When they spoke of this, one realized instinctively how in their souls they had never parted from that birthplace in spite of the fate that forced them to pass the greater part of their lives far away from it. And so, when my father retired, after a life filled with work, they returned at once there—to Horn.

My father was of the utmost good will, but of a temper—especially while he was still young—which could be passionately aroused. The work of a railway employee was to him a matter of duty; he had no love for it. While I was still a boy, he would sometimes have to remain on duty for three days and three nights continuously. Then he would be relieved for twenty-four hours. Thus life bore for him no bright colors; all was dull gray. He liked to keep up with political developments; in these he took the liveliest interest. My mother, since our worldly goods were not plentiful, had to devote herself to household duties. Her days were filled with loving care of her children and of the little home.

When I was a year and a half old, my father was transferred to Mödling, near Vienna. There my parents remained a half-year. Then my father was put in charge of the little station on the Southern railway at Pottschach in Lower Austria, near the Styrian border. There I lived from my second to my eighth year. A wonderful landscape formed the environment of my childhood. The view stretched as far as the mountains that separate Lower Austria from Styria: "Snow Mountain," Wechsel, the Rax Alp, the Semmering. Snow Mountain caught the sun's rays on its bare rocky summit, and what these rays foretold as they were reflected from the mountain down to the little railway station was the first greeting of dawn on beautiful summer days. The gray back of the Wechsel put one, by contrast, into a sober mood. It was as if the mountains rose up out of the smiling all-surrounding green of the friendly landscape. On the distant boundaries of the circle one had the majesty of the peaks, and close around the charm of nature.

At the little station, however, all interest was centered in the business of the railway. At that time the trains passed in this region only at rather long intervals; but, when they came, many of the people of the village who could spare the time were gathered at the station, seeking thus to bring some change into their lives, which they seemed to find otherwise very monotonous. The schoolmaster, the priest, the bookkeeper of the manor, and often the burgomaster as well, would be there.

It seems to me that passing my childhood in such an environment had a certain significance for my life. For my interest was strongly attracted by everything about me of a mechanical character; and I know that this interest tended constantly to overshadow in my childish soul the affection which went out to that charming and yet mighty nature into which the railway train, in spite of being in subjection to this mechanism, yet always disappeared in the distance.

In the midst of all this there was present the influence of a certain personality of marked originality, the priest of St. Valentin, a place that one could reach on foot from Pottschach in about three-quarters of an hour. This priest liked to come to the home of my parents. Almost every day he took his walk to our home, and he always stayed for some time. He belonged to the liberal type of Catholic cleric, tolerant and genial; a robust, broad-shouldered man. He was witty, liked to make puns, and was pleased when he drew a laugh from the people about him. And they kept on laughing over what he had said long after he was gone. He was a person of a practical way of life, and liked to give good practical advice. Such a piece of practical counsel produced a lasting effect in my family. There was a row of acacia trees (locusts) on each side of the railway at Pottschach. Once we were walking along the narrow footpath under these trees, when he remarked: "Ah, what beautiful locust blossoms are here!" He instantly climbed one of the trees and broke off a mass of the blossoms. Spreading out his huge red pocket-handkerchief—he was extremely fond of snuff—he carefully wrapped the booty in this, and put the bundle under his arm. Then he said: "How lucky you are to have so many locust blossoms!" My father was astonished, and answered: "Why, what good can they do us?" "Wh-a-a-t?" said the priest. "Don't you know that you can bake locust blossoms just like elder flowers, and that they taste much better than these because they have a far more delicate aroma?" From that time on, as opportunity offered from time to time, we frequently had in our family "baked locust blossoms."

In Pottschach a daughter and another son were born to my parents. There was never any further addition to the family.

As a very young child I showed a strange idiosyncrasy. From the time that I could feed myself, I had to be carefully watched. For I had formed the conviction that a soup bowl or a coffee cup was meant to be used only once; and so, every time that I was not watched, as soon as I had finished eating something, I would throw the bowl or the cup under the table and smash it to pieces. Then, when my mother appeared, I would call out to her: "Mother, I've already finished!"

This cannot have been a mania in me for destroying things, since I handled my toys with the greatest care, and kept them in good condition for a long time. Among these toys those that captivated me especially were of the kind which even now I consider particularly good. These were picture-books with figures that could be made to move by pulling strings attached to them at the bottom. One associated little stories with these figures, to which one gave part of their life by pulling the strings. Many a time have I sat by the hour poring over the picture-books with my sister. Besides, I learned from them quite spontaneously the first steps in reading.

My father was concerned that I should learn early to read and write. When I reached the compulsory age, I was sent to the village school. The schoolmaster was an old man to whom the work of "teaching school" was a burdensome business. Equally burdensome to me, however, was the business of being taught by him. I did not believe at all that I could learn anything from him. For he often came to our house with his wife and little son, and this son, according to my notion at the time, was a scamp. So I had this idea firmly fixed in my head: "Whoever has such a scamp for a son, nobody can learn anything from him." Besides, something else happened, "quite dreadful." This scamp, who also was in the school, played the prank one day of dipping a chip in all the ink-wells of the school and making circles around them with dabs of ink. His father noticed this. Most of the pupils had already gone. The teacher's son, a few other boys, and I were still there. The schoolmaster was beside himself; he railed in a frightful manner. I felt sure that he would actually roar but for the fact that his voice was always husky. In spite of his rage, he got an inkling from our behavior as to who the culprit was. But things then took a different turn. The teacher's apartment adjoined the schoolroom. The "lady head-mistress" heard the commotion and came into the schoolroom with wild eyes, waving her arms in the air. To her it was perfectly clear that her little son could not have played this trick. She put the blame on me. I ran away. My father was furious when I reported this matter at home. The next time the teacher and his wife came to our house, he told them with the utmost bluntness that the friendship between us was ended, and declared: "My boy shall never set foot in your school again." Now my father himself took over the task of teaching me; and so I would sit beside him in his little office by the hour, and was supposed to read and write while he at the same time attended to the duties of his office.

Neither with him could I feel any real interest in what I was expected to learn by way of direct instruction. I was interested in what my father was writing. I wished to imitate what he did. In this way I learned a good deal. To that which he prepared for me to do for my own improvement I could gain no relation. On the other hand I entered gradually, in a child's way, into everything that formed a part of the practical work of life. The routine of the railway office, everything connected with this, caught my attention. It was, however, more especially the laws of nature that attracted me, even in their tiny ramifications. When I wrote, it was because I was required to write, and I wrote, indeed, as fast as I could so that I should soon have a page filled. For then I could strew the sort of writing-sand that my father used over this writing. I would then be absorbed in watching how fast the sand dried up the ink, and what sort of mixture they made together. I would test the letters over and over with my fingers to discover which were already dry, which were not. My curiosity about this was very great, and for this reason I usually touched the letters too soon. Thus my handwriting took on a character that did not please my father at all, but he was good-natured, and reproved me only by frequently calling me an incorrigible little "smudger." But this was not the only thing that developed for me out of the writing lessons. What interested me more than the shapes of the letters was the formation of the pen itself. I could take my father's paper knife and force it into the slit in the point of the pen, and in this way carry on researches in physics concerning the elasticity of the pen. Afterwards, of course, I bent the pen back into shape, but the beauty of my handwriting suffered distinctly in this process.

This was also the time when, with my inclination toward the understanding of natural phenomena, I occupied a position midway between seeing into a combination of things, on the one hand, and the "limits of knowledge" on the other. About three minutes from the home of my parents there was a flour mill. The owners of the mill were the godparents of my brother and sister. We were always welcome in this mill. I often disappeared within it. For I "studied" with enthusiasm the operation of the mill. There I forced a way for myself into the "interior of nature." Still nearer us, however, there was a spinning mill. The raw material for this came to the railway station; the finished product went away from the station. Thus I participated in everything which disappeared within the factory and everything which came to manifestation out of it. I was strictly forbidden to take a peep at its "inside." This I never succeeded in doing. There were the "limits of knowledge." And how I wished to step across these limits! For almost every day the manager came to see my father on some matter of business. For me as a boy this manager was a problem, casting a veil of wonder as it were, over the "inside" of this establishment. He was spotted here and there with white tufts; his eyes had taken on a certain set look from working at machinery. He spoke hoarsely as if with a mechanical speech. "What is the connection between this man and everything that is surrounded by those walls?"—this was an insoluble problem facing my mind. But I never questioned any one regarding the mystery. For it was my childish conviction that it does no good to ask questions about a thing which is concealed from one's eyes. Thus I lived between the friendly flour mill and the unfriendly spinning mill.

Once something happened at the station that was "shocking." A freight train rumbled up. My father stood looking toward it. One of the rear cars was on fire. The crew had not noticed this at all. The train arrived at our station in flames. All that occurred as a result of this made a deep impression on me. Fire had started in the car by reason of some highly inflammable material. For a long time I was absorbed in the question how such a thing could occur. What those around me said to me about this was, as in many other cases, not to my satisfaction. I was filled with questions, and I had to carry these about with me unanswered. It was thus that I reached my eighth year.

During my eighth year the family moved to Neudörfl, a little Hungarian village. This village is just at the border over against Lower Austria. The boundary here was formed by the Laytha river. The station that my father had in charge was at one end of the village. Half an hour's walk led to the boundary stream. Still another half-hour brought one to Wiener-Neustadt.

The range of the Alps that I had seen near by at Pottschach was now visible only at a distance. Yet the mountains still stood there in the background to awaken our memories when we looked at lower mountains that could be reached in a short time from my father's new home. Moderate heights covered with beautiful forests bounded the view in one direction; in the other, the eye could range over a level region, decked out in fields and woodlands, in the direction of Hungary. Of all the mountains, I gave my unbounded love to one that could be climbed in three-quarters of an hour. On its crest there stood a chapel containing a painting of Saint Rosalie. This chapel came to be the objective of a walk which I often took at first with my parents and my sister and brother, and later loved to take alone. Such walks were filled with a special happiness because of the fact that, at the right time of the year, we could bring back with us rich gifts of nature. For in these woods there were blackberries, raspberries, and strawberries. One could often find a joyous satisfaction in an hour and half of berrying for the purpose of adding a delicious contribution to the family supper, which otherwise consisted merely of a piece of buttered bread or bread and cheese for each of us.

Still another pleasant thing came from rambling about in these forests, which were the property of the community. There the villagers got their supply of wood. The poor gathered it for themselves; the more well-to-do had hired men to do this. One became acquainted with all of them, for the most part, tender-hearted persons. They always had time for a chat when "Steiner Rudolf" met them. "Well, you wish again to take a little walk, Steiner Rudolf"—thus would they begin, and then they would talk about everything imaginable. The people did not think of the fact that they had a mere child before them, for at the bottom of their souls they also were only children, even when they could number sixty years. And so I really learned from the stories they told me almost everything that happened even inside the houses of the village.

Half an hour's walk from Neudörfl is Sauerbrunn, where there is a spring containing iron and carbonic acid. The road to this lies along the railway, and part of the way through beautiful woods. During vacation time, I went there every day early in the morning, carrying with me a "Blutzer." This is a water vessel made of clay. Mine held three or four liters. One could fill this at the spring without charge. Then at the midday meal the family could enjoy the delicious sparkling water.

Toward Wiener-Neustadt and farther on toward Styria, the mountains fall away to a level country. Through this level country the Laytha winds its way. On the slope of the mountains there was a monastery of the Order of the Most Holy Redeemer. I often met the monks on my walks. I still remember how glad I should have been if they had spoken to me. They never did. And so I carried away from these meetings an undefined but solemn feeling which remained constantly with me for a long time. It was in my ninth year that the idea became fixed in me that there must be weighty matters in connection with the duties of these monks which I ought to learn to know. There again I was filled with questions that I had to carry around unanswered. Indeed, these questions about all sorts of things made me as a boy very lonely.

On the foothills of the Alps two castles were visible: Pitten and Frohsdorf. In the second there lived at that time Count Chambord, who, at the beginning of the 'seventies, made claim to the throne of France as Henry V. Very deep were the impressions that I received from that fragment of life bound up with the castle Frohsdorf. The Count with his retinue frequently took the train for a journey from the station at Neudörfl. Everything connected with these men attracted my attention. Especially deep was the impression made by one man in the Count's retinue. He had but one ear. The other had been slashed off clean. The hair lying over this he had braided. At the sight of this I learned for the first time what a duel is. For it was in this manner that the man had lost one ear.

Then, too, a fragment of social life was unveiled to me in connection with Frohsdorf. The assistant teacher at Neudörfl, whom I was often permitted to see at work in his little chamber, prepared innumerable petitions to Count Chambord for the poor of the village and the country around. In response to every such appeal there came back a donation of one *gulden,* and from this the teacher was always permitted to keep six *kreuzer* for his service. This income he had need of, for the annual salary yielded him by his profession was only fifty-eight *gulden.* In addition, he had his morning coffee and his lunch with the "schoolmaster." Then, too, he gave extra lessons to about ten children, of whom I was one. For such lessons the charge was one *gulden* a month.

To this assistant teacher I owe a great deal. Not that I was greatly benefited by his lessons in the school. In that respect I had about the same experience as at Pottschach. As soon as we moved to Neudörfl, I was sent to school there. The school consisted of one room in which five classes of boys and girls all had their lessons. While the boys who sat on my row of seats were at their tasks of copying out the story of King Arpad, the little fellows stood at the blackboard, on which *i* and *u* had been written with chalk for them. It was simply impossible to do anything save to let the mind fall into a dull revery while the hands almost mechanically took care of the copying. Almost all the teaching had to be done by the assistant teacher alone. The "schoolmaster" appeared in the school only rarely. He was also the village notary, and it was said that in this occupation he had so much to take up his time that he could never keep school.

In spite of all this I learned earlier than usual to read well. Because of this fact the assistant teacher was able to bring into my life something which has influenced its whole course. Soon after my entrance into the Neudörfl school, I found a book on geometry in his room. I was on such good terms with the teacher that I was permitted at once to borrow the book for a time for my own use. I plunged into it with enthusiasm. For weeks at a time my mind was filled with the coincidence, the similarity, of triangles, squares, polygons; I racked my brains over the question: Where do parallel lines actually meet? The theorem of Pythagoras fascinated me.

That one can live within the mind in the shaping of forms perceived only within oneself, entirely without impression upon the external senses, became for me the deepest satisfaction. I found in this a solace for the unhappiness which my unanswered questions had caused me. To be able to lay hold upon something in the spirit alone brought me an inner joy. I am sure that I learned through geometry to know happiness for the first time.

In my relation to geometry I must perceive the first budding forth of a conception which later gradually evolved within me. This lived within me more or less unconsciously during my childhood, and about my twentieth year took a definite and fully conscious form.

I said to myself: "The objects and occurrences which the senses perceive are in space. But, just as this space is outside man, so there exists within man a sort of soul-space which is the scene of action of spiritual beings and occurrences. I could not look upon thoughts as something like images which the human being forms of things; on the contrary, I saw in them revelations of a spiritual world on this field of action in the soul. Geometry seemed to me to be a knowledge which appears to be produced by man, but which, nevertheless, has a significance quite independent of him. Naturally, I did not as a child say this to myself distinctly, but I felt that one must carry knowledge of the spiritual world within oneself after the manner of geometry.

For the reality of the spiritual world was to me as certain as that of the physical. I felt the need, however, for a sort of justification of this assumption. I wished to be able to say to myself that the experience of the spiritual world is just as little an illusion as is that of the physical world. With regard to geometry, I said to myself: "Here one *is permitted* to know something which the mind alone through its own power experiences." In this feeling I found the justification for speaking of the spiritual world that I experienced just as of the physical. And I spoke of it in this way. I had two conceptions which were, naturally, undefined, but which played a great rôle in my mental life even before my eighth year. I distinguished things and beings which "are seen" and those which are "not seen."

I relate these matters in accordance with the truth, in spite of the fact that those persons who are seeking for evidence to prove that Anthroposophy is fantastic will, perhaps, draw the conclusion from what has been said that even as a child I was marked by a gift for the fantastic: no wonder, then, that a fantastic philosophy should also have developed within me.

But it is just because I know how little I have later followed my personal inclination in the description of a spiritual world—having, on the contrary, followed only the inner necessity of the matter— that I myself can look back quite objectively upon the childlike, awkward way in which I confirmed for myself by means of geometry the feeling that I must speak of a world "which is not seen."

Only, I must say also that I loved to live in that world. For I should have been forced to feel the physical world as a sort of spiritual darkness if it had not received light from that side.

The assistant teacher of Neudörfl provided me, in his geometry textbook, with the confirmation of the spiritual world which I then needed.

In other ways also I owe much to him. He brought to me the element of art. He played the piano and the violin, and he drew a great deal. These things attracted me powerfully to him. Just as much as I possibly could be, I was with him. Of drawing he was especially fond, and even in my ninth year he interested me in drawing with charcoal crayons. I had in this way to copy pictures under his direction. Long did I sit, for instance, copying a portrait of Count Szedgenyi.

Very seldom at Neudörfl, but frequently in the neighboring town of Sauerbrunn, could I listen to the impressive music of the Hungarian gypsies.

All this played its part in a childhood which was passed in the immediate neighborhood of the church and the churchyard. The station at Neudörfl was but a few steps from the church, and between these lay the churchyard.

If one went along by the churchyard and then a short stretch further, one came into the village itself. This consisted of two rows of houses. One row began with the school and the other with the home of the priest. Between these two rows of houses flowed a little brook, along the banks of which grew stately nut trees. In connection with these nut trees an order of precedence grew up among the children of the school. When the nuts began to get ripe, the boys and girls assailed the trees with stones, and in this way laid in a winter's supply of nuts. In autumn almost the only thing any one of them talked about was the size of his harvest of nuts. Whoever had gathered most of all was the most looked up to, and then step by step was the descent all the way down—to me, the last, who as an "outsider in the village" had no right to share in this order of precedence.

Near the parsonage the row of the most important houses, in which the "big farmers" lived, was met at right angle by a row of some twenty houses owned by the middle class villagers. Then, beginning with the garden that belonged to the station, came a group of thatched houses belonging to the "small cottagers." These constituted the immediate neighborhood of our family. The roads leading out from the village went past fields and vineyards that were owned by the villagers. Every year I took part with the "small cottagers" in the vintage, and once also in a village wedding.

Next to the assistant teacher, the person whom I loved most among those who had to do with the direction of the school was the priest. He came regularly twice a week to give instruction in religion and often besides for inspection in the school. The image of this man was deeply impressed upon my mind, and he has come back into my memory again and again throughout my life. Among the persons whom I came to know up to my tenth or eleventh year, he was by far the most significant. He was a vigorous Hungarian patriot. He took an active part in the process of Magyarizing the Hungarian territory which was then going forward. From this point of view he wrote in the Hungarian language articles with which I became acquainted through the fact that the assistant teacher had to make clear copies of these and he always discussed their content with me, in spite of my youthfulness. But the priest was also an energetic worker for the Church. This once impressed itself deeply upon my mind through one of his sermons.

At Neudörfl there was a lodge of Freemasons. For the villagers this was shrouded in mystery, and they wove about it the most amazing legends. The leading rôle in this lodge belonged to the manager of a match-factory which stood at the end of the village. Next to him in prominence among the persons immediately interested in the matter were the manager of another factory and a clothing merchant. Otherwise the only significance attaching to the lodge was the fact that from time to time strangers from "remote parts" were visitors there, and these seemed to the villagers in the highest degree sinister. The clothing merchant was a curious person. He always walked with his head bowed over as if in deep thought. People called him the "pretender," and his singularity made it neither possible nor necessary that any one should approach him. The place in which the lodge met belonged to his house.

I could establish no sort of relation to this lodge. For the entire behavior of the persons about me in regard to this matter was such that here again I had to refrain from asking questions; besides the absurd way in which the manager of the match-factory talked about the Church made a repugnant impression upon me.

Now, one Sunday the priest delivered a sermon in his energetic fashion in which he set forth in due order the true significance of morality for human life and then spoke of the enemies of the truth in figures of speech framed to fit the lodge. He brought his address to a climax with the sentence: "Beloved Christians, bear in mind who is an enemy of this truth: for example, a Mason and a Jew." In the eyes of the people, the factory owner and the clothing merchant were thus authoritatively characterized. The vigor with which this had been uttered was especially pleasing to me.

I owe to this priest also, because of a certain profound impression made upon me, a great deal in the later orientation of my intellectual life. One day he came into the school, gathered around him in the teacher's little room the "more mature" children, among whom he included me, unfolded a drawing he had made, and with the help of this explained to us the Copernican system of astronomy. He spoke in this connection very vividly about the revolution of the earth around the sun, its rotation on its axis, the inclination of the axis, about summer and winter, as well as the zones of the earth. In all of this I was completely absorbed; I made similar drawings for days together, and then received from the priest special instruction about eclipses of the sun and moon. Thenceforth I directed all my craving for knowledge toward this subject.

I was then about ten years old, and I could not yet write without mistakes in spelling and grammar.

Of deep significance for my life as a boy was the nearness of the church and the churchyard beside it. Everything that happened in the village school was affected in its course by its relation to these. This was due not only to the dominant social and political relations then existing in that region, but primarily to the fact that the priest was an impressive personality. The assistant teacher was

at the same time organist of the church and custodian of the vest-
ments used at Mass and of the other church furnishings. He performed all the services of an assistant to the priest in his carrying out
of the rites of the church. We schoolboys had to perform the duties
of ministrants and choristers during Mass, rites for the dead, and
funerals. The solemnity of the Latin language and of the liturgy was
a thing in which my boyish soul found a vital happiness. Because of
the fact that, up to my tenth year, I took an earnest part in the services of the church, I was often in the company of the priest whom I
so deeply revered.

In the home of my parents I received no encouragement in this
matter of my relation to the church. My father took no part in this.
He was then a "freethinker." He never entered the church to which
I had become so deeply attached; and yet he also, as a boy and a
young man, had been equally devoted in the service of such a
church. In his case all this changed once more only when he went
back, as an old man on a pension, to Horn, his native region. There
he became again a "pious man." But by that time I had long ceased
to have any connection with my parents' home.

Out of my boyhood at Neudörfl I have the strongest impression
of the way in which the contemplation of the rites of the church,
in connection with the solemnity of liturgical music, causes the riddles of existence to rise in powerful suggestive fashion before the
mind. The instruction in the Bible and the catechism imparted by
the priest had far less effect upon my inner world than what he
accomplished as celebrant of the cultus in mediating between the
sensible and the supersensible world. From the first, all this was to
me no mere form, but a profound experience. It was all the more so
because of the fact that in this I was a stranger in the home of my
parents. Even in the atmosphere surrounding me in my home, my
spirit did not lose that vital experience which it had gained from the
liturgy. I passed my life amid the home environment without sharing in it. I was aware of it; but my real thoughts, feelings, and
experiences were continually in that other world. I can assert em-

phatically, however, in this connection that I was no dreamer, but became familiar as a matter of course with all practical affairs of life.

A complete counterpart of this world of mine was also my father's political arguments. He and another employee took turns on duty. This man lived at another railway station, for which he was responsible. He came to Neudörfl only every two or three days. During the free hours of the evening he and my father would talk politics. This would take place at a table which stood near the station under two huge and gorgeous linden trees. There our whole family and the other employee would assemble. My mother knitted or crocheted; my brother and sister busied themselves about us; I would often sit at the table and listen to the incessant political arguments of the two men. My interest, however, was never directed toward the meaning of what they were saying, but only toward the form that the conversation took. They were always on opposite sides; if one said "Yes," the other always contradicted him with "No." All this, however, though marked by the quality of intensity—indeed, even passion—was also characterized by the good humor which was a basic element in my father's nature.

In the little circle often gathered there, to which were frequently added some of the "notables" of the village, there appeared at times a doctor from Wiener-Neustadt. He had many patients in this place, where at that time there was no physician. He came from Wiener-Neustadt to Neudörfl on foot, and would come to the station after visiting his patients to wait for the train on which he went back. This man passed with my parents, and with most persons who knew him, as an odd character. He did not like to talk about his profession as a doctor, but all the more gladly did he talk about German literature. It was from him that I first heard of Lessing, Goethe, Schiller. At my home there was never any such conversation. Nothing was known of such things. Nor in the village school was there any mention of such matters. There the emphasis was all on Hungarian history. Priest and assistant teacher had no interest in the masters of

German literature. And so it happened that with the Wiener-Neustadt doctor a whole new world came within my range of vision. He gladly took an interest in me; often drew me aside after he had rested for a while under the linden trees, walked up and down with me by the station, and talked—not like an instructor, but enthusiastically—about German literature. In these talks he set forth all sorts of ideas about what is beautiful and what is ugly.

This also has remained as a picture with me, giving me many happy hours in memory throughout my life: the tall, slender doctor on one side, with his long, vigorous stride, always with his umbrella in his right hand held invariably in such a way that it dangled beside the upper part of his body, and I, a boy of ten years, on the other side, quite absorbed in what the man was saying.

Along with all these things, I was greatly interested in everything pertaining to the railway. I learned the principles of electricity first through observation in connection with the station telegraph. I learned also to telegraph as a boy.

As to language, I grew up in the dialect of German that is spoken in eastern Lower Austria. This was really the same as that still used then in those parts of Hungary bordering on Lower Austria. My relation to reading and that to writing were entirely different. In boyhood I passed rapidly over the words when reading; my mind went immediately to the percepts, the concepts, the ideas, so that I got from reading no feeling either for spelling or for writing grammatically. On the other hand, in writing I had a tendency to fix the word-forms in my mind by their sounds as I generally heard them spoken in the dialect. For this reason it was only after the most arduous effort that I gained facility in writing the literary language, whereas reading it was easy for me from the first.

Under such influences I grew up to the age at which my father had to decide whether to send me to the *Gymnasium*[1] or to the *Realschule*[1] in Wiener-Neustadt. From that time on I heard much

---

[1] The *Gymnasium* and the *Realschule* in Germany and Austria are secondary schools, in the former of which the curriculum emphasizes the humanities and in the latter science and the modern languages. (Translator.)

talk with other persons—between political discussions—as to my own future. My father was given this and that advice. I knew already: "He likes to listen to what others say, but he acts according to his own firmly felt determination."

II

THE DECISIVE fact for my father in determining whether I should be sent to the *Gymnasium* or the *Realschule* was that he intended to give me the right preparation for a "position" on the railway. His ideas finally concentrated into the decision that I should be a railway civil engineer. Hence his choice was the *Realschule*.

First, however, the question had to be settled whether, in passing from the village school of Neudörfl, to one of the schools in Wiener-Neustadt, I should be prepared at all for admission to such a school. So I was first taken to the higher elementary school for an entrance examination.

These events which were being initiated for my own future did not excite in me any great interest. At that age these questions concerning my "position" and whether the choice should fall on higher elementary school, *Realschule,* or *Gymnasium* were to me matters of indifference. Through what I observed around me and had thought out within me, I was conscious of undefined but burning questions about life and the world, and my wish was to learn something in order to be able to answer these questions of mine. I cared very little through what sort of school this should be brought about.

The entrance examination at the higher elementary school I passed very creditably. All the drawings I had made for the assistant teacher had been brought along, and these made such an impression upon the teachers who examined me that on this account my very defective knowledge was overlooked. I got through the examination with a "brilliant" record. There was unmingled rejoicing on the part of my parents, the assistant teacher, the priest, and many of the notabilities of Neudörfl. People were happy over the result of my examination because to many of them it was a proof that "the Neudörfl school can accomplish something."

For my father there came out of all of this the thought that I should not spend a preliminary year in the higher elementary school —seeing that I was already so far along—but should enter the *Realschule* at once. So a few days later I was taken to that school for another examination. In this case matters did not turn out so well; nevertheless, I was admitted. This was in October 1872.

I had now to go every day from Neudörfl to Wiener-Neustadt. In the morning I could go by train, but I had to come back in the evening on foot, since there was no train at the right time. Neudörfl was in Hungary; Wiener-Neustadt in Austria. So every day I went from "Transleithania" to "Cisleithania." (These were the official designations for the Hungarian and Austrian districts.)

During the noon recess I remained in Wiener-Neustadt. It so happened that a certain woman had come to know me during one of her stops at the Neudörfl station, and had learned that I was coming to Wiener-Neustadt to school. My parents had spoken to her of their concern as to how I was to pass the noon recess during my attendance at the Wiener-Neustadt school. She told them she would be glad to have me take lunch at her home without charge, and would welcome me there whenever I needed to come.

In summer the walk from Wiener-Neustadt to Neudörfl is very beautiful; in winter it was often hard. To get from the outskirts of the town to the village, one had to walk for a half-hour on a field path that had not been cleared of snow. There I often had to "wade" through the snow, which was knee-deep, and I would arrive at home a veritable "snow man."

The town life I could not share inwardly as I could the life of the country. I would fall into a brown study over the problem what might be happening in and between those houses jammed together side by side. Only in front of the book-sellers' shops in Wiener-Neustadt did I often linger for a long time.

What was brought forward in the school also, and what I had to do there, passed before my mind at first without awakening any lively interest. In the first two grades I had great difficulty in "keeping up." Only in the second half of the second grade did I get along better. Only then had I become a "good student."

I was conscious of one overwhelming need. I craved persons whom I could take as human models to follow. The teachers of the first two grades were not such persons.

In this school experience something now occurred which impressed me deeply. The principal of the school, in an annual report such as was issued at the close of each school year, published a paper entitled *Die Anziehungskraft betrachtet als eine Wirkung der Bewegung.*[1] As a child of eleven years I could at first understand almost nothing of the content of this paper, for it began at once with higher mathematics. Yet from single sentences I got hold of a certain meaning. There was formed in my mind a bridge between what I had learned from the priest concerning the cosmic system and these sentences in the paper. The paper referred also to a book which the principal had written, *Die allgemeine Bewegung der Materie als Grundursache aller Naturerscheinungen.*[2] I saved my money until I could buy that book. It now became my aim to learn as rapidly as possible everything that might lead me to an understanding of the content of the paper and the book.

The matter was like this. The principal considered the conception of forces acting at a distance from the substance exerting these forces an unjustified "mystical" hypothesis. He undertook to explain the "attraction" between the heavenly bodies as well as that between molecules and atoms without reference to such "forces." He said that between any two bodies there are many small bodies in motion. These, moving back and forth, strike against the larger bodies. Like-

[1] *Attraction Considered As an Effect of Motion.*
[2] *The General Motion of Matter As the Fundamental Cause of All the Phenomena of Nature.*

wise these larger bodies are struck from every direction on the sides turned away from each other. The thrusts on the sides turned away from each other are much more numerous than those in the space between the two bodies. It is for this reason that they approach each other. "Attraction" is not any special force, but only an "effect of motion." I came across two sentences on the first pages of the book: "1. There exist space and in space motion continuing for a long period of time. 2. Space and time are continuous homogeneous magnitudes; but matter consists of separate particles (atoms)." Out of the motions occurring in the manner described between the small and the great parts of matter, the author undertook to derive all physical and chemical occurrences in nature.

I had nothing within me that inclined me in any way to accept such a view; but I had the feeling that it would be very important for me if I could understand what was in this way expressed. I did everything I could to arrive at that point. Whenever I could in any way get hold of books on mathematics and physics, I seized the opportunity. Progress was slow. I set to work over and over again to read the paper and the book; each time there was some improvement.

Now something else happened. In the third grade I had a teacher who really fulfilled the "ideal" I had before my mind. He was a person whom I could emulate. He taught arithmetic, geometry, and physics. His teaching was wonderfully systematic and transparent. He built up everything so clearly out of its elements that it was in the highest degree beneficial to one's thinking to follow him.

A paper accompanying the second annual school report was written by him. It dealt with the theory of probabilities and calculations in life insurance. I buried myself in this paper also, though of this likewise I could not yet understand very much. But I soon came to grasp the idea of the theory of probabilities. A more important result for me, however, was that the exactness with which my favorite teacher had handled his material gave me a model for my own thinking in mathematics. This now brought about a very beautiful relation between this teacher and me. I was very happy to have this man through all the grades of the *Realschule* as teacher of mathematics and physics.

Through what I learned from him, I drew nearer and nearer to the riddle that had arisen for me through the writings of the principal.

With another teacher I came only after a long time into a more intimate inner relation. This was the one who taught geometrical drawing in the lower grades and descriptive geometry in the upper. He taught even in the second grade. But only during his course in the third grade did I come to an appreciation of the kind of man he was. He was a splendid constructor. His teaching also was a model of clarity and order. Drawing with compass, ruler, and triangle became for me, through his influence, a favorite occupation. Behind all that I was taking into myself from the principal, the teacher of mathematics and physics, and the teacher of geometrical drawing there arose in me, in a boyish way of thinking, the problem of what goes on in nature. My feeling was that I must grapple with nature in order to acquire a point of view with regard to the world of spirit which confronted me in self-evident perception.

I said to myself that it is possible after all to come to an understanding of the experience of the spiritual world through one's soul only if one's process of thinking itself has reached such a form that it can attain to the reality of being which is in the phenomena of nature. It was with such feelings that I lived through the third and fourth years of the *Realschule*. Everything that I learned I so applied as to bring myself nearer to the goal I have indicated.

Then one day I passed a bookstore. In the show-window I saw a copy of Kant's *Kritik der reinen Vernunft*,[1] in Reclam's edition. I did everything that I could to acquire this book as quickly as possible.

As Kant then entered the circle of my thinking, I knew nothing

[1] *Critique of Pure Reason.*

whatever of his place in the spiritual history of mankind. What any one whatever had thought about him, in approval or disapproval, was to me entirely unknown. My boundless interest in the *Critique of Pure Reason* had arisen entirely out of my own mental life. In my boyish way, I was striving to understand what human reason might be able to achieve toward a real insight into the nature of things.

The reading of Kant met with various obstacles in the external circumstances of my life. Because of the long distance I had to traverse between home and school, I lost every day at least three hours. In the evenings I did not get home till six o'clock. Then there was an endless quantity of home work to master. On Sundays I devoted myself almost entirely to geometrical designing. It was my ideal to attain to the greatest precision in carrying out geometrical constructions, and the most immaculate neatness in hatching and the laying on of colors.

Thus I had scarcely any time left just then for reading the *Critique of Pure Reason*. I found the following way out. Our history course was handled in such a way that the teacher appeared to be lecturing but was in reality reading from a book. Then from lesson to lesson we had to learn from our books what he had given us in this fashion. It occurred to me that I must take care of this reading of what was in my book while at home. From the teacher's "lecture" I got nothing at all. From listening to what he read I could not take in the least thing. I now took apart the single sections of the small Kant volume, fastened these inside the history book which I kept before me during the history lesson, and read Kant while the history was "taught" down to us from the professor's seat. This was, of course, from the point of view of school discipline a serious fault; yet it disturbed nobody, and it subtracted so little from what was expected of me that the grade I was given on my history lessons at that very time was "excellent."

During vacations the reading of Kant went forward briskly. Many a page I read more than twenty times in succession. I wished to reach a judgment as to the relation sustained by human thinking to the creative work of nature.

The feeling I had in regard to these strivings of thought was influenced from two directions. In the first place, I wished to build up thought within myself in such a way that every thought should be completely subject to survey, that no vague feeling should incline the thought in any direction whatever. In the second place, I wished to establish within myself a harmony between such thinking and the teaching of religion. For this also had at that time the very strongest hold upon me. In just this field we had truly excellent textbooks. From these books I took with the utmost devotion the system of dogmas and symbols, the description of the Church liturgy, the history of the Church. These teachings were to me a vital matter. But my relation to them was determined by the fact that for me the spiritual world counted among the contents of human perception. The very reason why these teachings penetrated so deeply into my mind was that in them I realized how the human spirit can find its way knowingly into the supersensible. I am perfectly sure that I did not lose my reverence for the spiritual in the slightest degree because of this relation to knowledge.

On the other hand, I was constantly occupied with the question of the scope of the human capacity for thinking. It seemed to me that thinking can be developed to a faculty which actually lays hold upon the things and occurrences of the world. A "substance" which remains outside of thinking, which we can merely reflect about, was to me an unendurable conception. Whatever is in things, this must enter into human thought, I said to myself again and again.

Against this feeling, however, there always opposed itself what I read in Kant. Yet I scarcely observed this conflict, for I desired more than anything else to attain through the *Critique of Pure Reason* essential facts, in order to understand my own thinking. Wherever and whenever I took holiday walks, I had to sit down quietly somewhere or other and once more afresh make clear to myself how one passes from simple, clear-cut concepts to conceptions in regard to natural phenomena. At that time my attitude toward Kant was quite uncritical, but no advance did I make by means of him.

By all this I was not drawn away from what has to do with the practical handling of every-day matters and the development of human skills. It so happened that one of the employees who took turns with my father in his work understood book-binding. I learned book-binding from him, and was able to bind my own school-books in the holidays between the fourth and fifth grades of the *Realschule.* In addition I learned stenography at this time during the vacation without a teacher. Nevertheless, I took later the course in stenography which was given from the fifth grade on.

Occasions for practical work were plentiful. My parents were allotted near the station a little garden with fruit trees and a small field for potatoes. Gathering cherries, taking care of the garden, preparing the potatoes for planting, making the ground ready, digging the potatoes,—all this work was done by my sister and brother and me. Buying the family groceries in the village, of this I would not let any one deprive me when the school left me free.

When I was about fifteen years old, I was permitted to come into a more intimate relation with the doctor at Wiener-Neustadt whom I have mentioned. I had conceived a great liking for him because of the way in which he talked to me during his visits to Neudörfl. So I often slipped past his home, which was on the ground floor of a building at the corner of two very narrow streets in Wiener-Neustadt. One day he was at the window. He called me into his room. I stood before what seemed to me then a great library. He talked again about literature; then took down Lessing's *Minna von Barnhelm* from the collection of books, and said I must read that and afterwards come back to him. In this way he gave me one book after another to read, and permitted me from time to time to come to see him. Every time that I had an opportunity to go back, I had to tell him my impression of what I had read. In this way he became really my teacher in poetical literature. For up to that time, both at my home and also at school, all this—except for some "extracts"—had been rather remote from me. In the atmosphere of this lovable doctor, sensitive to everything beautiful, I learned especially to know Lessing.

Another event deeply influenced my life. The mathematical books that Lübsen had prepared for home study became known to me. I was then able to teach myself analytical geometry, trigonometry, and even differential and integral calculus long before I learned these in school. This enabled me to return to the reading of those productions on *The General Motion of Matter As the Fundamental Cause of All the Phenomena of Nature*. For now I could understand them better through my knowledge of mathematics. Meanwhile instruction in chemistry had been added to that in physics, and this brought me a new set of riddles of knowledge to add to the older ones. The teacher of chemistry was a very fine person. He taught almost entirely by means of experiments. He spoke little. He let natural processes speak for themselves. He was one of our favorite teachers. There was something noteworthy in him which distinguished him in the eyes of his pupils from the other teachers. One felt that he stood in a closer relation to his science than did the others. The others we addressed with the title "Professor"; although he was just as much a professor, we called him "Doctor." He was the brother of the thoughtful Tyrolese poet Hermann von Gilm. He had an eye which held one's attention firmly. One felt that this man was accustomed to looking intently at the phenomena of nature and then retaining what he had perceived.

His teaching confused me a little. With the striving for unification which then characterized my state of mind, I could not always hold together the multiplicity of facts which he presented. Still he must have considered that I made good progress in chemistry, for he gave me from the first the mark "commendable," and I kept this mark throughout the grades of the school.

One day at that time I found at an antiquary's in Wiener-Neustadt Rotteck's *History of the World*. Till then, in spite of the fact that I received in the school the highest grade in the subject of history, it had always remained for me something external. Now it grew to be an inner thing. The warmth with which Rotteck conceived and set forth historical events fascinated me. His one sidedness of view I did not then perceive. Through him I was led to two other historians who, by reason of their style and their conception of the history of human life, made the deepest impression on me: Johannes von Müller and Tacitus. Amid such impressions it was hard for me to take any interest in the school lessons in history and literature, but I strove to give life to these lessons from all that I made my own out of other sources. In this manner I passed my time in the upper three grades of the seven years of the *Realschule*.

From my fifteenth year on, I tutored other pupils of the same grade as my own or of a lower grade. The teachers were very willing to assign me this tutoring, since I was rated as a "good student." Through this means I was enabled to contribute at least a very little toward what my parents had to spend out of their meager income for my education.

I owe much to this tutoring. In having to give to others in turn the matter which I had been taught, I myself became, so to speak, awake to this. For I cannot express the thing otherwise than by saying that I received in a sort of living dream the knowledge imparted to me by the school. I was awake to what I gained by my own effort and what I received from a spiritual benefactor, such as the doctor I have mentioned of Wiener-Neustadt. What I received thus in a fully conscious state of mind was noticeably different from what passed by me like dream-pictures in the class-room instruction. The development of what had thus been received in a half-waking state was now brought about by the fact that, in the periods of tutoring, I had to vitalize my own knowledge.

On the other hand, this experience compelled me at an early age to concern myself with practical psychology. Through my pupils I became acquainted with the difficulties in the development of the human mind.

For pupils of my own grade whom I tutored, the most important thing I had to do was to outline the German compositions. Since I had to write for myself also every such composition, I had to discover for each theme assigned to us various forms of development. Thus I often found myself in a rather difficult situation. I wrote my own composition only after I had already given away the best thoughts on the subject.

A rather strained relation existed between me and the teacher of the German language and literature in the three upper grades. The pupils considered him the "keenest professor" and especially strict. My compositions had always turned out to be unusually long. The briefer forms I had dictated to my fellow pupils. It took the teacher a long time to read my papers. After final examination, during the commencement exercises, when for the first time he was "in a genial mood" among us pupils, he told me how I had annoyed him with my long compositions.

Still another thing happened. I had the feeling that something was brought into the school through this teacher with which I must come to an understanding. When he discussed, for example, the nature of poetic representation, it seemed to me that there was something in the background behind what he said. After a time I found out what this was. He adhered to the philosophy of Herbart. He himself said nothing of this, but I discovered it. And so I bought an introduction to philosophy and a psychology both of which were written from the point of view of Herbart's philosophy.

And now began a sort of game of hide and seek between the teacher and me in my compositions. I began to understand much in him which he set forth with a coloring from Herbart's philosophy, and he found in my compositions all sorts of ideas that came from the same source. Only, neither he nor I mentioned Herbart as the source of our ideas. This was as if by tacit agreement. But one day I ended a composition in a way that was indiscreet in view of the situation. I had to write about some trait of character in human beings. At the end I used this sentence: "Such a person possesses psychological freedom." The teacher would discuss the compositions with the class after he had corrected them. When he came to the discussion of the composition just mentioned, he drew in the corners of his mouth with obvious irony, and said: "You say something here about psychological freedom. There is no such thing." I answered: "That seems to me to be a mistake, Professor. There really is a psychological freedom, only there is no 'transcendental freedom' in the ordinary state of consciousness." The folds around the teacher's mouth became smooth again. He looked at me with a penetrating glance and said: "I have noticed for a long while that you have a philosophical library. I would advise you not to read in it; you only confuse your thinking by so doing." I could not understand at all why I should confuse my thinking by reading the same books from which his own thinking was derived. And thus the relation between us continued to be somewhat strained.

His teaching gave me much to do. For he covered in the fifth grade the Greek and Latin poets, from whom selections were used in German translation. Then for the first time I began to regret once in a while that my father had put me in the *Realschule* instead of the *Gymnasium*. For I felt how little I was brought into contact with the special character of Greek and Roman art through the translations. So I bought Greek and Latin textbooks, and gave myself, without any mention of this, a private course of *Gymnasium* instruction, along with the *Realschule* course. This required much time, but it also laid the foundation by means of which I later met, although in unusual fashion yet quite correctly, the *Gymnasium* requirements. That is to say, when I was a student in the *Technische Hochschule*,[1] in Vienna, then indeed I did have to give many hours of tutoring, and I soon had a *Gymnasium* pupil to tutor. Circumstances of which I shall speak later brought it about that I had to

[1] The *Technische Hochschule* is an institution in the educational systems of Germany and Austria resembling the American Institute of Technology.

help this pupil by means of tutoring through almost the whole *Gymnasium* course. I gave him instruction also in Latin and Greek, so that in teaching him I had to go together with him through every detail of the *Gymnasium* instruction.

The teachers of history and geography who could give me so little in the lower grades became, nevertheless, important for me in the upper grades. The very one who had driven me to such unusual reading of Kant wrote once for a school report a paper on *Die Eiszeit und ihre Ursachen.*[2] I absorbed the content of this with great eagerness of mind, and retained from it a strong interest in the problem of the glacial age. But this teacher was also a good student of the distinguished geographer Friedrich Simony. This fact led him to explain in the upper grades the geological-geographical relations of the Alps with illustrative drawings on the blackboard. Then I certainly did not read Kant, but was all eyes and ears. In this field I got a great deal from the teacher whose lessons in history did not interest me at all.

In the last grade I had for the first time a teacher who gripped me with his instruction in history. He taught history and geography. In this class the geography of the Alps was continued in the same delightful fashion as had already been the case with the other teacher. In the history lessons the new teacher got a strong hold upon us. He was to us a personality in the full sense of the word. He was a partisan, enthusiastic for the progressive ideas of the Austrian liberal movement of the time. But in the school there was no evidence of this. He brought nothing from his partisan views into the classroom. Yet his teaching of history had, by reason of his own participation in life, a strong vitality. I listened to the temperamental historical analyses of this teacher with the results from my reading of the Rotteck volumes still in my memory. The experience produced a satisfying harmony. I cannot but think it was an important thing for me to have had the opportunity to assimilate precisely the history of modern times in this manner.

[2] *The Glacial Age and Its Causes.*

At home I heard much at that time about the Russo-Turkish war (1877-78). The employee who then took my father's place every third day was an original sort of person. When he came to relieve my father, he always brought along a huge carpet-bag. In this he had great packages of manuscripts. These were abstracts of the most varied assortments of scientific books. These abstracts he gave to me, one after another, to read. I devoured them. He would then discuss these things with me. For he really had in his head a conception, somewhat chaotic to be sure but comprehensive, about all these things that he had compiled. With my father, however, he talked politics. He delighted to take the side of the Turks; my father defended with passionate earnestness the Russians. He was one of those persons still grateful to Russia for the service she rendered to the Austrians at the time of the Hungarian uprising (1848). For my father was on no sort of terms with the Hungarians. He lived, indeed, in the Hungarian border town of Neudörfl during that period when the process of Magyarizing was going forward, and the sword of Damocles hung over his head—the danger that he might not be allowed to remain in charge of the station at Neudörfl because he could not speak Magyar. This language was quite unnecessary in that thoroughly German locality, but the Hungarian regime was endeavoring to bring it to pass that railway lines in Hungary should be manned with Magyar-speaking employees, even the privately owned lines. But my father wished to hold his place at Neudörfl long enough for me to finish at the school in Wiener-Neustadt. By reason of all this, he was not very well disposed toward the Hungarians. Thus, since he disliked the Hungarians, he liked in his simple way to think of the Russians as those who in 1848 had "shown the Hungarians who were their masters." This way of thinking manifested itself with exceptional earnestness, and yet in the extraordinarily amiable manner of my father toward his Turkophile friend in the person of the "alternate." The tide of discussion rose often very high. I was greatly interested in the reciprocal outbursts of the two personalities, but scarcely at all in their political opinions. For me a much more vital need at that time was that of finding an answer to the question: To what extent is it possible to prove that in human thinking real spirit is the agent?

III

My FATHER had been promised by the management of the Southern Railway that he would be assigned to a small station near Vienna as soon as I should have finished the *Realschule* and should attend the *Technische Hochschule*. In this way it was to be made possible for me to go to Vienna and return every day. So my family came to Inzersdorf am Wiener Berge. The station was at a distance from the town, and in unlovely natural surroundings.

My first visit to Vienna after we moved to Inzersdorf was used for the purpose of buying a greater number of philosophical books. What I was now especially devoted to was the first sketch of Fichte's *Wissenschaftslehre*.[1] I had got so far with my reading of Kant that I could form a notion, even though immature, of the advance which Fichte wished to make beyond Kant. But this did not greatly interest me. What interested me then was to express the living weaving of the human mind in a sharply outlined thought-picture. My strivings after concepts in natural science had finally brought me to see in the activity of the human ego the sole starting point for true knowledge. When the ego is active and itself beholds this activity, there is something spiritual present in utmost immediacy in one's consciousness—thus I said to myself. It seemed to me that what was thus perceived needed now only to be expressed in clear surveyable concepts. In order to find a way to do this, I devoted myself to Fichte's *Science of Knowledge*. And yet I had my own views. So I took the

[1] *The Science of Knowledge.*

Science of Knowledge and rewrote it, page by page. This made a lengthy manuscript. I had previously struggled hard to find concepts for the phenomena of nature from which one might derive a concept of the ego. Now I wished to do the opposite: from the ego to penetrate into nature's process of becoming. Spirit and nature were at that time present before my mind in their absolute contrast. There was for me a world of spiritual beings. That the ego, which itself is spirit, lives in a world of spirits was for me a matter of direct perception. But nature refused to enter into this spirit-world of my experience.

From my study of the *Science of Knowledge* I conceived a special interest in Fichte's *Über die Bestimmung des Gelehrten*[1] and *Über das Wesen des Gelehrten*.[2] In these writings I found a sort of ideal toward which I myself wished to strive. Along with these I read *Reden an die deutsche Nation*.[3] These aroused my interest in much lesser degree at that time than Fichte's other works.

But I wished now to come also to a better understanding of Kant than I had yet been able to achieve. In the *Critique of Pure Reason* this understanding refused to be revealed to me. So I attacked the Problem with the *Prolegomena zu einer jeden künftigen Metaphysik*.[4] Through this book I thought I recognized that a thorough penetration into all the questions which Kant had raised among thinkers was necessary for me. I now worked more consciously to the end that I might mould into the forms of *thought* the immediate *perception* of the spiritual world which I possessed. And while I was occupied with this inner work I sought to get my bearings with reference to the roads that had been followed by the thinkers of Kant's time and the succeeding epoch. I studied the dry, bald *Transcendentaler Synthetismus*[5] of Traugott Krug just as eagerly as I entered into the tragedy of knowledge at which Fichte had arrived when he wrote his *Bestimmung des Menschen*.[6] The history of philosophy

[1] *The Vocation of the Scholar.*
[2] *The Nature of the Scholar.*
[3] *Addresses to the German Nation.*
[4] *Prolegomena to Every Future Metaphysics.*
[5] *Transcendental Synthesism.*
[6] *The Vocation of Man.*

by Thilo, of the school of Herbart, broadened my view of the evolution of philosophical thought from the period of Kant onward. I fought my way through to Schelling, to Hegel. The contrast between the thinking of Herbart and that of Fichte confronted me in all its intensity.

The summer months of 1879, from the end of my *Realschule* course until my entrance into the *Technische Hochschule,* I spent entirely in such philosophical studies. In the autumn I was to decide my choice of studies with reference to my future livelihood. I decided to prepare to teach in a *Realschule.* The study of mathematics and descriptive geometry would have suited my inclination. But I had to give up the latter, for the study of this subject required a great many practice hours during the day in geometrical drawing, but in order to earn some money I had to have time to devote to tutoring. This was possible while enrolled for lectures whose subject matter, when it was necessary to be absent, could afterward be taken up in reading, but not possible when one had to spend hours assigned for drawing regularly in the school.

So I had myself enrolled for mathematics, natural history, and chemistry.

Of special import for me, however, were the lectures which Karl Julius Schröer gave at that time in the *Hochschule* on German literature. He lectured during my first year on "German Literature since Goethe" and "Schiller's Life and Works." From the very first lecture he captivated me. He developed a survey of the cultural life in Germany in the second half of the eighteenth century, and described in a dramatic way Goethe's first appearance in its effect upon this cultural life. The warmth of his manner of treatment, the inspiring way in which during his lectures he read from the poets, introduced one in an intensified way into the nature of poetry.

In addition, he had arranged for "practice in oral discourse and written exposition." The students had to deliver orally or read aloud what they themselves had prepared. Schröer would then give instructions growing out of these student performances as to style, manner of delivery, and the like. My first lecture dealt with Lessing's *Lao-koon*. Then I undertook a more comprehensive task. I worked up the theme: "To what extent is man in his actions a free being?" In connection with this task I got deeply involved in Herbart's philosophy. Schröer did not like this at all. He had not shared in the enthusiasm for Herbart which was then dominant in Austria both among professors of philosophy and also in pedagogy. He was completely devoted to Goethe's manner of thought. So everything that was derived from Herbart seemed to him pedantic and prosaic, although he acknowledged the discipline of thought characterizing this philosopher.

I was now able to attend also single lectures at the University. I had been looking forward with much pleasure to the Herbartian, Robert Zimmermann, who lectured on *"Praktische Philosophie."* [1] I attended that part of his lectures in which he developed the basic principles of ethics. I alternated, generally attending his lecture one day and the next that of Franz Brentano, who at the same time lectured in the same field. I could not keep this up very long, since I missed too much of the courses in the *Hochschule*.

It made a deep impression on me to become acquainted with philosophy now, not merely through books, but from the lips of philosophers themselves.

Robert Zimmermann was a strange personality. He had an extraordinarily high forehead and a long philosopher's beard. With him everything was measured, reduced to style. When he entered through the door and mounted to his desk, his steps seemed to be studied; yet, on the other hand, one felt that for this man it was a matter of course in his nature to be like this. In bearing and movement it seemed as if he had formed himself through long discipline according to the aesthetic principles of Herbart. And yet it was possible to sympathize entirely with all this. He then slowly sat down on the chair, cast a long glance through his spectacles over the auditorium, slowly and precisely took off his spectacles, looked once more for a

[1] *Practical Philosophy.*

long time without spectacles over the circle of auditors, and finally began his lecture, without manuscript, in carefully formed, artistically spoken sentences. There was something classic in his speech. Yet, owing to the long periods, one easily lost the thread of his discourse. He expounded Herbart's philosophy in a somewhat modified form. The close logic in the sequence of his ideas impressed me. But it did not impress the other hearers. During the first three or four lectures, the great hall in which he lectured was crowded. "Practical Philosophy" was required for the law students in the first year. They needed the signature of the professor on their cards. From the fifth or sixth lecture on, most of them stayed away; while listening to the classical philosopher, one was in a very small group of auditors in the front seats. To me these lectures afforded a powerful stimulus, and the difference between the views of Schröer and Zimmermann interested me deeply.

The little time I did not spend in attendance at the lectures or in tutoring I utilized either in the *Hofbibliothek* or the library of the *Hochschule*. There for the first time I then read Goethe's *Faust*. In fact, until my nineteenth year, when I was inspired by Schröer, I had never gone as far as this work. Then, however, it immediately won a strong claim upon my interest. Schröer had already published his edition of the First Part. Through it I first became acquainted with the First Part. Moreover, it happened that after a few lectures I became better acquainted with Schröer. He then often took me to his home, told me this or that in amplification of his lectures, gladly answered my questions, and sent me away with a book from his library, which he lent me to read. In this connection he said many things about the Second Part of *Faust,* an annotated edition of which he was just preparing. This also I read at that time.

In the libraries I spent my time on Herbart's metaphysics and with Zimmermann's *Aesthetik als Formwissenschaft*,[1] which was written from Herbart's point of view. Together with this I made a thorough study of Ernst Haeckel's *Generelle Morphologie*.[2] I can

[1] *Aesthetics As the Science of Form.*
[2] *General Morphology.*

well say that everything with which I felt myself confronted through the lectures of Schröer and Zimmermann, as well as the reading I have mentioned, became a matter of the deepest soul experience. Riddles of knowledge and of world views took shape within me from these things.

Schröer was a spirit who cared nothing for system. He thought and spoke out of a certain intuition. Besides, he gave the greatest possible care to the manner in which he clothed his views in language. It was probably for this reason that he never lectured without a manuscript. He needed to write things down undisturbed in order to satisfy himself in converting his thoughts into words to be spoken. He then read what he had written with a marked intensification of his way of speaking. Once, indeed, he did speak extemporaneously about Anastasius Grün and Lenau. He had forgotten his manuscript. In the next period, however, he treated the whole topic again, reading from the manuscript. He was not satisfied with the form he had been able to give to the matter *extempore*.

Through Schröer I became acquainted with many concrete examples of the beautiful; through Zimmermann there came to me a developed theory of beauty. The two did not harmonize well. Schröer, the intuitive personality with a certain scorn for the systematic, confronted me side by side with Zimmermann, the rigidly systematic theorist of the beautiful.

Franz Brentano, whose lectures on "Practical Philosophy" I attended also, particularly interested me through his personality. He was a keen thinker and at the same time given to revery. In his manner of lecturing there was something ceremonious. I listened to what he said, but I had also to observe every glance, every movement of his head, every gesture of his expressive hands. He was the perfect logician. Every thought must be absolutely transparent, and supported by many other thoughts. The forming of these thought-series was carried out with the most scrupulous attention to the requirements of logic. But I had the feeling that this thinking did not escape from the network woven by itself; nowhere did it break through into reality. And such also was the whole attitude of Bretano. He held the manuscript loosely in his hand as if at any moment it might slip from his fingers; with his glance he merely skimmed along the lines. This was the gesture suited to a merely superficial touch upon reality, not for a firm grasp of it. I could understand his philosophizing better from his "philosopher's hands" than from his words.

The stimulus which came from Brentano had a strong after-effect upon me. I soon began to study his writings, and in the course of later years I have read most of what he published.

I felt in duty bound at that time to seek for the truth through philosophy. I had to study mathematics and natural science. I was convinced that I should find no relation with them unless I could place their findings upon a solid foundation of philosophy. But I beheld a spiritual world *as reality*. In perfectly clear vision the spiritual individuality of every one was manifest to me. This had in the physical body and in action in the physical world merely its expression. It united itself with that which came as a physical germ from the parents. The dead human being I followed on his way into the spiritual world. After the death of a schoolmate, I wrote about this phase of my spiritual life to one of my former teachers who had continued to be a close friend of mine even after my *Realschule* days. He wrote back to me with unusual affection, but he did not deign to say one word about what I had written regarding the dead schoolmate.

And this is what happened to me always at that time in this matter of my perception of the spiritual world. No one would pay any attention to it. From this or that direction persons would come forward at most with all sorts of spiritistic ideas. With this I, in turn, would have nothing to do. To me it was utterly distasteful to approach the spiritual in such a way.

It then chanced that I became acquainted with a simple man of the people. Every week he went to Vienna by the same train that I took. He gathered medicinal plants in the country and sold them to apothecaries in Vienna. We became fast friends. With him it was possible to talk about the spiritual world as with one who had his own experience in this world. He was a personality of inner piety. He was quite without schooling. To be sure, he had read many mystical books, but what he said was not at all influenced by this reading. It was the outflow of a soul-life which was marked by its own quite elementary creative wisdom. It was easy to see that he had read those books only because he wished to find in others what he knew for himself. But it did not satisfy him. He impressed one as if he, as a personality, were only the mouthpiece for a spiritual content which sought for utterance out of hidden worlds. When with him, it was possible to look deeply into the mysteries of nature. He carried on his back the bundle of medicinal plants, but in his heart he bore the findings which he had won from the spirituality of nature in the gathering of these herbs. I have seen many a person smile who now and then made a third party while I walked through the streets of Vienna with this "initiate." No wonder; for his manner of expression was not to be understood at once. One had first, in a certain sense, to learn his "spiritual dialect." To me also he was at first unintelligible. But from our first acquaintance I was in deepest sympathy with him. And so I gradually came to feel as if I were in the company of a soul of the most ancient times who—quite unaffected by the civilization, science, and general conceptions of the present age—brought to me an instinctive knowledge of earlier eras.

According to the usual conception of "learning," one might say that it was impossible to "learn" anything from this man. But, if one possessed in oneself the perception of a spiritual world, very deep glimpses could be obtained into this world through another who had a firm footing there.

Moreover, anything in the nature of mere illusionary enthusiasm was utterly foreign to this personality. Upon entering his home, one was in the midst of the soberest and simplest family of country folk. Above the entrance to his home were the words: "All that matters is the blessing of God." One was entertained just as by other village people. I always had to drink coffee there, not from a cup, but from a porridge bowl which held nearly a liter; with this I had to eat a piece of bread of enormous dimensions. Nor did the villagers by any means look upon the man as a mere visionary. His manner of life in his home place repelled any possible mockery. Besides, he possessed a sound, wholesome humor, and knew how to chat, when he met young or old village folk, in a way that delighted the people. There no one smiled like those persons who walked with him and me through the streets of Vienna, most of whom saw in him something quite foreign to themselves.

This man always continued to be, even after life had taken me again away from him, very close to me in soul. He appears in my Mystery Dramas in the person of Felix Balde.

It was no light matter for my mental life at that time that the philosophy which I learned from others could not in its thinking be carried all the way to the perception of the spiritual world. Out of the difficulties which I experienced in this respect, a kind of "theory of knowledge" began to take form within me. The life of thought came gradually to seem to me the reflection radiated into the physical human being of what the soul experiences in the spiritual world. Thought-experience was for me existence in a reality which—as something actually experienced through and through—doubt dared not approach. The world of the senses did not seem to me so completely a matter of experience. It is present; but one does not lay hold upon it as upon thought. In it or behind it there might be a reality concealed. Yet man himself is set in the midst of this world. Therefore, the question arose: Is *this* world, then, a reality complete in itself? When the human being weaves thoughts out of his inner being in connection with it which bring light into this world of the senses, is he actually bringing into this world something foreign to it? This certainly does not at all accord with the experience that we have when we confront the world of the senses and break into it by means of our thoughts. Thought then surely appears to be that by means of which the world of the senses expresses *its own nature*. The further development of this reflection was at that time an important part of my inner life.

But I wished to be prudent. To pursue a course of thinking too hastily all the way to the building up of a philosophical view of one's own appeared to me dangerous. This drove me to a thorough study of Hegel. The way in which this philosopher sets forth the reality of thought was congenial to my own thinking. That he made his way through only to a thought-world—although a living one—and not to the perception of a world of concrete spirit,—this repelled me. The assurance with which one philosophizes when advancing from thought to thought attracted me. I saw that many persons hold there is a difference between experience and thinking. To me thinking itself was experience, but such experience that one lives in it, not such that it confronts one from without. Thus for some time Hegel was very valuable to me.

As to my required studies, which in the midst of these philosophical interests would necessarily have been neglected, it was fortunate that I had already occupied myself a great deal with differential and integral calculus and with analytical geometry. Because of this, I could remain away from many lectures in mathematics without losing my connection. Mathematics retained its importance for me as the foundation also under my whole striving after knowledge. For mathematics provides a system of percepts and concepts which have been arrived at independently of any external sense-impression. And yet, I said to myself constantly at that time, one approaches sense-reality with these percepts and concepts and through them discovers its laws. Through mathematics one learns to know the world, and yet in order to do this it is necessary first to evoke mathematics out of the human mind.

A decisive experience came to me at that time precisely from the side of mathematics. The conception of space gave me the greatest inner difficulty. As the illimitable, all-encompassing void—the form in which it lay at the basis of the dominant theories of contemporary science—it could not be conceived in any definite manner. Through the more recent (synthetic) geometry, which I learned through lectures and in private study, there came into my mind the perception that a line prolonged infinitely toward the right hand would return again from the left to its starting point. The infinitely distant point on the right is the same as the point infinitely distant on the left.

It occurred to me that by means of such conceptions of the more recent geometry it might be possible to form a conception of space, which otherwise remained fixed in a void. The straight line returning upon itself like a circle seemed to me to be a revelation. I left the lecture at which this had first passed before my mind as if a great load had fallen from me. A feeling of liberation came over me. Again, as in my early boyhood, something joy-bestowing had to come to me out of geometry.

Behind the riddle of space stood at that time in my life the riddle of time. Ought a conception to be possible there also which would contain within itself in idea a return out of the past by means of an advance into the "infinitely distant" future? My happiness over the space conception caused me profound unrest over that of time. But there was then no visible way out. All efforts of thought led only to the realization that I must beware of applying the perceptible spacial concepts to the problem of time. All the disappointments which can arise from the striving for knowledge were experienced in connection with the riddle of time.

The stimulus which I had received from Zimmermann toward the study of aesthetics led me to read the writings of the famous specialist in aesthetics of that time, Friedrich Theodor Vischer. I found in a passage of his works a reference to the fact that the more recent scientific thinking rendered necessary a change in the concept of time. A special pleasure was evoked in me when I found in another person a sense of cognitional needs which had presented themselves to me. In this case, it seemed to me like a justification of my struggle toward a satisfactory conception of time.

The lectures for which I was enrolled in the *Technische Hoch-schule* had always to be finished with a corresponding examination. For a scholarship had been granted to me, and I could continue to draw my allowance only if I showed each year positive results from my studies.

But my craving for knowledge, especially in the field of natural science, was but little satisfied by these required studies. It was possible at that time, however, in connection with the technical institutes of Vienna both to attend lectures as an auditor and also to pursue laboratory courses. I found everywhere those who met me half-way when I sought thus to foster my scientific life, even so far as to the field of medicine.

I may state that I never permitted my insight into the spiritual to become a disturbing factor while engaged in the endeavor to learn the sciences as they were then developed. I applied myself to what was taught, and only in the background of my mind did I have the hope that some day the blending of natural science with the knowledge of the spirit would result for me.

Only from two sides was I disturbed in this hope.

The sciences of organic nature—wherever I could occupy myself with them—were steeped in Darwinian ideas. To me Darwinism appeared at that time as scientifically impossible. I had little by little reached the stage of forming for myself a conception of the inner being of man. This was of a spiritual nature. I thought of it as a member of the world of spirit. It was conceived as dipping down out of the world of spirit into the existence in nature, uniting with the organism in order by means of this to perceive and to act in the world of the senses.

Even the fact that I felt a certain respect for the course of thought characterizing the evolutionary theory of organisms did not render it possible for me to sacrifice anything from this conception. The derivation of higher out of lower organisms seemed to me a fruitful idea, but the reconciling of this idea with that which I knew as the spiritual world appeared immeasurably difficult.

The studies in physics were permeated throughout by the mechanical theory of heat and the wave theory of the phenomena of light and color.

The study of the mechanical theory of heat had taken on for me the charm of a personal coloring because in this field of physics I attended lectures by a personality to whom I was quite extraordinarily devoted. This was Edmund Reitlinger, the author of the beautiful book *Freie Blicke*.[1]

This man was of the most captivating lovableness. When I became his student, he was already seriously ill with tuberculosis. For two years I attended his lectures on the mechanical theory of heat, physics for chemists, and the history of physics. I worked under him in the physics laboratory in many fields, especially in that of spectral analysis.

Of special importance for me were Reitlinger's lectures on the history of physics. He spoke in such a way that one felt as if, on account of his illness, every word became difficult for him. And yet his lectures were in the best possible sense inspiring. He was a man of strongly inductive method in research. For all methods in physics, he liked to cite the book of Whewel on inductive sciences. Newton marked for him the climax in research in physics. The history of physics he set forth in two parts: the first from the earliest times to Newton; the second from Newton to modern times. He was a universal thinker. From the historical consideration of problems in physics, he always passed over to general cultural-historical perspectives. Indeed, quite general philosophical ideas would appear in his lectures on natural science. In this way he treated the problems of optimism and pessimism, and spoke most stimulatingly about the legitimacy of setting up scientific hypotheses. His exposition of Keppler, his characterization of Julius Robert Mayer, were masterpieces of scientific discourse.

I was stimulated at that time to read almost all the writings of Julius Robert Mayer, and I was privileged to experience the truly

[1] *Free Outlook.*

great pleasure of frequent personal conversations with Reitlinger about the content of these.

I was filled with deep sorrow when, only a few weeks after I had passed my final examination on the mechanical theory of heat under Reitlinger, my beloved teacher succumbed to his grievous illness. Just a short time before his death he had given me, like a legacy, recommendations for persons who could provide me with pupils for private tutoring. This had most fortunate results. No small part of what came to me in the following years as means of livelihood I owed to Reitlinger after his death.

Through the mechanical theory of heat and the wave theory of the phenomena of light and of the action of electricity I was impelled to a study of theories of knowledge. At that time the external physical world was conceived as motion-processes in matter. Sensations appeared to be only subjective experiences, the effects of pure motion-processes upon the senses of the human being. Out there in space, it was assumed, occur motion-processes in matter; if these processes affect the human sense for heat, the sensation of heat is experienced. *Outside* of man are wave-processes in ether; if these affect the optic nerve, light and color sensations are generated *within* the human being.

This conception met me everywhere. It caused me unspeakable difficulties in my thinking. It banished all spirit from the objective external world. It was clear to me that, if the observation of natural phenomena leads to such assumptions, one possessed of a vision of the spirit could not arrive at these assumptions. I saw how seductive these assumptions were for the trend of thinking at that time, developed by the natural sciences. Even so I could not yet resolve to oppose a manner of thinking of my own, even for myself alone, against that which then prevailed. But just this caused me bitter soul battles. Again and again the criticism I could easily formulate against this way of thinking had to be suppressed within me to await a time when more comprehensive sources and ways of knowledge could give me greater assurance.

I was deeply stirred by the reading of Schiller's letters concerning the aesthetic education of man. His reference to the fact that human consciousness oscillates, as it were, back and forth between different states afforded me a connection with the picture I had formed of the inner working and weaving of the human soul. Schiller distinguishes two states of consciousness in which man develops his relation with the world. When he surrenders himself to what affects him through the senses, he lives under the compulsion of nature. The senses and instincts determine his life. If he subjects himself to the logical laws and principles of reason, he is living under a rational compulsion. But he can develop an *intermediate* state of consciousness. He can develop the "aesthetic mood," which is not given over one-sidedly either to the compulsion of nature or to the necessity of reason. In this aesthetic mood, the soul lives through the senses; but into the sense-perception and the action set on foot by sense-stimuli the soul brings over something spiritual. One perceives through the senses, but as if the spiritual had streamed over into the senses. In action one surrenders oneself to the gratification of the present desire; but one has so ennobled this desire that to it the good is pleasing and the evil displeasing. Reason has entered into intimate union with the sensible. The good becomes an instinct; instinct can safely direct itself, for it has taken on the character of the spiritual. Schiller sees in this state of consciousness that condition of the soul in which man can experience and produce works of beauty. In the development of this state he sees the awakening in man of the true human being.

These thoughts of Schiller's were to me very attractive. They implied that man must first have his consciousness in a certain condition before he can attain to such a relation with the phenomena of the world as corresponds with his own being. Something was here given to me which brought to greater clarity the questions that confronted me as a result of my observation of nature and my spiritual experience. Schiller spoke of the state of consciousness which must be present in order that one may experience the *beauty* of the world.

Might not one think also of a state of consciousness which would mediate to us the truth in the nature of things? If this is granted, one must not, then, after the manner of Kant, observe the existing state of human consciousness and inquire whether this can enter into the true nature of things. On the contrary, one must first seek to discover the state of consciousness through which man places himself in such a relation with the world that things and phenomena reveal their essential nature to him.

And I believed that I knew that such a state of consciousness is reached up to a certain degree when the human being has not only thoughts which reproduce external things and occurrences, but thoughts that he *experiences as thoughts themselves*. This living in thoughts revealed itself to me as quite different from that in which the human being ordinarily exists and also carries on ordinary scientific research. If one penetrates deeper and deeper into thought-experience, one finds that spiritual reality comes to meet this thought-experience. One takes the path of the soul to the spirit. But, on this inner way of the soul, one arrives at a spiritual reality which one finds again also within nature. One gains a deeper knowledge of nature when one then faces nature after having in living thoughts beheld the reality of the spirit.

It became clearer and clearer to me that, through going forward beyond customary abstract thoughts to those spiritual visions—which, however, retain the circumspection and clarity of thought—the human being becomes acquainted with a reality from which ordinary consciousness separates him. This ordinary state has, on the one hand, the living quality of sense-perception, on the other the abstractness of thought-conceiving. Spiritual vision perceives spirit as the senses perceive nature; but it does not stand apart in thinking from the spiritual percept as the ordinary state of consciousness stands in *its* thinking apart from the sense-percept. On the contrary, spiritual vision thinks while it experiences spirit, and experiences while it sets to thinking the awakened spirituality in man.

A spiritual vision confronted my soul which did not rest upon obscure mystical feeling. It took its course rather in a spiritual activity which, in its transparency, might be compared completely with mathematical thinking. I was approaching a state of mind in which I felt that I might consider that the perception of the spiritual world which I bore within me was justified also before the forum of natural-scientific thinking.

When these experiences passed through my mind, I was in my twenty-second year.

IV

FOR THE FORM of experience of spirit which I then desired to establish upon a firm foundation within me, music came to have a crucial significance. There was in process at that time in the most intense fashion in the cultural environment in which I lived the "battle over Wagner." During my boyhood and youth I had seized every opportunity to improve my understanding of music. The attitude I held toward thinking rendered this inevitable. For me thinking had *content* in itself. It did not acquire this merely through the percept which it expresses. This, however, led over inevitably into the experience of the pure musical tone-form as such. The world of tones in itself was to me the revelation of an essential aspect of reality. That music, beyond the tone-forming, should "express" something, as was then maintained in every possible way by the adherents of Wagner, seemed to me utterly "unmusical."

I was always of a social disposition. Because of this I had even in my school-days in Wiener-Neustadt, and then again in Vienna, formed many friendships. In opinions I seldom agreed with these friends. This, however, did not mean at all that these friendships did not possess an intimacy and strong mutual stimulation. One of these friendships was with a young man delightfully idealistic. With his blond locks and frank blue eyes, he was the very type of a German youth. He was at the time quite enraptured by Wagnerism. Music that lived in itself, that would only weave in tones, was to him an outmoded world of wretched Philistinism. What revealed itself in the tones as a kind of speech—that for him gave the tone-form its value. We attended together many concerts and operas. We always held different views. My limbs grew heavy as lead when "expressive music" inflamed him to ecstasy; and he was horribly bored by music that did not pretend to be anything else than music.

The debates with this friend stretched out endlessly. In long walks together, in protracted sessions over our cups of coffee, he drew out his "proofs," expressed in animated fashion, that only with Wagner had true music really been born, and that everything which had gone before was only a preparation for this "discoverer of music." This led me to assert my own convictions in drastic manner. I spoke of the barbarism of Wagner, the graveyard of all true understanding of music.

On special occasions the argument grew particularly vehement. One day my friend very noticeably formed the habit of directing our almost daily walks to a certain narrow little street and passing with me up and down it many times discussing Wagner. I was so absorbed in our argument that it only gradually dawned upon me how he had got this bent. At a window of one of the little houses on the narrow alley there sat at the time of our walk a charming young girl. There was no relation between him and the girl except that he saw her sitting at the window almost every day and at times thought that a glance she let fall on the street was intended for him.

At first I noticed only that his championship of Wagner—which in any case was fiery enough—was fanned to a glowing flame in this little alley. When I became aware of what tributary stream flowed from that vicinity into his inspired heart, he grew confidential in this matter also, and I came to share in the tenderest, most beautiful, most enthusiastic young love. The relation between the two never went much beyond what I have described. My friend, who came of people not blessed with worldly goods, had soon after to take a petty journalistic job in a provincial city. He could not think of any closer tie with the girl. Neither was he strong enough to master the existing conditions. I kept up a correspondence with him for a long time. A melancholy note of resignation marked his letters. That from which he had been forced to cut himself off was still living in his heart.

Long after life had brought to an end my correspondence with this friend of my youth, I chanced to meet a person from the same city in which he had found a place as a journalist. I had continued to be fond of him, and I asked about him. This person said to me: "Yes, things turned out badly for him; he could scarcely earn his bread. Finally he became a clerk in my employ, and then he died of tuberculosis." The news stabbed me to the heart, for I knew that the fair-haired youth had severed his relation with his young love of that time, under the compulsion of circumstances, with the feeling that it would make no difference to him what life might further bring. He considered it of no value to lay the basis for a life which could not be such as had hovered before him as an ideal during our walks in that little alley.

In intercourse with this friend my anti-Wagnerism of that period only came to expression in more emphatic form. But, in other respects also, it played a great rôle in my inner life at that time. I strove in all directions to find my way into the element of music which had nothing to do with Wagnerism. My love for "pure music" increased for a number of years; my horror at the "barbarism" of "music as expression" became steadily greater. And in this matter it was my lot to get into a human environment in which almost every one was an admirer of Wagner. This all contributed much toward the fact that it became very hard for me—much later—to struggle through to an understanding of Wagner, which is, of course, the obviously human attitude toward so significant a cultural phenomenon. This struggle belongs, however, to a later period of my life. During the time I am now describing, a performance of *Tristan,* for example, to which I had to accompany one of my pupils was to me "mortally boring."

To this time belongs still another youthful friendship very significant for me. This was with a young man who was in every way the opposite of the fair-haired youth. He felt that he was a poet. With him, too, I spent a great deal of time in stimulating talk. He had a great enthusiasm for everything poetic. At an early age he entered upon important undertakings. When we became acquainted, he had already written a tragedy, *Hannibal,* and much lyric verse.

I was together with both these friends also in the "practice in oral discourse and written exposition" which Schröer conducted in the *Hochschule.* From this course we three, and many others, received the greatest stimulation. We young people could present what we had arrived at in our minds and Schröer talked over everything with us and elevated our mood by his splendid idealism and his noble capacity for enthusiasm.

My friend often accompanied me when I had the privilege of calling at the home of Schröer. There he always grew animated, whereas elsewhere a note of burden was manifest in his life. Because of an inner discord, he could not come to terms with life. No calling was so attractive to him that he would gladly have entered upon it. He was altogether taken up with his poetical interest, and apart from this his life found no satisfying relation with existence. At last he had to take a position to which he was utterly indifferent. With him also I continued my connection by means of letters. The fact that even in his poetry he could not find real satisfaction preyed upon his spirit. Life for him was not filled with anything possessing worth. I had to observe to my sorrow how in his letters and also in his conversation the belief grew upon him little by little that he was suffering from an incurable disease. Nothing sufficed to dispel this groundless suspicion. So one day I had to receive the distressing news that the young man who was so very close to me had made an end of himself.

An intimate friendship I formed at this time with a young man who had come from the German Transylvania to the Vienna *Hochschule.* Him also I had first met in Schröer's exercise periods. There he had delivered a lecture on pessimism. Everything that Schopenhauer had presented in favor of this view of life was revived in that lecture. In addition there was the personal pessimistic temperament

of the young man himself. I offered to present an opposing statement. I "refuted" pessimism with veritable words of thunder, calling
Schopenhauer already at that time a "narrow-minded genius," and
wound up my discourse with the sentence: "If the gentleman who
delivered that lecture were right in his attitude with respect to pessimism, I had rather be the wooden board on which my feet now tread
than to be a man." These words were for a long time repeated mock-
ingly about me among my acquaintances. But they made of the
young pessimist and me intimately united friends. We now passed
much time together. He also felt himself to be a poet, and many a
time I sat for hours in his room listening with pleasure to the reading
of his poems. In my spiritual strivings of that time he also took a
warm interest, although he was moved less by the thing itself with
which I was concerned than by his personal affection for me. He
was united in many delightful friendships and also youthful love
affairs. He needed this in his life, which was very hard. At Hermannstadt he had gone through school as a poor boy and even then
had to make his living by tutoring. He then conceived the clever
idea of continuing to instruct by correspondence from Vienna the
pupils he had gained at Hermannstadt. The sciences in the *Hochschule* interested him very little. Nevertheless, one day he wished to
pass an examination in chemistry. He had never attended a lecture
nor opened a single one of the pertinent books. On the last night
before the examination, he had a friend read to him a digest of the
entire subject matter. Finally he fell asleep over this. Yet he went
with his friend to the examination. Both made "brilliant" failures.

This young man had boundless faith in me. For a long time he
treated me almost as a father confessor. He opened to my view an
interesting, often melancholy life, enthusiastic for all that is beautiful. He gave to me so much friendship and love that it was really
hard at times not to cause him bitter disappointment. This happened
especially for the reason that he often felt I did not show him enough
attention. And yet this could not be otherwise, since I had so many
spheres of interest for which I found in him no real understanding.

All this, however, only contributed in the end toward making the friendship more and more intimate. He spent his summer vacations at Hermannstadt. There he sought for students to be tutored by correspondence the following year from Vienna. I always received long letters during these periods from him. He was grieved because I seldom or never answered them. But, when he returned to Vienna in the autumn, he hurried to me like a boy, and the united life began again. I owed it to him at that time that I was able to mingle with many persons. He liked to take me to meet all the people with whom he was associated. And I was thirsting for sociability. This friend brought much into my life that gave me joy and warmth.

Our friendship lasted throughout life till my friend died a few years ago. It stood the test of many storms of life, and I shall still have much to say of it.

In retrospective consciousness much comes to mind in the form of human and life relations which continues its full existence within me, bound up with feelings of love and gratitude. Here I must not relate everything in detail, but must leave quite unmentioned much that was, indeed, very close to me precisely in my personal experience, and has continued to be so.

My youthful friendships in the time of which I am speaking had a peculiar relation to the course of my life. They forced me into a sort of double life of the soul. The struggle with the riddles of knowledge which then filled my mind more than anything else aroused in my friends always, to be sure, a strong interest, but very little active participation. In the experience of these riddles, I remained rather lonely. On the other hand, I shared completely in whatever arose in the existence of my friends. Thus there flowed along in me two parallel currents of life: one that I followed like a lone wanderer, and one that I shared in vital companionship with persons bound to me by ties of affection. But the experiences of the second kind were also in many instances of profound and lasting significance in my development.

In this connection I must mention especially a friend who had already been a schoolmate of mine in Wiener-Neustadt. During that time, however, we were far apart. Only in Vienna, where he visited me often and where he later lived as an official, did he come into a close relation with me. And yet even in Wiener-Neustadt, without an external relation between us, he had already had a significance for my life. Once I was with him in a gymnasium period. While he was exercising, and I had nothing to do, he left a book lying by me. It was Heine's book on the romantic school and the history of philosophy in Germany. I glanced into it. The result of this was that I myself read the book. I found many stimulating things in it, but was vitally opposed to the manner in which Heine treated the content of life which was dear to me. In the perception of a way of thinking and type of feeling utterly at variance with those taking form in me I received a powerful stimulation toward self-reflection regarding the inner orientation of life that was necessary for me according to my mental predisposition.

I then had a talk with my schoolmate in relation to the book. In this talk, his inner life came to the fore and led later to the establishing of a lasting friendship. He was an uncommunicative person who confided in very few people. He was thought by most to be an odd character. With those few in whom he was willing to confide he became quite expressive, especially in letters. He thought himself called by inner endowments to be a poet. He was of the opinion that he bore within him a great treasure. He was at the same time inclined to dream himself into relations with other persons, especially feminine personalities, rather than actually to form such relations in external fact. At times he was close to such a relation, but he could not bring it to actual experience. In conversation with me he would then live through his dreams with fervor and enthusiasm, as if they were actualities. It was inevitable, therefore, that he experienced bitter emotions when the dreams always melted away.

This produced in him a soul life that had not the slightest relation to his outer existence. And this life again was to him the occasion for tormenting reflections about himself, which were mirrored in many letters to me and in conversations. Thus he once wrote me a long dissertation about the way in which the least or the greatest experience became to him a symbol and how he lived with such symbols.

I loved this friend, and in my love for him I entered into his dreams, although I always had the feeling while with him: "We are moving about in the clouds and have no ground under our feet!" For me, who ceaselessly busied myself for the very purpose of finding a firm support for life in knowledge, this was a peculiar experience. Again and again I had to slip outside my own being and leap across into another skin, as it were, when in company with this friend. He liked to share his life with me; at times he even set forth extensive theoretical reflections concerning the "difference between our two natures." He was quite unaware how little our thoughts harmonized, because the attitude of friendship carried him above all thoughts.

The situation was similar in my relation with another Wiener-Neustadt schoolmate. He belonged to the next lower grade in the *Realschule,* and we first came into closer contact when he entered the *Hochschule* in Vienna a year after me. Then, however, we were often together. He also entered but little into what inwardly concerned me in the sphere of knowledge. He studied chemistry. The natural-scientific views with which he was then confronted prevented him from showing himself in any other light than as a sceptic in regard to the spiritual conception with which I was imbued. Later in life I found in the case of this friend how close to my state of mind he had been in his innermost being even then, but at the time he never allowed his innermost being to become manifest. Thus our long and lively arguments became for me a "battle against materialism." To my avowal of the spiritual essence of the world he always opposed all the refutations that are supposed to be derived from natural science. I then had always to array everything I possessed by way of insight in order to drive from the field the objections drawn from the materialistic orientation of thinking against a knowledge of the world in keeping with the spirit.

Once we were arguing the question with great zeal. Every day, after attending the lectures in Vienna, my friend went back to his home, which was still in Wiener-Neustadt. I often accompanied him through the *Alleegasse* in Vienna to the station of the Southern Railway. One day we reached a sort of climax in the argument over materialism after we had already arrived at the station and the train was almost due to leave. I then put together what I still had to say in the following words: "So, then, you maintain that, when you say 'I think,' this is merely the necessary effect of processes in your brain-nerve system. These processes alone are reality. So it is likewise when you say 'I see this or that,' 'I walk,' and so forth. But observe this. You do not say, 'My brain thinks,' 'My brain sees this or that,' 'My brain walks.' If, however, you had really come to the opinion that what you theoretically maintain is actually true, you would have to correct your form of expression. When you continue, nevertheless, to speak of 'I,' you are really lying. But you cannot do otherwise than to follow your sound instinct against the insinuations of your theory. You experience a different state of affairs from that which your theory defends. Your consciousness calls your theory a lie." My friend shook his head. He had no time to reply. As I went back alone, I could not but think that opposing materialism in this crude way did not correspond with a particularly exact philosophy. But what then really concerned me was not so much to furnish, five minutes before the train left, a philosophically convincing proof as to express my certitude from inner experience of the nature of the human ego. To me this ego was an inwardly observable experience of a *reality* present in the experience. This reality seemed to me no less certain than any recognized by materialism. But in it there is absolutely nothing material. This thorough-going insight into the reality and the spirituality of the ego has in the succeeding years helped me to rise above all temptations to materialism. I have always known that the ego is unshakeable. And it has been clear to me that no one really knows the ego who considers it as a phenomenal form, a result of other processes. *The fact* that I had this as an inner spiritual perception was what I wished to express to my friend. We fought together many times thereafter on this battle-field. But in general conceptions of life we had so many similar sentiments that the vehemence of our theoretical battling never resulted in the least misunderstanding in our personal relation.

During this time I entered more deeply into the student life of Vienna. I became a member of the German Reading Hall at the *Hochschule*. In the assembly and in smaller gatherings the political and cultural phenomena of the time were thoroughly discussed. These discussions brought out all possible—and impossible—points of view such as young people could hold. Especially when officers were to be elected, opinions clashed against one another quite vio-lently. Very stimulating and exciting was much that came to expres-sion among the youth in connection with events in the public life of Austria. It was the time when national parties were becoming stead-ily more sharply defined. Everything that led later more and more to the disruption of the Empire, and which appeared in its results after the World War, could then be experienced in germ.

I was first chosen librarian of the Reading Hall. As such I found out all possible authors who had written books that I thought might be of value to the student library. To such authors I wrote begging letters. I often wrote in a single week fully a hundred such letters. Through this "work" of mine the library was rapidly enlarged. But this had a secondary effect for me. It was possible for me in this way to become acquainted in comprehensive fashion with the scientific, artistic, culture-historical, political literature of the time. I was an eager reader of the books given.

Later I was chosen president of the Reading Hall. This, however, was for me a burdensome office. For I was confronted by the most diverse party view-points and I saw in all of these their relative justification. Yet the adherents of the various parties would come to me, and each would seek to convince me that his party alone was right. At the time when I was elected, every party had voted for me. For until then they had only *heard* that in the assemblies I had taken the part of what was justified. After I had been president for a half-year, all voted against me. They had then found that I could not decide as positively for any party as that party desired.

My craving for companionship found abundant satisfaction in the Reading Hall. Moreover, an interest was developed in a broader field of public life through the reflection of its events in the community life of the students. In this way I came to attend very interesting parliamentary debates, sitting in the gallery of the Austrian Chamber of Deputies or of the Upper House.

Apart from measures adopted by Parliament—which often affected life profoundly—I was especially interested in the personalities in the House of Deputies. There stood every year at the end of his row of seats, as chief budget expositor, the keen philosopher Bartolemäus Carneri. His words were a hailstorm of slashing accusations against the Taaffe ministry; they were in defence of Germanism in Austria. There stood Ernst von Plener, the dry speaker, unexcelled authority in matters of finance. One felt chilled while he criticized the expenditures of the Minister of Finance, Dunajewski, with the coldness of a calculator. There the Ruthenian Thomaszuck thundered against nationality-politics. One had the feeling that what he was bent upon was the discovery of an especially well coined word for that moment in order to foster antipathy against the ministers. There argued in peasant-sly fashion, always intelligently, the clerical Lienbacher. His slightly bowed head caused what he said to seem like the outflow of clarified conceptions. There argued in his cutting style the Young Czech Gregr. One felt in him a half-demagogue. There stood Rieger, of the Old Czechs, in a deeply characteristic sense altogether the embodiment of the Czech people as they had been built up during a long period and had come in the second half of the nineteenth century to self-consciousness— a man strangely shut up in himself, a powerful mind and a steadfast will. There spoke on the right side of the chamber in the midst of the Polish seats Otto Hausner—often only wittily setting forth the results of reading, often sending shafts well aimed to all sides of the house, with a certain sense of satisfaction in himself. A thoroughly self-satisfied but clever eye sparkled behind a monocle; the other always seemed to express a satisfied "yes" to the sparkle. A speaker, however, who even then at times uttered prophetic words as to the future of Austria. What he then said ought to be read today; one would be amazed at the keenness of his vision. People then laughed, indeed, over much which years later became bitter earnest.

V

CONCERNING public life in Austria I could not then bring myself to reflections which might have taken a deeper hold in any way whatever upon my mind. I merely continued to observe the extraordinarily complicated conditions. Discussions which won my deeper interest I could have only with Karl Julius Schröer. I had the pleasure of being in his home often at that time. His own destiny was closely bound up with that of the Germans of Austria-Hungary. He was the son of Tobias Gottfried Schröer, who conducted a German college in Pressburg and wrote dramas as well as books on historical and aesthetic subjects. The latter appeared under the name Christian Oeser, and were favorite textbooks. The poetical writings of Tobias Gottfried Schröer, although they are doubtless significant and received marked recognition within restricted circles, did not become widely known. The sentiment that breathes through them was opposed to the political current dominant in Hungary. They had to be published without the author's name, partly in German regions outside Hungary. Had the trend of the author's thinking been made known in Hungary, he would have risked, not only dismissal from his post, but also severe punishment.

Karl Julius Schröer thus experienced oppression of Germanism even as a young man in his own home. Under this oppression, he developed his intimate devotion to the German nature and German literature, as well as a great devotion to everything belonging to

Goethe or pertaining to him. The history of German imaginative literature by Gervinus had a profound influence upon him.

In the fourth decade of the nineteenth century he went to Germany to pursue his studies in the German language and literature at the Universities of Leipzig, Halle, and Berlin. After his return, he was occupied in teaching German literature in his father's college and in conducting a teacher-training course. He now became acquainted with the Christmas folk-plays which were enacted every year by the German colonists in the region of Pressburg. There he was face to face with Germanism in a form deeply congenial to him. The Germans who had migrated from more westerly regions into Hungary hundreds of years before had brought with them these plays from their native land, and continued to perform them as they had done in days of old during the Christmas festival in regions which probably lay in the neighborhood of the Rhine. The Paradise story, the birth of Christ, the coming of the three kings were alive in popular form in these plays. Schröer published them, as he had heard them or had read them in old manuscripts he was able to look into at the homes of peasants, using the title *Deutsche Weihnachtspiele aus Ungarn*.[1]

Loving absorption in the German folk-life took an ever stronger hold on Schröer's mind. He made journeys for the purpose of studying German dialects in the most widely separated regions of Austria. Wherever the German folk was scattered in Slavic, Magyar, or Italian regions of the Danubian Monarchy, he wished to learn its individual character. Thus came into existence his dictionaries and grammars of the Zipser dialect, which was native to the south of the Carpathians; of the Gotschee dialect, which survived with a small fragment of German folk in Krain; the language of the Heanzes, which was spoken in western Hungary.

For Schröer these studies were never a mere scientific task. He lived with his whole soul in the manifestations of the folk nature, and wished by word and writing to bring its character to the conscious-

[1] *German Christmas Plays Out of Hungary.*

ness of those who had been uprooted from it by life. He then became a professor in Budapest. There he could not be comfortable in the presence of the then dominant current of thought; so he moved to Vienna, where at first he was entrusted with the direction of the Evangelical schools, and where he later became professor of the German language and literature. When he already occupied this position, I had the privilege of becoming acquainted with him and of entering into a close association with him. At the time when this occurred, all his reflections and his life were directed toward Goethe. He was engaged in editing the Second Part of *Faust,* and writing an introduction for this, and had already published the First Part.

When I went to call at Schröer's little library, which was also his study, I felt that I was in a spiritual atmosphere in the highest degree beneficial to my inner life. I knew even then how Schröer, on account of his writings, and especially on account of his *Geschichte der deutschen Dichtung im neunzehnten Jahrhundert,*[1] had been attacked by those who adhered to the prevailing literary-historical methods. He did not write, for instance, like the members of the Scherer school, who treated literary phenomena after the fashion of the natural scientists. He had certain sentiments and ideas about literary phenomena, and he expressed these in a purely human way, without turning his eyes much, at the moment of writing, to the "sources." It had even been said that he had written his exposition with superficial fluency.

This interested me very little. I experienced a spiritual warmth when I was with him. I had the privilege of sitting by his side for hours. Out of his inspired heart the Christmas plays lived on his lips, the spirit of the German dialects, the course of the life of literature. The relation between dialect and cultured speech became perceptible to me in a practical way. I experienced a real joy when he spoke to me, as he had already done in his lectures, of the poet of the Lower Austrian dialect, Joseph Misson, who wrote the splendid poem *Da Naaz, a niederösterreichischer Bauernbua, geht ind*

[1] *History of German Literature in the Nineteenth Century.*

Fremd.[1] Schröer was constantly giving me books from his library through which I could pursue further what had been the subject matter of our conversation. In truth, when I sat there alone with Schröer, I always had the feeling that still another was present—the spirit of Goethe. For Schröer lived so strongly in the spirit and work of Goethe that, with every sentiment or idea which entered his mind, he asked himself the question: "Would Goethe have felt or thought thus?"

I listened with the utmost sympathy of mind to everything that came from Schröer. Yet I could not do otherwise even in relation with him than to build up quite independently in my own mind that toward which I was striving in my innermost spirit. Schröer was an Idealist, and the world of ideas as such was for him that which acts as a propulsive force in the creative work of nature and of man. For me, the idea was the shadow of a wholly living world of spirit. I found it truly difficult at that time to express in words for myself the difference between Schröer's way of thinking and my own. He spoke of ideas as the propelling forces in history. He felt life in the existence of ideas. For me, the life of the spirit was *behind* the ideas, and these were only the manifestation of that life in the human mind. I could then find no other term for my way of thinking than "Objective Idealism." I wished thereby to denote that, for me, the essential truth as regards the idea is *not* the fact that this appears in the human subject but the fact that, just as color appears on a physical object, so the idea appears on the *spiritual object* and that the human mind—the subject—perceives it there as the eye perceives color on a living being.

My conception Schröer very largely satisfied, however, in the form of expression he used when we talked about that which reveals itself as the "folk-soul." He spoke of this as of a real spiritual being which comes to manifestation in the totality of the individual human beings who belong to one folk. In this matter his words took on a character which did not belong to the mere denoting of ideas ab-

[1] *Ignatius, a Peasant Boy of Lower Austria, Goes Abroad.*

stractly held. And it was thus that we both observed the structure of ancient Austria and the individualities of the several folk-souls active there.

In this aspect, it was possible for me to form ideas about the state of public affairs which penetrated more deeply into my mind.

Thus my experience at that time was strongly bound up with my relation to Karl Julius Schröer. What was more foreign to his interests, however, but that by means of which I strove most of all for an inner explanation, was the natural sciences. I wished to know that my Objective Idealism was in harmony also with the science of nature.

It was during the period of my most vital intercourse with Schröer that the question of the relation between the spiritual and natural worlds came before my mind in a new form. This happened at first quite independently of Goethe's way of thinking in the natural sciences. For Schröer also could tell me nothing decisive about this field of Goethe's work. He was happy whenever he found in one or another natural scientist a benevolent recognition of Goethe's observations on the nature of plant and animal; as to Goethe's theory of color, however, he was met on all sides among scientifically educated persons with decisive disapproval. Thus in this direction he developed no special opinion.

My relation to natural science was not at this time of my life influenced from this direction, although in my intercourse with Schröer I came into close touch with Goethe's intellectual life. My relation was determined much more by the difficulties I experienced when I had to think through the facts of optics in the sense of the physicists.

I found that light and sound, as conceived in the natural sciences, were thought of in an analogy which is inapplicable. The expressions "sound in general" and "light in general" were used. The analogy lay in the following conception. The individual tones and sounds were viewed as specially modified air-vibrations, and the objective element in sound, outside of man's experience of the sensation of sound, was viewed as a state of vibration of air. Light was thought of similarly. What occurs outside the human being when he perceives a phenomenon caused by light was defined as vibration in ether. The colors, then, are specially formed ether-vibrations. This analogy became at that time an actual torment for my mental life. For I believed myself perfectly clear in the perception that the concept "sound" is merely an abstract combination of the individual occurrences in the sphere of sound, whereas "light" signifies in itself a concrete entity, in contrast with the phenomena of the illuminated world. "Sound" was for me a composite abstract concept; "light" a concrete reality. I said to myself that light is really not perceived by the senses; "colors" are perceived *by reason of* light, which is everywhere manifest in the color-percept but is not itself sensibly perceived. "White" light is not light, but is also a color.

Thus light became for me a real entity *in the sense world,* which, however, is itself extrasensory. I recalled now the opposition between Nominalism and Realism, as this was developed in Scholasticism. The Realists maintained that concepts are real entities which exist in things and are simply drawn out of these by human cognition. The Nominalists maintained, on the contrary, that concepts are mere names, formed by the human being, which combine the manifoldness in things but have no existence in things themselves. It now seemed to me that the sound-experience must be viewed in the Nominalist manner and the experiences which proceed from light in the Realist manner.

I applied this orientation to the optics of the physicists. I had to reject much in this science. Then I arrived at views which paved a way for me to Goethe's color theory. From this side I opened a door for myself to Goethe's writings on natural science. I first took to Schröer brief papers I had written on the basis of my conceptions in natural science. He could make but little of them; for they were not yet worked out in accordance with Goethe's mode of conception, but I had introduced at the end only the remark that, not until people came to the point of thinking about nature in the manner I had set forth would proper credit be given among scientists to Goethe's research. Schröer felt intensely pleased when I made such a statement, but beyond this nothing came of the matter. The situation in which I then found myself is illustrated through the following incident. Schröer related to me one day that he had spoken with a colleague who was a physicist. The man said: Well, Goethe opposed Newton, and Newton was "such a genius." To which Schröer replied: But Goethe "also was a genius." Thus I felt again that I had a riddle to solve which I faced entirely alone.

The conceptions at which I had arrived in physical optics seemed to me to form a bridge between what is revealed to insight into the spiritual world and what is derived from research in the natural sciences. I felt a need at that time to test through *sense-experience,* by means of certain experiments in optics arranged by myself, the *ideas* I had formed regarding the nature of light and that of color. It was not easy for me to buy the things needed for such experiments; for the means of livelihood I derived from tutoring were little enough. Whatever was in any way possible for me I did in order to arrive at such arrangements for experimenting with regard to the theory of light as would lead to an unprejudiced insight into the facts of nature in this field.

With the physicist's usual arrangements for experimentation I was familiar through my work in Reitlinger's physics laboratory. With the mathematical treatment of optics I was familiar, for I had pursued thorough courses in just this field. In spite of all objections raised by the physicists against Goethe's theory of color, I was driven by my own experiments further away from the customary view and toward Goethe. I became aware that all such experimentation is only the establishment of certain facts in connection with light—to use an expression of Goethe—and not experimentation with light itself. I said to myself that colors are not, as Newton thinks, produced out of light; they come to manifestation when obstructions hinder the free unfolding of light. It seemed to me that this was to be inferred directly from the experiments.

But light was thus removed for me from the category of truly physical elements of reality. It presented itself as a midway stage between the realities perceptible to the senses and those visible to the spirit.

I was not inclined to engage in merely philosophical processes of thinking about these things. But I laid strong emphasis upon *reading the facts of nature aright*. It then became constantly clearer to me that light itself does *not* enter the realm of the sense-perceptible, but remains on the farther side of this, while colors appear when the sense-perceptible is brought into the realm of light.

I now felt compelled afresh to press forward toward a knowledge of the natural sciences from the most diverse directions. I was led again to the study of anatomy and physiology. I observed the members of the human, animal, and plant organisms in their formations. In this study I came in my own way upon Goethe's theory of metamorphosis. I became more and more aware that the picture of nature which is attainable through the senses penetrates through to that which was visible to me in a spiritual way.

If in this spiritual way I directed my look to the soul activity of the human being, to thinking, feeling, and willing, the "spiritual man" took form for me even as a clearly visible image. I could not linger in the abstractions of which it is customary to think when speaking of thinking, feeling, and willing. In these inner manifestations of life I saw creative forces which placed the "human being as spirit" spiritually before me. If I then directed my look to the sense-appearance of man, this was supplemented to my reflective contemplation through the spirit-form which holds sway in the sense-perceptible.

I came upon the *sensible-supersensible form* of which Goethe speaks, which is interposed, both for true natural vision and also for spiritual vision, between what the senses grasp and what the spirit perceives.

Anatomy and physiology struggled through, step by step, to this sensible-supersensible form. In this struggling through my look fell, at first in a very imperfect way, upon the threefold organization of the human being, about which—after having pursued my studies concerning it for thirty years in silence—I first began to speak publicly in my book *Von Seelenrätseln*.[1] At the beginning, it became clear to me that, in the portion of the human organization in which the formation is directed chiefly to the nerves and the senses, the sensible-supersensible form also stamps itself most strongly upon the sense-perceptible. The head organization appeared to me as that in which the sensible-supersensible also becomes most strongly manifest in the sensible form. On the other hand, I was forced to look upon the organization consisting of the limbs as that in which the sensible-supersensible most completely conceals itself, so that in this organization the forces active in nature external to man continue their work in the shaping of the human body. Between these two poles of the human organization everything seemed to me to exist which expresses itself in a rhythmic way, the processes of breathing, circulation, and the like.

At that time I found no one to whom I could have spoken of these perceptions. If I intimated here or there something about them, they were looked upon at once as the result of a philosophical idea, whereas I was certain that they were disclosed to me out of anatomical and physiological empirical knowledge free of preconception.

For the soul-depressing mood which grew out of this isolation in the matter of my perceptions, I found inner release only when I read again and again the conversation that Goethe had with Schiller as the two went away from a meeting of the Society for Scientific Research in Jena. They were both of the opinion that nature should not be considered in such piecemeal fashion as had been done in a lecture by the botanist Batsch which they had heard. Goethe sketched before the eyes of Schiller with a few strokes his "archetypal plant." This represented, in a sensible-supersensible form, the plant as a whole, out of which leaf, blossom, and so forth, reproducing the whole in detail, take form. Schiller, because he had not yet overcome the Kantian point of view, could see in this "whole"

[1] *Riddles of the Soul.*

only an "idea" formed by human reason through the observation of the details. Goethe would not allow this to pass. He "saw" the whole *spiritually* as he saw the group of details with his senses, and he admitted no difference in principle between the spiritual and the sensible perception, but only a transition from one to the other. To him it was clear that both had the right to a place in empirical reality. Schiller, however, did not cease to maintain that the archetypal plant was no experience but an idea. Goethe then replied, on the basis of his way of thinking, that in this case he saw his idea before him with his eyes.

I derived comfort after a long struggle of the mind from what came to me out of the understanding of these words of Goethe, to which I felt that I had penetrated. Goethe's way of viewing nature appeared to me as in keeping with spirit.

Impelled now by an inner necessity, I had to study in detail all of Goethe's scientific writings. At first, I had no thought of undertaking an interpretation of these writings, such as I soon afterward published in the introductions to them in Kürschner's *Deutsche Nationalliteratur*.[1] I thought, rather, of setting forth independently some field or other of natural science as this science now appeared before me in a form in keeping with the spirit.

The circumstances of my external life were at that time not suited to such an undertaking. I had to do tutoring in the most diverse subjects. The "pedagogical" situations into which I had to find my way were complex enough. For example, there appeared in Vienna a Prussian officer who for some reason or other had been compelled to leave the German military service. He wished to prepare himself to enter the Austrian army as an officer of engineers. Through a peculiar course of destiny, I became his teacher in mathematics and natural-scientific subjects. I found in this "instructing" the deepest satisfaction; for my "pupil" was an extraordinarily lovable man who craved human intercourse with me when we had put behind us the mathematical and scientific developments he needed for his

[1] *German National Literature.*

preparation. In other cases also, as in those of students who had completed their work and were preparing for their doctoral examinations, I had to give instruction especially in mathematics and natural science.

Because of this necessity of working again and again through the natural sciences of that time, I had ample opportunity to immerse myself in contemporary views in those fields. In teaching I could give out only those views; what was of greatest interest to me in relation to the science of nature I had still to carry locked up within myself.

My activity as a tutor, which afforded me at that time the sole means of livelihood, preserved me from one-sidedness. I had to learn many things in order to be able to teach them. Thus I found my way into the "mysteries" of book-keeping, for I found opportunity to give instruction in just this subject.

I derived from Schröer the most fruitful stimulus also in the field of pedogogical thinking. He had worked for years as director of the Evangelical schools in Vienna, and he had set forth his experiences in the charming little book *Unterrichtsfragen*.[1] What I read in this could then be discussed with him. In matters of education and instruction, he often spoke against the mere imparting of information and in favor of the development of the full and entire being of man.

[1] *Problems of Teaching.*

VI

IN THE DOMAIN of pedagogy destiny brought me a special task. I was recommended as tutor in a family where there were four boys. To three I had to give only the preparatory instruction of the elementary school and then assistance in the work of the secondary school. The fourth, who was almost ten years old, was entrusted to me for all his education. He was the child of sorrow to his parents, especially to his mother. When I went to live in the home, he had scarcely learned the most rudimentary elements of reading, writing, and arithmetic. He was considered so abnormal in his physical and mental development that the family had doubts as to his capacity for being educated. His thinking was slow and dull. Even slight mental exertion caused a headache, lowering of vital functions, pallor, and alarming mental symptoms.

After I had come to know the child, I formed the opinion that an education suited to such a bodily and psychic organism must awaken the sleeping faculties, and I proposed to the parents that they leave the child's training to me. The mother had enough confidence to accept this proposal, and I was thus able to set myself this special educational task.

I had to find access to a soul which was, as it were, in a state resembling sleep, and which must gradually be enabled to gain the mastery over the bodily manifestations. In a certain sense, one had first to fit the soul into the body. I was thoroughly convinced that the boy really had great mental capacities, though they were then hidden.

This made my task a profoundly satisfying one. I was soon able to bring the child into a loving attachment to me. This caused the mere intercourse between us to awaken his sleeping faculties of soul. For his instruction I had to devise special methods. Every fifteen minutes beyond a certain time allotted for instruction caused injury to his health. To many subjects of instruction, the boy had great difficulty in relating himself.

This educational task became a source from which I myself learned very much. Through the method of instruction that I had to employ, there was laid open to my view the association between the spirit-soul element and the bodily element in the human being. It was then that I went through my real course of study in physiology and psychology. I became aware that instructing and educating must become an art having its foundation in a genuine knowledge of the human being. I had with great care to follow out an economic principle. I frequently had to spend two hours in preparing for half an hour's instruction in order to get the material for instruction into such a form that, in the least time and with the least strain upon the mental and physical powers of the child, I might reach his highest capacity for achievement. The order of the subjects of instruction had to be carefully considered; the division of the entire day into periods had to be properly determined. I had the satisfaction of seeing the child in the course of two years catch up in the work of the elementary school and successfully pass the examination for entrance into the *Gymnasium*. Moreover, his condition of health had materially improved. The existing hydrocephalic condition was markedly diminishing. I was able to advise the parents to send the child to a public school. It seemed to me necessary that he should find his life development in company with other boys. I continued to be a tutor for several years in the family, and gave special attention to this boy, who was wholly dependent upon making his way through school in such a manner that his home activities should be carried through in the spirit in which they had been begun. I then had the inducement, in the way I have already mentioned, to increase my knowledge of Latin and Greek, for I was responsible for tutoring this boy and another in the family for the *Gymnasium* lessons.

I must needs feel grateful to destiny for having brought me into such a life relationship. For through this means I gained in a living way a knowledge of the nature of the human being which I do not believe I could have developed so vitally in any other way. Moreover, I was taken into the family in an extraordinarily affectionate manner; we came to live a beautiful life in common. The father of this boy was a sales-agent for Indian and American cotton. I was able to get a glimpse into the working of business, and of much that is connected with this. In this way also I learned a great deal. I had an inside view of the conduct of a branch of an unusually interesting import business, and could observe the intercourse between business friends and the interlinking of many commercial and industrial activities.

My young charge was successfully guided through the *Gymnasium:* I continued with him till the next to the last class. By that time he had made such progress that he no longer needed me. After completing the *Gymnasium,* he entered the School of Medicine, became a physician, and in this capacity was later a victim of the World War. The mother, who had become a true friend of mine because of what I had done for her boy, and who clung to this child of sorrow with the most devoted love, soon followed him in death. The father had already gone from this world.

A good portion of my youthful life was bound up with the task which had thus come about for me. For a number of years I went every summer with the family of the children whom I had to tutor to the Attersee in the Salzkammergut, and there became familiar with the noble Alpine nature of Upper Austria. I was gradually able to eliminate the private lessons I had continued to give to others even after beginning this tutoring. Thus I had time left for prosecuting my own studies.

Before coming into this family, I had enjoyed little opportunity in my life for sharing in the games of children. Thus it came about that my "play-time" came after my twentieth year. I had then to learn also how to play games, for I had to direct the games. This I did with great enjoyment. Indeed, I think that I have played no less during my life than other men; only, in my case what is usually completed in this sphere before the tenth year had to be made up from the twenty-third to the twenty-eighth.

It was during this period that I was occupied with the philosophy of Eduard von Hartmann. As I studied his theory of knowledge, continual opposition was aroused within me. The opinion that the genuinely real exists as the unconscious beyond conscious experience, and that the latter is nothing more than an unreal pictorial reflection of the real, was to me profoundly repugnant. In opposition to this I postulated that the experiences of consciousness can, through the strengthening of the inner life of the soul, become immersed in the truly real. It was clear in my own mind that the divine-spiritual reveals itself in man if he himself makes this revelation possible through his own inner life.

The pessimism of Eduard von Hartmann deemed to me the result of an utterly erroneous questioning of human life. I had to conceive man as striving toward the goal of obtaining from the source of his own inner being that which will fill his life in a manner satisfying to him. I asked myself the question: If, through the world order, a "best life" were simply allotted to man from the beginning, how could he make of this inner fountain a flowing stream? The external world order arrives at a stage in evolution at which it has conferred good and bad on things and phenomena. Only then does the human being awake to his own consciousness and guide the evolution further, but in such a way that this evolution takes the direction it is freely to follow, not from things and phenomena, but only from the fountain head of being. The mere raising of the question of pessimism or optimism seemed to me to run counter to the free being of man. I frequently said to myself: "How could man be the free creator of his highest happiness if a measure of happiness were allotted to him through the external world order?"

On the other hand, Hartmann's work *Phänomenologie des sittlichen Bewusstseins*[1] attracted me. There, I found, the moral evolution of man is traced according to the clue of what is empirically observable. Speculative thinking is not linked there—as is the case in Hartmann's theory of knowledge and metaphysics—to unknown being existing beyond consciousness; on the contrary, what can be experienced as morality is grasped in its phenomenal form. And it was clear to me that philosophical speculation must not think *beyond* the phenomena if it seeks to arrive at the truly real. The phenomena of the world manifest of themselves this truly real if only the conscious soul makes itself ready to grasp this reality. He who takes into consciousness only what is apprehensible to the senses may seek for real being in a Beyond realm, outside of consciousness; but one who apprehends the spiritual in his perception speaks of this as something on this side, not as existing in a Beyond, in an epistemological sense. Hartmann's reflection about the moral world seemed to me acceptable, because in this reflection his Beyond standpoint withdraws wholly into the background, and he confines himself to what can be observed. Through a deeper penetration into phenomena, even to the point where these disclose their spiritual essential nature—it was in this way, I believed, that knowledge of real being, of existence, is achieved, not through inferential reasoning as to what is "behind" phenomena.

Since I was always striving to appreciate a human achievement in its positive aspect, Eduard von Hartmann's philosophy became valuable to me, in spite of the fact that its fundamental tendency and its conception of life were repugnant to me; for it cast a penetrating light upon many phenomena. Even in those writings of the "philosopher of the unconscious" from which I dissented in principle I found, nevertheless, much that was immensely stimulating.

[1] *The Phenomenology of Moral Consciousness.*

So it was also with the popular writings of Eduard von Hartmann which dealt with cultural-historical, pedagogical, and political problems. I found in this pessimist "sound" conceptions of life such as I could not discover in many an optimist. It was just in connection with him that I experienced what I needed: to be able to appreciate even when I had to oppose.

It was thus that I sat many times at the Attersee till late in the evening—after I could leave my boys to themselves and after the starry heavens had been admired from the balcony of the house— in studying *The Phenomenology of Moral Consciousness* and *Das religiöse Bewusstsein der Menschheit in der Stufenfolge seiner Entwicklung*.[1] While reading these writings, I attained to an ever increasing assurance as to my own epistemological standpoints.

Upon the recommendation of Schröer, Joseph Kürschner invited me in 1884 to edit Goethe's scientific writings with introductions and running explanatory comments, as part of an edition of *German National Literature* planned by him. Schröer, who had taken responsibility for Goethe's dramas in the large collective work, was to preface the first volume assigned to me with an introductory foreword. (In this he analyzed the way in which Goethe, as poet and as thinker, was related to the contemporary cultural life. In the world view introduced by the age of natural science that followed after Goethe he saw a falling away from the spiritual height upon which Goethe had been standing. The task which had been assigned to me in the editing of Goethe's scientific writings was characterized in a comprehensive way in this foreword.)

For me this task included the fixing of my relation with natural science, on the one hand, and with Goethe's entire world view, on the other. Now that I had to present to the public such an exposition, it was necessary for me to bring to a certain conclusion all that I had thus far acquired in the form of a world view.

Until that time I had occupied myself as a writer with nothing more than a few articles for the press. It was not easy for me to

[1] *The Religious Consciousness of Humanity in the Stages of Its Evolution.*

reduce to written form what constituted a vital experience in a way that I could consider worthy of publication. I always had the feeling that what had been developed within appeared in paltry form when I had to present it as a finished exposition. Thus all literary endeavors became for me a source of continual inner dissatisfaction.

The way of thinking which has been dominant in natural science since the beginning of its great influence upon the civilization of the nineteenth century seemed to me ill adapted for reaching an understanding of what Goethe strove to achieve for the science of nature, and actually did in large measure achieve.

I beheld in Goethe a personality who, by reason of the special spiritual relation in which he placed man with reference to the world, was in a position also to relate the science of nature in the right way to the total realm of human creative action. The mode of thinking of the period into which I had grown up appeared to me fit for forming ideas only regarding lifeless nature. I considered it incapable of entering with powers of cognition into the realm of living nature. I said to myself that, in order to arrive at ideas which can mediate knowledge of the organic, it is necessary first to endue with life the intellectual concepts themselves which are adapted for an understanding of inorganic nature. For these concepts seemed to me dead, and fit, therefore, for grasping only that which is dead.

How ideas became endued with life in Goethe's mind, how they became idea-formations, this was what I sought to set forth in order to interpret Goethe's view of nature.

What Goethe thought and elaborated in detail as to this or that field of the science of nature appeared to me of less importance than the *central* discovery that I had to attribute to him. This I saw in the fact that he discovered how one must think about the organic in order to grasp it in knowledge.

I found that the science of mechanics satisfies the need for knowledge in that it develops concepts in a rational manner in the human mind which it then finds realized in the sense-experience of that which is lifeless. Goethe was to me the founder of the science of *organics,* which in like manner is applicable to what is alive. When I looked back in the history of the modern intellectual life to Galileo, I had to observe how he, by the development of concepts about the inorganic, had given to modern natural science its present form. What he had achieved for the inorganic Goethe had striven to attain for the organic. Goethe became for me the Galileo of the organic.

For the first volume of Goethe's writings on natural science, I had first to elaborate his ideas on metamorphosis. It was difficult for me to express the relation between the *living idea-form* through which the organic can be known and the *formless idea* suited to enable one to grasp the inorganic. But it seemed to me that my whole task depended upon making this point perfectly clear in the right way.

In cognizing the inorganic, concept is linked to concept in order to survey the correlation of forces which bring about an effect in nature. In the case of the organic, it is necessary so to cause one concept to grow out of another that, in the progressive living metamorphosis of concepts, there come to light images of that which appears in nature as an entity that has taken form. This Goethe strove to do in that he sought to hold fast in his mind an image-in-idea of a leaf that is not a fixed lifeless concept but such a one as might present itself in the most varied forms. If these forms in the mind are permitted to proceed one out of another, the whole plant is thus constructed. One creates in the mind, in the form of ideas, the process whereby nature in actual fashion shapes the plant.

If the effort is made in this way to conceive the plant entity, one thus stands much nearer in spirit to the world of nature than in conceiving the inorganic by means of formless concepts. For the inorganic, only a mental fantasm is conceived of that which is present in nature in a manner that is void of spirit. But in a plant's coming into existence there is something remotely resembling what arises in the human mind as a conception of the plant. One becomes aware of how nature, in bringing forth the organic, is herself bringing into action within herself essential being similar to the spirit.

In the introduction to Goethe's botanical writings, I desired to show how in his theory of metamorphosis he took the direction of conceiving the workings of organic nature as similar to those of spirit.

Still more like the spirit, for Goethe's way of thinking, seemed the working of nature in the realm of the animal and in the natural substratum of the human being.

In relation to the animal-human, Goethe began by seeing through an error he had observed among his contemporaries. These sought to ascribe a special position in nature to the organic bases of the human being by finding individual distinctions between man and animal. They found such a distinction in the intermaxillary bone possessed by animals, in which their upper incisor teeth are imbedded. In man, they said, such a special intermediary bone in the upper jaw is lacking; that his upper jaw consists of a single piece.

This seemed to Goethe an error. For him the human form was a metamorphosis of the animal to a higher stage. Everything that appears in the formation of the animal must be present also in that of the human being, only in a higher form so that the human organism may become the bearer of the self-conscious spirit.

In the elevation of the whole form of man Goethe saw the distinction from the animal, not in details.

Step by step does one perceive the organic creative forces become more spirit-like as one rises from consideration of the plant entity to the varied forms of the animals. In the organic form of man, creative forces are active which bring about the highest metamorphosis of the animal shape. These forces are present in the coming of the human organism into existence; and they finally become manifest as the human spirit, after having formed in the natural basic parts a vessel fit to receive them in their form of existence free from nature.

In this conception of the human organism it seemed to me that Goethe had anticipated everything justifiable which was later asserted on the basis of Darwinism, concerning the relation of the human being to the animal. But it seemed to me also that everything unjustifiable had been rejected. The materialistic interpretation of what Darwin discovered leads to the adoption of conceptions based upon the kinship of man and animal which deny the spirit where it appears in its highest form in earthly existence—in man. Goethe's conception leads one to see a spiritual creation in the animal form which has simply not yet arrived at the stage at which spirit as such can *live*. That which *lives* in man as spirit *creates* in the animal form at a preliminary stage; and, in the case of man, it metamorphoses this form in such a way that it can then appear, not only as creative, but also as self-experiencing.

Viewed in this way, Goethe's way of conceiving nature becomes one which, by tracing the natural development from the inorganic to the organic, leads natural science over into a spiritual science. To bring out this fact was my chief endeavor in working up the first volume of Goethe's writings on natural science. For this reason I caused my introduction to come to a close in the statement that Darwinism establishes a one-sided view which must be restored to wholeness by Goethe's way of thinking.

How one must cognize in order to penetrate into the phenomena of life,—this is what I wished to show in discussing Goethe's view of the organic. I soon came to feel that this way of presenting the matter required a basis to support it. The nature of cognition was then represented by my contemporaries in a way that could never arrive at Goethe's view. The epistemologists had in mind natural science as it then existed. What they said in regard to the character of knowledge held good only for a comprehension of inorganic nature. There could be no agreement between what I must say as to Goethe's kind of knowledge and the theories of knowledge generally held at that time.

What I had set forth, therefore, on the basis of Goethe's theory of the organic sent me afresh to the theory of knowledge. I had in mind such theories as that of Otto Liebmann, which expressed in the most varied forms the proposition that human consciousness can never get outside itself; that it must, therefore, be content to live with what reality sends into the human mind, and that which becomes manifest within in spiritual form. If one views the matter in this way, it is impossible to affirm, after the manner of Goethe, that one perceives in organic nature something akin to spirit. It is necessary to look for spirit within human consciousness and to consider a spiritual conception of nature inadmissible.

I discovered that there was no theory of knowledge fitting Goethe's form of knowledge. This induced me to sketch, at least, such a theory. I wrote my *Erkenntnistheorie der Goethe'schen Weltanschauung*[1] out of an inner need before I proceeded to prepare the other volumes of Goethe's writings on natural science. The brochure was finished in 1886.

[1] *The Theory of Knowledge Implicit in Goethe's World-Conception.*

VII

I wrote down the ideas of a *Theory of Knowledge Implicit in Goethe's World-Conception*[1] at a time when destiny had led me into a family which made it possible for me to spend many happy hours and a fortunate chapter of my life within its circle. Among my friends there had been for some time one whom I had come to hold very dear because of his gay and sunny disposition, his accurate observations upon life and persons, and his whole manner, so open and loyal. He introduced me and other mutual friends into his home. There we met, in addition to this friend, two daughters of the family, his sisters, and a man whom we soon had to recognize as the fiancé of the older daughter.

In the background in this family hovered something unknown that we were never able to see. This was the father of the brother and sisters. He was there, and yet not there. We learned from the most various sources something about the man who was to us unknown. According to what we were told, he must have been something extraordinary. At first, the brother and sisters never spoke of their father, even though he must have been in the next room. Only gradually did they begin to make one or another remark about him. Every word was inspired by feelings of genuine reverence. One felt that in this man they honored a significant human being. But one felt also that they were anxious lest by chance we should happen to see him.

[1] Anthroposophic Press, New York.

Our conversation in the family circle was generally of a literary character. In order, then, to refer to one thing or another, many a book was brought by the brother or sisters from the father's library, and this circumstance brought it about that I became acquainted, little by little, with much which the man in the next room read, although I never had the opportunity to see him.

At last I could no longer do otherwise than to inquire about much that concerned the unknown man. And thus, from the words of the brother and sisters—which held back much, and yet revealed much —there gradually arose in my mind an image of the strange personality. I loved the man, who to me also seemed a significant person. I came finally to reverence in him a man whom the hard experiences of life had brought to the pass of dealing thenceforth only with the world within himself and of foregoing all human intercourse.

One day we visitors were told that the man was ill, and soon afterwards the news of his death had to be conveyed to us. The brother and sisters entrusted to me the funeral address. I said what my heart impelled me to say about a personality whom I had come to know only in the way I have described. It was a funeral at which only the family, the fiancé of the elder daughter, and my friends were present. The brother and sisters said to me that I had given a true picture of their father in the funeral address; and, from the way in which they spoke and from their tears, I could not but feel that this was their real conviction. Moreover, I really knew that the man was as near to me in spirit as if I had had much intercourse with him.

Between the younger daughter and me there gradually came about a beautiful friendship. She really had in her something of the primal type of the German maiden. She bore within her nothing of an education acquired by routine, but manifested an original and charming naturalness together with a noble reserve. This reserve of hers caused a like reserve in me. We loved each other, and both of us were fully aware of this; but neither of us could overcome the diffidence which kept us from saying that we loved each other. Thus the love lived between the words we spoke to each other, and not in the words themselves. I felt the relation as to our souls was of the most intimate character, but it found no possibility of taking even a single step beyond what is of the soul.

I was happy in this friendship; I felt my friend as something sun-like in my life. Yet this life later bore us far apart. In place of hours of happy companionship there remained only a short-lived correspondence, followed by the melancholy memory of a beautiful period of my past life—a memory, however, which through all my later life has arisen again and again from the depths of my soul.

It was at this time that I once went to Schröer. He was altogether filled with an impression which he had just received. He had become acquainted with the poems of Marie Eugenie delle Grazie. She had published at that time a volume of poems; an epic, *Herman;* a drama, *Saul;* and a story, *Die Zigeunerin.*[1] Schröer spoke enthusiastically of these poetical writings. "And all these have been written by a young person before completing her sixteenth year!" he said. Then he added that Robert Zimmermann had declared she was the only real genius he had known in his life.

Schröer's enthusiasm now led me also to read the productions in rapid succession. I wrote an article about the poet. This brought me the great pleasure of being permitted to call upon her. During this call I had the opportunity for a conversation with the poet which has often come to mind during my life. She had already begun to work upon an undertaking in the grand style, her epic *Robespierre.* She discussed the main ideas of this composition. Even then there was manifest in her conversation a basic mood of pessimism. I felt her temperament to be such that, in a personality like *Robespierre,* she wished to represent the tragedy involved in all idealism. Ideals arise in the human heart, but they have no power against the cruel destructive action of nature, empty of all ideas, who utters against everything ideal her pitiless cry: "Thou art mere illusion, a fantasm of my own, which ever again I hurl back into nothingness."

This was her conviction. The poet then spoke to me of a further

[1] *The Gypsy Woman.*

poetic plan, for a *Satanide*. She wished to represent the Antitype of God as the Primal Being which is the Power revealing itself to man in cruel, ruinous nature, void of ideas. She spoke with genuine inspiration of this Power from the abyss of being, dominant over all being. I went away from the poet profoundly shocked. The greatness with which she had spoken remained impressed upon me; the content of her ideas was the opposite of everything that I had in mind as a conception of the world. But I was never inclined to withhold my admiration and interest from what seemed to me great, even when it repelled me utterly by its content. Indeed, I said to myself that such antitheses in the world must surely somewhere find their reconciliation. And this enabled me to enter into what repelled me just as if it lay in the same direction as the conception held by my own mind.

Shortly after this I was invited to the home of delle Grazie. She was to read from her *Robespierre* before a number of persons, among whom were Schröer and his wife and also a woman friend of his family. We listened to scenes of lofty poetic rhythm, but with a pessimistic undertone, characterized by a richly colored naturalism: life depicted in its most terrible aspects. Great human beings, inwardly deceived by Fate, rose to the surface and sank below in deeply moving tragedy. This was my impression. Schröer became indignant. For him, art must not descend into such abysses of the "terrible." The women withdrew. They had experienced a sort of convulsion. I could not agree with Schröer, for he seemed to me wholly filled with the idea that what is terrible in the experience of a human being must never become the content of poetic art, even though the terrible is sincerely experienced. Delle Grazie soon afterward published a poem in which Nature is celebrated as the Highest Power, but in such a way that she mocks at everything ideal, which she calls into existence only in order to delude man, and which she hurls back into nothingness when this delusion has been accomplished.

In relation to this composition, I wrote a paper entitled *Die Natur und unsere Ideale,*[1] which I did not publish but had privately printed in a small number of copies. In this I discussed the apparent correctness of delle Grazie's view. I said that to me a view which does not shut out the hostility manifested by nature against human ideals is of a higher order than a "superficial optimism" which blinds itself to the abysses of existence. But I said also in regard to this matter that *the free inner being of man* creates out of itself that which gives meaning and content to life, and that this being could not fully unfold itself if a prodigal nature bestowed upon it from without what should arise within.

Because of this paper I had a painful experience. When Schröer had received it, he wrote me that, if I thought in such a way about pessimism, we had never understood each other, and that any one who spoke in such a way about nature as I had done in the paper showed thereby that he was unable to take in a sufficiently profound sense Goethe's words: "Know thyself, and live at peace with the world."

I was affected to the bottom of my soul when I received these lines from the person to whom I felt the most devoted attachment. Schröer could be passionately aroused when he became aware of a sin against the harmony in art manifest as beauty. He turned away from delle Grazie when, according to his conception, he was forced to observe this sin. And he considered the admiration that I retained for the poet as a breaking away both from him and also from Goethe. He failed to see in my paper what I said about the *human spirit* which overcomes from within itself the hindrances of nature; he was offended because I said that external nature could not be the creator of true inner satisfaction for man. I wished to set forth the meaninglessness of pessimism in spite of its correctness within certain limits; Schröer saw in every inclination toward pessimism something that he called "the slag of burned-out spirits."

In the home of Marie Eugenie delle Grazie I passed some of the happy hours of my life. On Saturdays she always received visitors.

[1] *Nature and Our Ideals.*

Those who came were persons of divers spiritual tendencies. The poet formed the center of the group. She read aloud from her poetical works; she spoke in the spirit of her world view in most positive language. The light of these ideas she cast upon human life. It was by no means the light of the sun. Always, in truth, only the somber light of the moon. Threatening, overcast skies. But from human dwellings arose flames of fire into the murky air, as if carrying the passions and illusions in which men are consumed. All this, nevertheless, humanly gripping, always fascinating, the bitterness enveloped in the noble magic of a wholly spiritualized personality.

At delle Grazie's side was Laurenz Müllner, a Catholic priest, teacher of the poet and later her discreet and noble friend. He was at that time professor of Christian philosophy in the theological faculty of the University. The impression he made, not only by his face but in his whole figure, was that of one whose intellectual development had been accompanied by an ascetic life of the soul. A sceptic in things philosophical, thoroughly grounded in all aspects of philosophy, in views on art and literature. He wrote for the Catholic clerical journal *Vaterland* stimulating articles on artistic and literary subjects. The poet's pessimistic view of the world and of life fell always from his lips also.

Both were united in a violent antipathy toward Goethe; on the other hand their interest was directed toward Shakespeare and the later writers, children of the sorrowful burden of life and of the naturalistic aberrations of human nature. Dostoevski they loved warmly; Leopold von Sacher-Masoch they looked upon as a brilliant writer who shrank from no truth in representing what was growing up in the morass of modern life, as all too human and worthy of destruction. In Laurenz Müllner the antipathy to Goethe took on something of the color of the Catholic theologian. He praised Baumgarten's monograph, which characterized Goethe as the antithesis of what is deserving of human aspiration. In delle Grazie there was something like a deep personal antipathy to Goethe.

About the two were gathered professors of the theological faculty, Catholic priests of the very finest scholarship. Always most intensely stimulating of all was the priest of the Cistercian Order of the Holy Cross, Wilhelm Neumann. Müllner justly esteemed him because of his comprehensive scholarship. He said to me once when, in the absence of Neumann, I spoke with enthusiastic admiration of his comprehensive scholarship: "Yes, indeed, Professor Neumann knows the whole world and three villages besides." I liked to accompany the learned man when we went away from delle Grazie's at the same time. I thus had many conversations with this "ideal" of a scientific man who was at the same time a "true son of the Church." I should like to mention here only two of these. One was in regard to the being of Christ. I expressed my view to the effect that Jesus of Nazareth, by reason of supramundane influence, received the Christ into himself, and that Christ, as a spiritual Being, has lived with human evolution since the Mystery of Golgotha. This conversation remained deeply imprinted upon my mind, for it was profoundly significant for me. There were really three persons engaged in that conversation: Professor Neumann and I, and a third unseen, the personification of Catholic dogmatic theology, visible to the eye of the spirit, who appeared as if threatening while accompanying Professor Neumann from behind, always reprovingly tapping him on the shoulder whenever the subtle logic of the scholar led him too far in agreement with me. It was curious how often the first clause of the latter's sentences would be reversed in the second clause. There I was face to face with the Catholic way of life in one of its best representatives. It was through him that I learned to esteem it, but also to know it through and through.

Another time we discussed the question of repeated earth lives. The professor then listened to me, spoke of all sorts of literature in which something on this subject could be found; he often shook his head slightly but evidently had no inclination to enter into the substance of a topic which seemed to him queer. And yet this conversation also became important for me. The uncomfortableness with which Neumann *felt* the opinions he did not utter in response to my statements was deeply impressed on my memory.

The historians of the Church and other theologians were Saturday callers. Besides, there came now and then the philosopher Adolf Stöhr, Goswine von Berlepsch, the deeply sensitive story-teller Emilie Mataja (who bore the pen-name Emil Mariot), the poet and writer Fritz Lemmermayer, and the composer Stross. Fritz Lemmermayer, with whom I was later on terms of intimate friendship, I came to know during one of delle Grazie's afternoons. A quite peculiar person. Whatever interested him he expressed with inwardly measured dignity. In his outward appearance he resembled equally the musician Rubinstein and the actor Lewinsky. He had developed almost a religious worship of Hebbel. He had definite views on art and life born out of a sagacious and understanding heart, and these were unusually fixed. He has written the interesting and profound novel, *Der Alchimist*,[1] and much besides that is characterized by beauty and depth of thought. He knew how to place the least things in life at the point of view of the important. I recall how I once visited him in his charming little room in a side street in Vienna, together with other friends. He himself had just prepared his meal— two soft-boiled eggs in an instantaneous boiler, together with bread. He remarked with emphasis while the water was boiling to cook the eggs for us: "This will be delicious!" In a later phase of my life I shall have occasion again to speak of him.

Alfred Stross, the composer, was a gifted man but one by nature deeply pessimistic. When he took his seat at the piano in delle Grazie's home and played his études, one had the feeling: Anton Bruckner's music reduced to airy tones that would fair flee this earthly existence. Stross was little understood; Fritz Lemmermayer was inexpressibly devoted to him.

Both Lemmermayer and Stross were intimate friends of Robert

[1] *The Alchemist.*

Hamerling. Through them I was led later into brief correspondence with Hamerling, to which I shall refer again. Stross died of grievous illness in a state of mental derangement.

The sculptor Hans Brandstädter also appeared at delle Grazie's. Unseen, however, there hovered over this whole company, by reason of frequent wonderful descriptions almost like hymns of praise, the historian of theology, Werner. Delle Grazie loved him most of all. Never once did he appear on a Saturday when I was able to be present. But his admirer showed us the picture of the biographer of Thomas Aquinas from ever new angles, the picture of the good, lovable scholar who remained naive even to extreme old age. One was shown a human being so selfless, so absorbed in the matter about which he spoke as a historian, so exact, that one said to oneself: "If only there were many such historians!"

A veritable magic spell ruled over these Saturday gatherings. After it had grown dark, a ceiling lamp under a shade of some red fabric was lit, and we sat in a space of light which made the whole company solemn. Then delle Grazie would often become extraordinarily talkative—especially when those less closely connected with her had gone—and one was permitted to hear many a word that sounded like a sigh from the depths in the after-pangs of grievous days of fate. But one listened also to genuine humor over the perversities of life and tones of indignation over the corruption in the press and elsewhere. Intermingled with this were the sarcastic, often caustic, remarks of Müllner on all sorts of philosophical, artistic, and other themes.

Delle Grazie's home was a place in which pessimism revealed itself in direct and living power, a place of anti-Goetheanism. Every one listened whenever I spoke of Goethe, but Laurenz Müllner held the opinion that I imaginatively ascribed to Goethe things which really had little to do with the actual minister of the Grand Duke Karl August. Nevertheless for me every visit at this home—and I knew that I was welcomed there—was something for which I am inexpressibly indebted. I felt that I was in a spiritual atmosphere which was of genuine benefit to me. For this purpose I did not need agreement in ideas; I needed earnest and striving humanity, susceptible to the spiritual.

I was now placed between this house which I visited with so much pleasure and my teacher and fatherly friend Karl Julius Schröer, who, after the first visits, never again appeared at delle Grazie's. My feeling life, drawn in both directions by sincere love and esteem, was actually torn in two.

But it was just at this time that the initial thoughts came to maturity in me for my *Philosophie der Freiheit*,[1] published later. In the unpublished paper on delle Grazie mentioned above, *Nature and Our Ideals,* lies the original germ of this book, in the sentences: "Our ideals are no longer so superficial as to be satisfied with reality often so flat, so empty. Yet I cannot believe that there are no means whereby to rise above the profound pessimism which comes from this knowledge. This elevation comes to me when I look into our inner world, when I enter more intimately into the nature of our world of ideals. This is a self-contained world, perfect in itself, which can neither win anything nor lose anything by reason of the transitoriness of the external. Do not our ideals, if these are really living individualities, possess an existence for themselves independent of the kindness or unkindness of nature? Even though the lovely rose may be forever shattered by the pitiless gusts of the wind, it has fulfilled its mission, for it has rejoiced hundreds of human eyes; if tomorrow it should please murderous nature to destroy the whole starry sky, yet men have gazed up reverently toward it for thousands of years, and this is enough. Not the existence in time—no, but the inner being of things—constitutes their perfection. The ideals of our spirit are a world in itself which must also live its own life, and which can gain nothing from the cooperation of a beneficent nature. What a pitiable creature man would be if he could not gain satisfaction *within* his own ideal world but must first to this end have the cooperation of nature! Where would divine freedom exist if nature

---

[1] *Philosophy of Freedom*, Anthroposophic Press, New York.

guided and guarded us like helpless children tied to leading strings?
No; she must *deny* us everything, in order that, when happiness
comes to us, this shall be wholly the creation of our free selves. Let
nature destroy every day what we shape, in order that we may every
day experience anew the joy of creating. We would fain owe *nothing*
to nature, *everything* to ourselves.

"Yet this freedom, one might say, is only a dream! While we think
that we are free, we obey the iron necessity of nature. The loftiest
thoughts that we conceive are merely the fruit of the blind power
of nature within us. But surely we should finally admit that a being
who knows himself *cannot* be unfree! . . . We see the web of law
holding sway over things, and this it is that constitutes *necessity*. In
our capacity of cognition we possess the power to separate natural
laws from things, and must we, nevertheless, be the slaves of these
laws, without a will of our own?"

These thoughts I did not develop in a spirit of controversy, but
I was forced to set forth what my perception of the spiritual world
said to me in opposition to a view of life which I had to consider
as at the opposite pole from my own, but which I none the less profoundly reverenced because it was revealed to me from the depths
of true and earnest souls.

At the very time during which I enjoyed so many stimulating experiences at the home of delle Grazie, I had the privilege of entering
also a circle of young Austrian poets. Every week we met for free
expression and mutual sharing together of whatever one or the other
had produced. The most varied characters met in the gathering.
Every view of life and every temperament was represented, from
the optimistic, naive painter of life to the leaden-weighted pessimist. Fritz Lemmermayer was the soul of the group. There was present something of the storm which the Hart brothers, Karl Henckel,
and others had unleashed "over there" in the German Empire
against "the old" in the cultural life of the time. But all this was
tinged with Austrian "amiability." Much was said about how the
time had arrived in which new tones must sound forth in all do-

mains of life; but this was done with that disapproval of radicalism which characterizes the Austrian.

One of the youngest of this circle was Joseph Kitir. He devoted his efforts to a form of lyric to which he had been inspired by Martin Greif. He did not wish to bring subjective feelings to expression; he wished to set forth an event or situation "objectively," and yet as if this had been observed, not with the senses, but with the feelings. He did not wish to say that he was enchanted; but, rather, he would paint the enchanting event, and its enchantment should arise in the hearer or the reader without the poet's statement. Kitir did really beautiful things in this way. He was a naive soul. For a short time he bound himself more closely to me.

In this circle I now heard a German-Austrian poet spoken of with great enthusiasm, and I also became acquainted with some of his poems. These made a deep impression on me. I endeavored to meet the poet. I asked Fritz Lemmermayer, who knew him well, and also some others whether the poet could not be invited to our gatherings. But I was told that he could not be dragged there with a four-horse team. He was a strange character, they said, and would not mingle with people. But I was deeply desirous of knowing him. Then one evening the whole company set out and roamed over to the place where the "knowing ones" could find him. It was a little wine-shop in a street parallel to the Kärtnerstrasse. There he sat in one corner, his glass of red wine—not a small one—before him. He sat as if he had sat there for an indefinitely long time and wished to continue to sit indefinitely long. Already a rather old gentleman, but with shining youthful eyes, and a countenance which revealed the poet and idealist in the most delicate and speaking features. He did not see us as we entered. For it was clear that, in the nobly shaped head, a poem was taking form. Fritz Lemmermayer had first to take him by the arm; then he turned his face in our direction and looked at us. We had disturbed him. His perplexed glance could not conceal this; but he showed it in the most amiable manner. We took our places around him. There was not space enough for so many of us to sit in the cramped little room. It was now remarkable how the man who had been described as a "strange character" showed himself in a very short while as spiritedly talkative. We all had the feeling that, with what our minds were then exchanging in conversation, we could not remain in the dull closeness of this room. And there was now not much difficulty in bringing the "recluse" with us to another *Lokal*. Except for him and one other acquaintance of his, who had for a long time mingled with our circle, we were all young; yet it soon became evident that we had never been so young as on this evening when the old gentleman was with us, for he was really the youngest of us all.

I was completely captivated by the charm of this personality. It was at once clear to me that this man must have produced things far more significant than what he had published, and I made bold to question him as to this. He answered almost timidly: "Yes, I have besides at home some cosmic things." I succeeded in persuading him to promise that he would bring these the next time we could see him.

It was thus that I became acquainted with Fercher von Steinwand. A poet from Carinthia, pithy, full of ideas, idealistic in his sentiments. He was the child of poor people and had passed his youth amid great hardships. The distinguished anatomist Hyrtl came to know his worth, and made possible for him the sort of existence in which he could devote himself wholly to poetic creation, thinking, and musing. For a considerable time, the world knew little of him. After the appearance of his first poetical creation, *Gräfin Seelenbrand,* Robert Hamerling gave him the fullest recognition.

After that night we never needed again to go for the "strange character." He appeared almost regularly on our evenings. It was a source of great happiness to me that, on one of these evenings, he brought along his "cosmic things." These were the *Chor der Urtriebe* and the *Chor der Urträume,*[1] poems in which feelings live in swinging rhythm which seem as if they drew close to the very

---

[1] *Chorus of the Primal Impulses* and *Chorus of the Primal Dreams.*

creative forces of the world. There ideas weave as if actual beings in splendid harmony, affecting one like pictures of the Powers which in the beginning created the world. I consider the fact that I was permitted to know Fercher von Steinwand as one of the important events of my youth; for his personality made the impression of that of a sage who manifests his wisdom in genuine poetry.

I had struggled with the riddle of man's repeated earth lives. Many a conception in this direction had dawned upon me when I came close to men who, in the habit of their lives, in the impress of their personalities, revealed clearly the indications of a content within their beings which one could not expect to find in what they had inherited through birth and acquired afterward through experience. But in the play of countenance, in every gesture, of Fercher I saw the essence of a soul which could only have been formed in the time from the beginning of the Christian evolution, while Greek paganism was still influencing this evolution. One does not arrive at such a perception when thinking only of those manifestations of a personality which force themselves immediately upon one's attention; it is aroused in one, rather, by the intuitively perceived marks of the individuality which seem to accompany such direct manifestations, but which in reality deepen these expressions immeasurably. Moreover, one does not attain to such a perception when one seeks for it while in the presence of the personality, but only when the strong impression remains active in retrospect, becoming like a life-filled memory in which what is essential in the external life falls away and the "unessential" begins to speak a deeply significant language. Whoever "observes" men in order to solve the riddle of their previous earth lives will certainly not reach his goal. Such observation one must feel to be an offence to the person observed; only then can one hope for the present disclosure of the long past of a human being as if through a dispensation of destiny coming from the outer spiritual world.

It was in the very time of my life I am now describing that I succeeded in attaining to definite perceptions of the repeated earth lives of man. Before this time I was not far from them but they had not yet come out of indeterminate lines into sharply defined impressions. Theories, however, in regard to such things as repeated earth lives I did not form in my own thoughts; I took them into my intellect, of course, out of literature or other sources of information as something intelligible, but I did not myself theorize about them. And only because I was conscious within myself of real perception in this region was I in a position to have the conversation mentioned above with Professor Neumann. No one is to be blamed if he becomes convinced of the truth of repeated earth lives and other insights which can be attained only in supersensible ways; for a complete conviction in this region is possible also to the sound and unprejudiced human intellect, even though one has not attained to actual vision. Only, the way of theorizing in this region was not my own way.

During the time when concrete perceptions were more and more forming within me in regard to repeated earth lives, I became acquainted with the Theosophical Movement, which had been initiated by H. P. Blavatsky. Sinnett's *Esoteric Buddhism* came into my hands through a friend to whom I had spoken about these things. This book, the first from the Theosophical Movement with which I became familiar, made upon me no impression whatever. I was glad that I had not read the book before having experienced perceptions out of the life of my own soul. For the content of this book was repellent to me, and my antipathy against this way of representing the supersensible world might well have prevented me from advancing further at once upon the road that had been pointed out to me.

VIII

URING this time—about 1888—I was impelled, on the one hand,
by the inner life of my mind to intense spiritual concentration;
on the other hand, life itself brought me into social intercourse with
a wide circle of acquaintances. Because of the detailed introduction
which I had to prepare for the second volume of Goethe's scientific
writings, to be edited by me, I felt an inner necessity to set forth
my perception of the spiritual world in a form transparently clear
to thinking. This required an inner withdrawal from all with which
I was united by the outer life. I owe much to the fact that such a
withdrawal was possible. I could at that time sit in a coffee-house
with the greatest excitement all round me and yet be absolutely tran-
quil within, my thinking concentrated upon the task of writing
down in a rough draft what later composed the introduction I have
mentioned. In this way I led an inner life which had no relation
whatever with the outer world, although my interests were, on the
other hand, intimately bound up with that world.

This was a time when these interests, in the Austria of that period,
were forced to turn to the critical phenomena appearing in public
affairs. Persons with whom I was in frequent contact were devoting
their strength and efforts to the discussions then occurring among
the nationalities of Austria. Others were occupied with the social
question. Still others were in the midst of a struggle for the reju-
venation of the artistic life.

When I was living inwardly in the spiritual world, I often had the feeling that the strivings toward all these objectives must play themselves out fruitlessly because they refused, after all, to come into contact with the spiritual forces of existence. Consideration of these spiritual forces seemed to me the thing needed first of all. But I could find no clear consciousness of this in the kind of spiritual life which surrounded me.

At that time Robert Hamerling's satirical epic *Homunculus* was published. In this a mirror was held before the times in which were reflected purposely caricatured images of its materialism, its interests centered on the outer life. A man who can live only in mechanistic, materialistic conceptions and activities enters into matrimony with a woman whose nature lies, not in a real world, but in a realm of the fantastic. Hamerling wished to represent the two aspects in which civilization has become malformed. On one side he perceived the utterly unspiritual striving which conceives the world as a mechanism and would shape human life mechanically; on the other side, the soulless fantasy which cares not at all whether its make-believe spiritual life enters into any true relation whatever with reality.

The grotesque pictures drawn by Hamerling repelled many who had esteemed him for his earlier works. Even in delle Grazie's home, where Hamerling had enjoyed unmeasured admiration, there was a certain reserve after the appearance of this epic.

Upon me, however, the *Homunculus* made a deep impression. It showed, so I thought, those spiritually darkening forces which are dominant in modern civilization. I found in it an earnest warning to the age. But I also had difficulty in establishing a relation with Hamerling, and the appearance of the *Homunculus* at first increased this difficulty in my own mind. In Hamerling I saw a person who was himself a special manifestation of the age. I looked back to the period when Goethe and those who worked with him had brought Idealism to a height worthy of humanity. I recognized the need to pass through the gateway of this Idealism into the world of real spirit. To me this Idealism seemed the noble shadow, not cast into man's soul by the sense-world, but falling into his inner being from a spiritual world, and creating the obligation to go forward from this shadow to the world which had cast it.

I loved Hamerling, who had painted this idealistic shadow in such mighty pictures. But it was a great deprivation for me that he remained at that stage—that his look was directed backward to the shadows of a spirituality destroyed by materialism, rather than forward to a new way of breaking into the world of spirit. Yet the *Homunculus* attracted me. Though it did not show how man enters into the spiritual world, still it indicated the pass to which men come when they limit themselves to the unspiritual.

My preoccupation with the *Homunculus* happened at a time when I was pondering over the problem of the nature of artistic creation and of beauty. What was then passing through my mind is recorded in the brochure *Goethe als Vater einer neuen Aesthetik*,[1] which reproduces a lecture I had given before the Goethe Society in Vienna. I wished to discover the reasons why the Idealism of a bold philosophy, such as had spoken so impressively in Fichte and Hegel, had nevertheless failed to penetrate to the living spirit. One of the ways by which I sought to discover these causes was my reflection regarding the errors of a merely Idealistic philosophy in the sphere of aesthetics. Hegel and those who thought in his way found the content of art in the appearance of the "idea" in the sense-world. When the "idea" appears in the substance of the senses, it is manifest as the beautiful—this was their opinion. But the succeeding period refused to recognize any reality in the "idea." Since the idea of the Idealistic world view, as this existed in the consciousness of the Idealists, did not point to a world of spirit, it could not maintain itself, therefore, with the successors of these Idealists as something possessing reality. Thus arose the "realistic" aesthetics, which

[1] *Goethe as Father of a New Aesthetics.* Translated under title *Goethe as Founder of a New Science of Aesthetics.* Anthroposophic Press, New York.

saw in the work of art, not the appearance of the idea in sense-form, but only the sense-image which, because of the needs of human nature, takes on in the work of art an unreal form.

My view was that the essential thing in a work of art is that which appears to the senses. But the way taken by the true artist in his creative work appeared to me as a way leading to real spirit. He begins with what is perceptible to the senses, but he transforms this. In this transformation, he is not guided by a merely subjective impulse, but seeks to give to the sensibly apparent a form that causes it to look as if the spirit were there present. Not the appearance of the idea in sense-form is the beautiful, so I said to myself, but the representation of the sensible in the form of the spirit. Thus I saw in the existence of art the placing of the world of spirit within the world of the senses. The true artist more or less unconsciously confesses the spirit. And it is only necessary—so I then said to myself over and over again—to metamorphose the powers of the soul, which in the case of the artist work upon matter, to pure spiritual vision, free of the senses, in order to penetrate to a knowledge of the spiritual world.

At that time true knowledge, the manifestation of the spiritual in art, and the moral will in man united for me as members to form a single whole. I could not but recognize in the human personality a central point at which this personality is conjoined in the most immediate unity with the Primordial Being of the world. It is from this central point that the will takes its rise. If the clear light of the spirit is effective at this central point, the will is free. Man is then acting in harmony with the spiritual nature of the world, which creates, not by reason of necessity, but in the realization of its own nature. At this central point in man the motives of action arise, not out of obscure impulses, but out of "moral intuitions," out of intuitions which are just as transparent in character as the most transparent thought. In this way I desired, by means of a perception of the free will, to find that spirit through which man as an individual *exists* in the world. By means of a feeling for true beauty, I desired to behold the spirit which is active within man when he so works in the sensible as to express his own being, not merely spiritually, as a free deed, but in such a way that this spiritual being of his flows forth into the world, which is, indeed, of the spirit but does not directly manifest it. Through a perception of the true, I desired to *experience* the spirit which manifests itself in its own being, whose spiritual reflection is moral action, and toward which artistic creation aspires in the shaping of a sensible form.

A "philosophy of freedom," a life-conception of the sense-world thirsting for the spirit and striving toward it through beauty, a spiritual vision of the living world of truth hovered before my mind.

It was in the year 1888 also that I was introduced into the home of the Protestant pastor Alfred Formey, in Vienna. Once a week groups of artists and writers gathered there. Alfred Formey himself had come out as a poet. Fritz Lemmermayer, speaking out of the heart of a friend, thus described him: "Warm-hearted, intimate in his feeling for nature, rhapsodic, almost drunk with faith in God and blessedness, so does Alfred Formey write verse in mellow resounding harmonies. It is as if his tread did not touch the hard earth, but as if he dozed and dreamed high in the clouds." Such was Alfred Formey also as a man. One felt quite carried away from the earth when one entered the rectory and found at first only the host and hostess. The pastor was a person of childlike piety; but this piety passed over in his warm disposition in the most natural way into a lyric mood. One was immediately surrounded by an atmosphere of cordiality as soon as Formey had spoken a few words. The lady of the house had exchanged the life of the stage for the rectory. No one would ever have discovered the former actress in the lovable wife of the pastor, entertaining her guests with such delightful charm. She took care of the pastor in an almost motherly way, and motherly was almost every word one heard her speak to him. In each of them a delightful contrast existed between sweetness of soul and the utmost stateliness in appearance. Into this mood of the rectory, so other-worldly, the guests now brought "the world" from all directions of the cultural compass. There from time to time appeared the widow of Friedrich Hebbel. Her appearance was always the signal for a festival. In high old age she developed an art of declamation which took possession of one's heart with a happy fascination and completely captivated one's artistic sensibilities. And when Christine Hebbel told a story, the whole room was permeated with warmth of soul. At these Formey evenings I became acquainted also with the actress Wilborn. An interesting person, with a brilliant voice in declamation. Lenau's *Drei Zigeuner*[1] one could hear from her lips with constantly renewed pleasure. It soon came about that the group which had assembled at the home of Formey would from time to time gather also at that of Frau Wilborn. But how different it was there! Fond of the world, lovers of life, thirsty for humor— such were the same persons who at the rectory remained serious even when the "Vienna Folk Poet," Friedrich Schlögl, read aloud his jolly drolleries. He had, for instance, written a skit when the practice of cremation had been introduced among a small circle of Viennese. In this he told how a husband who loved his wife in a somewhat crude manner had always shouted to her whenever anything did not please him: "Old woman, off to the crematorium!" At Formey's such things would call forth remarks which formed a sort of chapter in the cultural history of Vienna; at Wilborn's people laughed till the chairs rattled. At Wilborn's Formey looked like a man of the world; Wilborn at Formey's like an abbess. One could pursue the most penetrating studies in the metamorphosis of human beings, even to the point of facial expression.

To Formey's came also Emilie Mataja, who, under the pen-name Emil Mariot, wrote her novels marked by penetrating observation of life: a fascinating personality, who in her way of life revealed the hardness of human existence clearly, with genius, often provocatively. An artist who knew how to present life when it mingles its riddles with every-day affairs, when it hurls the tragedy of fate ruinously among human beings.

We often had the opportunity also to hear the four women

---

[1] *Three Gypsies.*

artists of the Austrian Tschamper quartette; there Fritz Lemmermayer melodramatically recited over and over again Hebbel's *Hei-
deknabe* to a fiery piano accompaniment by Alfred Stross.

I loved this rectory where one could find so much warmth. There
the noblest humanity was actively manifest.

During the same period it came about that I must occupy myself
in detail with public affairs in Austria. For, in 1888, I was entrusted
for a brief period with the editorship of the *Deutsche Wochenschrift*.
The journal had been founded by the historian Heinrich Fried-
jung. My brief editorial experience came during a time when the
conflict among the races in Austria had reached a specially violent
character. It was not easy for me to write each week an article on
public events, since I was in truth at the furthest possible remove
from all partisan conceptions of life. What interested me was the
evolution of culture in the progress of humanity; and I had so to
present the point of view resulting from this fact that, even if I justified it fully, my article would not seem to be the production of a
"world-estranged idealist." Besides, it happened that the "educational reform" then being introduced into Austria, especially by
Minister Gautsch, seemed to me injurious to the interests of culture.
My comments in this field seemed on one occasion questionable
even to Schröer, who felt, after all, a strong sympathy always for
partisan points of view. I praised the expedient plans which the
Catholic clerical Minister Leo Thun had brought about in the Austrian secondary *Gymnasia* as early as the 'fifties, as opposed to the
unpedagogical measures of Gautsch. When Schröer had read my
article, he said: "Do you wish, then, to have again a clerical educational policy in Austria?"

This editorial activity, though brief, was for me very important.
It directed my attention to the style in which public affairs were discussed at that time in Austria. To me this style was intensely anti-
pathetic. Even in discussing such matters I wished to bring in something which would be marked by its comprehensive relation to the
great cultural and human objectives. This I missed in the style of

the daily papers in those days. How to bring this characteristic into play was then my daily problem, and it had to be a problem, for at that time I did not possess the power which a rich life experience in this field would have given me. I had really entered quite unprepared into this editorial work. I thought I could see whither we ought to steer in the most varied departments of life, but I had not the formulations so systematized as to be intelligible to newspaper readers. So the preparation of each week's issue was for me a difficult struggle.

Thus I felt as if I had been relieved of a great burden when this activity came to an end through the fact that the owner of the paper got into a controversy with the founder over the question of the initial purchase payment.

Yet this work brought me into rather close relations with persons whose activities had to do with the most various phases of public life. I became acquainted with Victor Adler, who was then the undisputed leader of the Socialist party in Austria. In this slender unassuming man there resided an energetic will. When he conversed over a cup of coffee, I always had the feeling: "The content of what he says is unimportant, commonplace, but his way of speaking marks a will that can never be bent." I became acquainted with Pernerstorffer, who was then changing from a German nationalist to a Socialist partisan. A strong personality possessed of comprehensive knowledge. A keen critic of misconduct in public affairs. He was then editing the monthly, *Deutsche Worte*. I found this stimulating reading. In company with these persons, I met with others who, either for scientific or for partisan reasons, were advocates of Socialism. Through these I was led to take up the study of Karl Marx, Friedrich Engels, Rodbertus, and other writers on social economics. To none of these could I gain any inner relation. It was a matter of personal distress to me to hear men say that the material-economic forces in human history carry forward man's real evolution, and that the spiritual is only a superstructure in ideas over this substructure of the "truly real." I knew the reality of the spiritual.

The assertions of the theorizing Socialists meant for me the closing of men's eyes to genuine reality.

In this connection, however, it became clear to me that the "social question" itself was of immense importance. But it seemed to me the tragedy of the times that this question was dealt with by persons wholly possessed by the materialism of contemporary civilization. It was my conviction that just this question could be rightly put only from the standpoint of a spiritual world view.

Thus as a young man of twenty-seven years I was filled with "questions" and "riddles" regarding the outer life of humanity, whereas the nature of the soul and its relation with the spiritual world had presented itself before my inner being in a perception complete in itself, taking on more and more definite forms. I could work spiritually only from this perception. And this work took increasingly the direction which some years later led to the composition of *The Philosophy of Freedom.*

IX

IT was at this time (1888) that I made my first journey into Germany. This was occasioned through the invitation to collaborate in the Weimar edition of Goethe, which was to be prepared by the Goethe Archives under a commission from the Arch Duchess Sophie of Saxony. Some years earlier, Goethe's grandson, Walther von Goethe, had died. He had left as a legacy to the Grand Duchess the manuscripts of Goethe. She had thereupon founded the Goethe Archives and, in conjunction with a number of Goethe specialists—chief among whom were Herman Grimm, Gustav von Loeper, and Wilhelm Scherer—had determined to prepare an edition of Goethe in which his already known works should be combined with those in the legacy as yet unpublished.

My publications in the field of Goethe literature were the occasion for my being requested to prepare a part of Goethe's writings on natural science for this edition. I was called to Weimar to make a general survey of the natural-scientific part of the literary legacy and to take the first steps required by my task.

My sojourn for some weeks in Goethe's city was a festival time in my life. For years I had lived in the thoughts of Goethe; now I was permitted to be in the places where these thoughts had arisen. I passed these weeks in the inspiring impression arising from this feeling.

I was able to have before my eyes day after day the papers in which were contained the supplements to what I had already prepared for the edition of Goethe for the Kürschner *German National Literature*.

My work in connection with this edition had given me a mental picture of Goethe's world view. Now the question to be settled was how this picture would stand since hitherto unpublished material dealing with natural science was to be found in these literary remains. With the utmost intensity I worked my way into this portion of the Goethe legacy.

I soon thought I could recognize that the hitherto unpublished material afforded an important contribution especially toward a more exact insight into Goethe's mode of cognition.

In my writings published up to that time I had conceived this mode of cognition as consisting in the fact that Goethe was permeated by the conception that, in the ordinary state of consciousness, man is at first a stranger to the true nature of the world by which he is surrounded. Out of this remoteness arises the impulse first to develop, *before* cognizing the world, powers of knowledge which are not present in ordinary consciousness.

From this point of view, it was highly significant for me to come upon such a statement as the following among Goethe's papers:

"In order to get our bearings to some extent in these different kinds [Goethe is referring to the different kinds of knowledge in man and his different relations to the outer world] we may classify these as utilizing, knowing, perceiving, and all-encompassing.

"1. Utilizing, profit-seeking, demanding persons are the first who, so to speak, outline the field of science and seize upon the practical. Consciousness gives them certitude through experience, and their requirements give them a certain breadth.

"2. Knowledge-craving persons require a serene look, free from personal objectives, a restless curiosity, a clear intellect, and they stand always in relation with the former. They likewise elaborate what already exists, only in a scientific sense.

"3. The perceptive are even in their attitude productive; and cognizing, as it ascends, calls for perception without being conscious of this, and passes over into perception; and, no matter how much the knowers may cross themselves as a shield against imagination, yet they must none the less—even before they are aware of this—call in the aid of productive imagination.

"4. The all-encompassing, whom one might call in a proud sense the creative, are in their attitude in the highest sense productive; beginning as they do with the idea, they already express thereby the unity of the whole, and it is the business of nature, as it were, thereupon to conform with this idea."

It becomes clear from such comments that Goethe considered man in his ordinary consciousness as standing *outside* the being of the external world. He must pass over into another form of consciousness if he desires to unite in cognition with this being. During my sojourn in Weimar the question arose within me in more and more decisive form: How must one build further upon the foundations of knowledge laid by Goethe in order to lead over in thinking from Goethe's mode of perception to that mode which can take up into itself *spiritual experience* as this had resulted for me?

Goethe began with what is acquired on the lower stages of knowledge, by "utilizing" persons and by those "craving knowledge." Upon this he causes to shine in his mind whatever can shine in the "perceptive" and the "all-encompassing" through productive powers of the mind, upon the content of the lower stages of knowledge. When he stood thus with the lower knowledge in the mind in the light of the higher perception and comprehension, he felt that he was in union with the nature of things.

To experience knowingly in the spirit is, to be sure, not yet achieved in this way; but the road to this is pointed out from one side—from that side which results from man's relation to the outer world. It was clear to my mind that satisfaction could come only with a grasp upon the other side, which arises from man's relation with himself.

When consciousness becomes *productive*—that is, when it brings forth from within itself something to add to the first pictures of reality—can it then still remain within a reality, or does it float out of this to lose itself in the unreal? What confronts consciousness in its "product"—it is this that must be looked into. Human consciousness must first effect an understanding with itself; then can man find a confirmation of what is experienced purely spiritually. Such were the paths taken by my thoughts, repeating in clearer manner their earlier form, as I pored over Goethe's papers in Weimar.

It was summer. Little was to be seen of the contemporary art life of Weimar. It was possible to yield oneself in complete serenity to that artistic element which was present like a memorial to Goethe's work. One did not live in the present; one was transported back to the time of Goethe. At the moment it was the age of Liszt in Weimar, but the representatives of this age were not there.

The hours after work I passed with those who were connected with the Archives. In addition, there were others sharing in the work who came from elsewhere for longer or shorter visits. I was received with extraordinary kindness by Bernhard Suphan, director of the Goethe Archives; and in Julius Wahle, a permanent collaborator, I found a dear friend. All this, however, took on a more definite form only when I went there two years later for a longer period, and it must be narrated at the point where I shall have to tell about that period of my life.

More than anything else at that time I craved to know personally Eduard von Hartmann, with whom I had corresponded for years about philosophical matters. This was to take place during a brief stay in Berlin which followed that in Weimar.

I had the privilege of a long conversation with the philosopher. He was reclining on a sofa, with his legs stretched out and his upper body erect. It was in this posture that he passed by far the greater part of his life from the time when his knee ailment began. I saw before me a forehead that was the evident manifestation of a clear and keen intellect, and eyes which revealed in their glance the assurance felt in the innermost being of the man as to that which he knew. A mighty beard framed the face. He spoke with complete positiveness, which showed how he had cast certain basic thoughts over the whole world picture and thus in his way illuminated it. In these thoughts everything that came to him from other points of view was immediately covered with criticism. Thus I sat facing him while he sharply passed judgment on me, but in reality never inwardly listened to me. For him the being of things lay in the unconscious, and must remain hidden there so far as concerns human consciousness; for me the unconscious was something that could be more and more lifted into consciousness through the exertions of the soul-life. During the course of the conversation about this, it occurred to me to say that a mental representation (*Vorstellung*) must not be assumed beforehand to be something severed from reality and standing only for an unreality in consciousness: that such a view could never be the starting point for a theory of knowledge. For, I said, such a view shuts one off from access to all reality in that it is possible, with this view, to believe only that one is living in mental representations and that there can be no approach toward reality except through hypothetical representations—that is, in an unreal manner. It was necessary, rather, first to investigate, I said, whether this view of the mental representation as unreal is tenable, or whether it merely rises out of a preconception. Eduard von Hartmann replied that there could be no argument as to this; that in the very definition of the term *representation* lay the evidence that nothing real is to be found there. When I received such an answer, I was chilled to the soul. Definitions of terms to be the point of departure for conceptions of life! I realized how far removed I was from contemporary philosophy. While I sat in the train on my return journey, buried in thoughts and recollections of this visit, which was nevertheless so valuable to me, I felt again that chilling of the heart. It was something that affected me for a long time afterwards.

Except for the visit to Eduard von Hartmann, the brief stops I made in Berlin and Munich, while passing through Germany after my stay in Weimar, were given over entirely to absorption in the art that these places afforded. The broadening of the scope of my views in this direction seemed to me at that time especially enriching to my inner life. So this first lengthy journey that I was able to take was of comprehensive significance in the development of my conceptions as to art. A fullness of vital impressions remained with me when I spent some weeks just after this visit in the Salzkammergut with the family whose sons I had already been teaching for many years. I was still dependent upon finding an external activity in tutoring, and I was also inwardly kept engaged in this because I desired to bring forward to a certain point in life the boy whose education had been entrusted to me some years before, and in whom I had succeeded in awaking the soul from a completely sleeping state.

Soon after my return to Vienna, I had the opportunity to mingle a great deal with a group of persons bound together by a woman whose mystical theosophical type of mind made a profound impression upon all the members of this group. The hours that I spent in the home of this woman, Marie Lang, were in high degree useful to me. An earnest trend of life-conception and life-experience was manifest in nobly beautiful form in Marie Lang. A profound inner experience came to expression in her sonorous and impressive voice. A life that struggled hard with itself and with the world could find in her, only through a mystical seeking, a kind of satisfaction though not complete. Thus she seemed almost as if created to be the soul of a group of seeking human beings. Into this circle had penetrated the theosophy which had been initiated by H. P. Blavatsky at the close of the last century. Franz Hartmann, who by reason of his numerous theosophical works, and his relations with H. P. Blavatsky, had become widely known, had introduced his theosophy into this circle also. Marie Lang had absorbed much of this theosophy. The thought contents that she was able to find there seemed in many respects to harmonize with the trend of her mind. Yet what she took from this source had become attached to her only superficially from without. But within herself she had a mystical possession which had been lifted into the realm of consciousness in a quite elementary manner out of a heart tested by life.

The architects, writers, and other persons whom I met in the home of Marie Lang would scarcely have been interested in the theosophy imparted by Franz Hartmann had not Marie Lang to some extent participated in this. Least of all should I myself have been interested in it; for the way of relating oneself to the spiritual world which was manifest in the writings of Franz Hartmann was absolutely opposite to the bent of my own mind. I could not concede that it rested upon real inner truth. I was less concerned with its content than with the way in which it affected persons who were, nevertheless, true seekers.

Through Marie Lang I became acquainted with Frau Rosa Mayreder, who was a friend of hers. Rosa Mayreder was one of those persons for whom in the course of my life I have conceived the greatest veneration, and in whose development I have had the greatest interest. I can well imagine that what I have to say here will please her very little; yet such is my feeling as to what came into my life through her. Of the writings of Rosa Mayreder which since that time have justly made so great an impression upon many persons, and which undoubtedly give her a very conspicuous place in literature, nothing had at that time appeared. But what is revealed in these writings lived in Rosa Mayreder in a spiritual form of expression to which I had to respond with the strongest possible inner sympathy. This woman impressed me as if she possessed each of the gifts of the human mind in such measure that these, in their harmonious interaction, constituted the right manifestation of humanness. She combined various artistic gifts with a free, penetrating power of observation. Her paintings are just as much marked by individual unfoldings of life as by devoted absorption in the objective world. The stories with which she began her literary career are perfect harmonies, a blending of personal struggles and wholly objective observations. Her later works show this character more and more. Most clearly of all does this come to light in her more recently published two-volume work, *Kritik der Weiblichkeit*.[1] I consider it a beautiful

---

[1] *A Survey of the Woman Problem.*

treasure in my life to have spent many hours during the time about which I am here writing together with Rosa Mayreder in the years of her seeking and inner strivings.

Here again I have to look back upon one of my human relations which took their rise and reached a vital intensity above the sphere of thought-content, and, in a sense, quite independently of this. For my world view and even more the trend of my feelings were not those of Rosa Mayreder. The way in which I ascend from what is at present recognized as scientific into an experience of the spiritual cannot possibly be congenial to her. She seeks to use the essence of the scientific as the foundation for ideas which have as their goal the complete development of human personality without permitting knowledge of a world of pure spirit to find access to this personality. What is to me in this direction a necessity means to her almost nothing. She is wholly devoted to the requirements of the immediately present human individuality, and pays no attention to the action of spiritual forces within the individuality. Through this method of hers she has achieved the most significant exposition yet produced of the nature of womanhood and the vital needs of woman.

Neither could I ever satisfy Rosa Mayreder in respect of the view she formed of my attitude toward art. She thought that I misunderstood true art, whereas I strove, on the contrary, to comprehend this specific entity of art by means of the conception which arose in my mind through my experience of the spiritual. She maintained that I could not sufficiently penetrate into the manifestations of the sense-world and, for this reason, could not arrive at the reality of art, whereas I was seeking just this thing—to penetrate into the full truth of the sensible forms. But all this did not detract at all from the intimate friendly interest in this personality which developed in me at the time during which I owed to her some of the most valuable hours of my life—an interest which, in truth, remains undiminished even to the present day.

At the home of Rosa Mayreder I was often privileged to share in conversations for which highly intellectual persons gathered there.

Very quiet, seemingly with his gaze directed inward upon himself rather than listening to those about him, sat Hugo Wolf, who was an intimate friend of Rosa Mayreder. One listened inwardly to him even though he spoke very little. For what he experienced was communicated in mysterious manner to those who could be with him. With heartfelt affection was I attached to the husband of Frau Rosa, Karl Mayreder, so fine a person both as man and as artist, and also to his brother, Julius Mayreder, so enthusiastic about art. Marie Lang and her circle and Friedrich Eckstein, who was then wholly given over to the spiritual current and world view of theosophy, were also present.

This was the time when my *Philosophy of Freedom* was taking more and more definite forms in my mind. Rosa Mayreder is the person with whom I talked most about these forms at the time when my book was thus coming into existence. She relieved me of part of the inner loneliness in which I had lived. She was striving for a conception of the immediately present human personality; I toward a revelation of the world which this personality may seek in the depths of the soul by means of the opened spiritual eye. Between the two there were many bridges. Often in later life has there risen before my mind in most grateful memory one or another picture from this experience—such, for example, as a walk through the noble Alpine forests, during which Rosa Mayreder and I discussed the true meaning of human freedom.

X

As I look back upon the course of my life, the first three decades appear to me as a chapter complete in itself. At the close of this period, I removed to Weimar, to work for almost seven years at the Goethe-Schiller Archives. The time I spent in Vienna between the first journey into Germany, which I have described, and my later settling down in the city of Goethe I look upon as a period that brought to a certain conclusion what my mind had until then been striving toward. This conclusion found expression in the preparation of my book *The Philosophy of Freedom*.

An essential part of the area of ideas in which I then expressed my views consisted in the fact that the sense-world did not pass with me as true reality. In books and papers published at that time I always gave expression to the view that, when engaged in thinking not drawn from the sense-world but unfolded as an activity above the level of sense-perception, the human soul appears as a true reality. This "sense-free" thinking I set forth as that which places the mind within the spiritual essence of the world.

But I emphasized strongly also that, while the human being lives within this sense-free thinking, he is really consciously within the primordial spiritual grounds of existence. All talk about limits of knowledge was for me without meaning. Knowing meant for me rediscovering within the world as perceived the spiritual content experienced in the soul. When any one spoke of limits of knowledge, I saw therein the admission that he was unable to experience spiritually within himself the true reality, and for this reason could not discover this reality in the world as perceived.

The first consideration with me in presenting my own insight was the problem of refuting the conception of the limitation of knowledge. I wished to reject that road to knowledge which looks toward the sense-world and would then break through the sense-world outward into a true reality. I desired to make clear that true reality is to be sought, *not* by such a breaking through in an outer direction, but by sinking down into the inner being of man. Whoever seeks to break through in an outer direction, and discovers that this is impossible—such a person speaks of limitations of knowledge. But the reason for this impossibility does not consist in a limitation of man's capacity for knowledge, but in the fact that one is seeking for something of which, upon adequate self-reflection, there can be no discussion. While endeavoring to press farther into the sense-world, one is seeking for a continuation of the sensible behind what is perceived. It is as if a human being living in illusions should seek in further illusions for the causes of the illusions.

The sense of my explanations at that time was as follows: While man is developing in the earthly life from birth onward, he confronts the world in the activity of cognizing. He attains first to sense-perception. But this is only an outpost of the process of knowing. In this perception is not at once revealed all that is in the world. The world, in its essential nature, is real being, but man does not at first attain to this reality of being. He still remains closed to this. Since he has not as yet confronted the world with his own being, he forms for himself a world-conception that is void of real being. This world-picture is in truth an illusion. In sense-perception, man faces the world as illusion. But, when from within man himself sense-free thinking follows after sense-perception, illusion is then permeated with reality; it ceases to be illusion. The human spirit, experiencing itself within, then meets the Spirit of the World, now no longer *concealed from man behind the sense-world, but living and moving within the sense-world.*

Finding the spirit in the world I did not view at that time as a matter of logical reasoning, or a projecting of sense-perception, but as something which results when the human being develops himself from perceiving to the experiencing of sense-free thinking.

What I wrote in 1888, in the second volume of my edition of Goethe's scientific writings, is permeated with such conceptions: "Whoever recognizes as an attribute of thinking its capacity of perception extending beyond apprehension through the senses must necessarily also attribute to thinking objects existing beyond the limits of mere sense-perceptible reality. But these objects of thinking are Ideas. As thinking takes possession of the Idea, it merges with the primordial foundation of the world; that which works without enters into the spirit of man; he becomes one with objective reality at its highest potency. *Becoming aware of the Idea within reality is the true communion of man.*

"Thinking has the same significance in relationship to Ideas as the eye has for light, the ear for sound: *it is the organ of perception.*" [1]

I was then less concerned to represent the world of the spiritual as it becomes manifest when sense-free thinking advances by way of the experience of itself to spiritual perception than to show that the being of nature as revealed to sense-perception is the spiritual. I wished to express the truth that nature is in reality spiritual.

This was due to the fact that my destiny led me to reach conclusions about contemporary formulations of theories of knowledge. These assumed, to begin with, a nature void of spirit; their task, therefore, was to show to what extent man is justified in forming in his mind a spiritual conception of nature. I wished to oppose to this an entirely different theory of knowledge. I wished to show that man, *in think-ing,* does not form conceptions regarding nature while standing outside her, but that knowing means *experiencing,* so that, while knowing, man is *inside* the being of things.

Moreover, it was my destiny to link my own views with those of Goethe. In this linking, there were, of course, many opportunities

[1] *Goethe the Scientist,* page 95. Anthroposophic Press, New York.

to show that nature is spiritual, because Goethe himself strove toward a spiritual view of nature; but one does not in the same way have the opportunity to speak of the world of pure spirit as such, since Goethe did not carry his spiritual view of nature all the way to the direct perception of spirit.

In a secondary degree, I was then concerned to bring to expression the idea of freedom. When man acts under the influence of his instincts, impulses, passions, and so forth, he is not free. Then impulses which become conscious in him as do the impressions from the sense-world determine his action. But his true being, likewise, is then not acting. He is acting at a level where his true being by no means comes to manifestation. He is then disclosing himself as man just as little as the sense-world discloses itself to mere sense-observation. Now, the sense-world is not really an illusion, but is only made such by man. But man, in his action, can cause the sense-related instincts, impulses, and so forth, to become real, as illusions; he is then permitting something illusionary associated with himself to act; it is not *he himself* that acts. He permits the unspiritual to act. His spiritual being does not act until he finds the impulses for action as moral intuitions in the realm of his sense-free thinking. He alone then acts; nothing else. Then is he a free being, acting from within himself.

I desired to show that whoever rejects sense-free thinking as something purely spiritual in man can never arrive at a comprehension of freedom; but that such a comprehension comes about the moment one gains an insight into the reality of sense-free thinking.

In this realm also I was at that time less intent upon representing the world of pure spirit, in which man experiences his moral intuitions, than to emphasize the spiritual character of these intuitions themselves. Had I been concerned with the former, I should have been obliged to begin the chapter on Moral Imagination in *The Philosophy of Freedom* in the following way: "The free spirit acts upon his impulses; these are intuitions experienced by him apart from the natural existence, in the world of pure spirit, without his being aware of this spiritual world in the ordinary state of consciousness." But it was my concern then only to set forth the spiritual character of moral intuitions. I referred, therefore, to the existence of these intuitions within the totality of the world of human ideas, and said accordingly: "The free spirit acts upon his impulses, which are intuitions selected by means of thinking from the totality of his world of ideas." One who does not direct his look toward a world of pure spirit, and who could not, therefore, write the first statement, can also not wholly admit the second. But allusions to the first postulate are to be found in ample number in my *Philosophy of Freedom;* for example: "The highest stage of the individual life is thinking in concepts without reference to a specific content of perception. We determine the content of a concept by means of pure intuitions out of the sphere of ideas. Such a concept then contains no reference to definite percepts." Here sense-percepts are intended. Had I then desired to write about the spiritual world, and not merely about the spiritual character of moral intuitions, I should have been forced to refer to the contrast between sensible and spiritual perceiving. But I was concerned only to emphasize the non-sensible character of moral intuitions.

My world of ideas was moving in this direction when the first chapter of my life came to a close, with the end of my third decade, with my entrance upon the Weimar period.

XI

A T THE CLOSE of this first chapter of my life, it became a matter of inner necessity for me to arrive at a clearly defined position in relation to certain orientations of the human mind. One of these orientations was mysticism. As this passed in review before my mind in the various epochs of the spiritual evolution of humanity—in Oriental Wisdom, in Neo-Platonism, in the Christian Middle Ages, in the endeavors of the Cabalists—it was only with difficulty that I, with my particular constitution of mind, could establish a relation with it.

The mystic seemed to me to be a person who failed to establish a right relation with the world of Ideas, in which for me the spiritual was manifest. I felt that it was a deficiency in real spirituality when, in order to arrive at inner satisfaction, one wishes to plunge with one's ideas into an inner world void of ideas. In this I could see no road to light, but rather a way to spiritual darkness. It seemed to me an impotence in cognition when the mind seeks through an escape from ideas to reach spiritual reality, which, although it does not itself weave in ideas, can be experienced by the human being through ideas.

And yet something also attracted me in the mystical strivings of humanity. This was the *nature* of the inner experience of the mystics. They desire a living union in their own inner being with the sources of human existence, not merely a view of these, as something external, by means of reflection in ideas. But it was also clear to me that the same kind of inner experience is arrived at when one sinks into the depths of the soul *accompanied by* the full and clear content of the world of ideas, instead of stripping off this content when sinking into one's depths. I desired to carry the light of the world of ideas into the warmth of the inner experience. The mystic seemed to me to be a person who cannot perceive the spirit in ideas and who is, therefore, inwardly chilled by ideas. The coldness that he experiences in connection with ideas drives him to seek through an escape from ideas for the warmth of which his soul has need.

As for myself, the warmth of my mind's experience came about precisely when I shaped into definite ideas the hitherto indefinite experiences of the spiritual world. I often said to myself: "How these mystics fail to understand the warmth, the intimacy of soul, that one experiences while living in association with ideas saturated with the spiritual!" To me, this living association had always been like a personal intercourse with the spiritual world.

The mystic seemed to me to strengthen the position of the materialistically minded observer of nature instead of weakening it. The latter rejects the consideration of the spiritual world, either because he does not admit the existence of such a world or because he considers human knowledge as adapted only to the physically visible one. He sets up boundaries of knowledge at the line where lie the boundaries of sense-perception. The ordinary mystic is of the same opinion as the materialist in regard to human knowledge through ideas. He maintains that ideas do not extend to the spiritual, and that knowledge through ideas, therefore, must always remain outside the spiritual. Since, however, he desires to attain to the spiritual, he turns to an inner experience void of ideas. He thus agrees with the materialistic observer of nature in that he limits cognition through ideas to that pertaining to the merely natural world.

But, if a person enters into the interior of his own soul without taking ideas with him, he arrives at the inner region of mere feeling. Such a person then says that the spiritual cannot be reached by a way which in ordinary life is called a way of knowledge, but that one must sink down from the sphere of knowledge into the sphere of the feelings in order to experience the spiritual.

With such a view a materialistic observer of nature can declare himself in agreement, unless he considers all talk about the spiritual as a fantastic playing with words that signify nothing real whatever. He then sees in his system of ideas directed toward the things of the senses the sole justifiable basis for knowledge, and in mystical relations of man with the spiritual something purely personal, to which one is either inclined or not inclined according to one's disposition, but which can never come under discussion in the same way as the content of "positive knowledge." Man's relation to the spiritual must be relegated entirely, he thinks, to the sphere of "subjective feeling."

While I fixed my attention upon this fact, the forces in my mind which stood in opposition to mysticism grew steadily stronger. The perception of the spirit in inner experience of the mind was to me far more certain than perception of the things of the senses; to place limits of knowledge before this experience of the mind was to me quite impossible. I objected with all positiveness to mere feeling as a way to the spiritual.

And yet, when I thought of the *nature* of the mystic's experience, I felt once more a remote kinship between this and my own attitude toward the spiritual world. I sought association with the spirit, by means of spirit-illuminated ideas, in the same way as the mystic seeks this through association with what is void of the idea. I also could say that my view rests upon "mystical" experience of ideas.

To achieve for this mental conflict within myself the clarification which at length lifts one above it was not a matter of great difficulty; for the real perception of the spiritual casts a light upon the range of applicability of ideas, and assigns proper limits to the personal. As an observer of the spiritual, one knows that the personal ceases to function in man when the very soul-being itself becomes an organ of perception for the spiritual world.

The difficulty consisted, however, in the fact that I had to find forms in which to express in my writings what I beheld. It is by no means easy to find a new mode of expression for an observation unfamiliar to the reader. I had to choose between putting what I found it needful to say either in those forms customarily applied in the field of nature-observation, or in forms used by writers more inclined to mystical experiences. The difficulties resulting from the latter method seemed to me to be insuperable.

I reached the conclusion that the form of expression in the domain of the natural sciences consists in content-filled ideas, even though the content is materialistically conceived. I desired to form ideas that bear upon the spiritual world in the same way as natural-scientific ideas bear upon the physical. In this way I could maintain the idea-character of what I had to say. With the use of mystical forms this seemed to me impossible; for these do not in essence refer to reality *outside* of man, but describe only subjective experiences within man. My purpose was not to describe human experiences, but to show how a spiritual world is revealed *in* man through spiritual organs.

Out of such fundamental considerations came about the forms of ideas from which my *Philosophy of Freedom* later developed. In the forming of these ideas, I desired that no mystical impulses become dominant within me, although it was clear to me that the ultimate experience of that which was to manifest itself in ideas must be of the same character within the soul as the inner perceiving of the mystic. Yet there was the difference that in my presentation man surrenders himself and brings the external spiritual world itself to objective manifestation within him, whereas the mystic strengthens his own inner life and in this way effaces the true form of the objective spiritual.

XII

THE TIME that I expended in presenting Goethe's natural-scientific ideas for Kürschner's *German National Literature* was very protracted. I commenced this task in the beginning of the 'eighties and I had not finished even when I entered upon the second chapter of my life with the removal from Vienna to Weimar. The reason for this lay in the difficulties described in connection with the natural-scientific and the mystical form of expression.

While I was laboring to reduce to correct idea-forms Goethe's attitude toward natural science, I had to advance also in the formulation of what had confronted my mind in spiritual experiences in viewing the world processes. I was thus constantly driven from Goethe to the presentation of my own world view and back again to him, in order the better to interpret his thoughts by means of the thoughts to which I myself had attained. I felt that the most essential thing in Goethe was his refusal to be content with any kind of theoretically easily surveyable thought picture as contrasted with the knowledge of the immeasurable richness of reality. Goethe becomes rationalistic when he wishes to describe the manifold forms of plants and animals. He strives for ideas which are manifest as active in nature's process of development when he wishes to comprehend the geologic structure of the earth and the phenomena of meteorology. But his ideas are not abstract thoughts; they are pictures living in the manner of thoughts in the mind.

When I grasped what he has set forth in such pictures in his natural-scientific works, I had before me something that satisfied me to the bottom of my soul. I looked upon a content of idea-pictures regarding which I could not but believe that this content—if developed further—represents a true reflection within the human mind of what occurs in nature. It was clear to me that the mode of thinking prevailing in the natural sciences must be raised to this of Goethe's.

At the same time, however, in this grasping of Goethe's knowledge of nature lay the obligation to present the nature of the content of idea-pictures in relation to spiritual reality itself. The idea-pictures are not justifiable unless they point to a spiritual reality underlying the reality of the senses. But Goethe, in his reverent awe before the immeasurable richness of reality, refrains from entering upon a presentation of the spiritual world after having in his mind brought the sense-world to the picture form in keeping with the spirit.

I had now to show that, although Goethe could *live* the life of the soul in advancing from sense-nature to spirit-nature, anyone else can wholly *understand* the life of Goethe's mind only by going beyond him and carrying knowledge forward to the comprehension in ideas of the spiritual world itself.

When Goethe spoke of nature, he was standing within the spirit. He feared that he would become abstract if he advanced further beyond this standing-within to a living in thoughts *concerning* this standing-within. He desired to sense himself within the spirit; but he did not desire to *think* himself within the spirit.

I often felt that I should be false to Goethe's way of thinking if I should, nevertheless, present thoughts *about* his world view. In regard to almost every detail that I had to interpret in connection with Goethe, I had again and again to master the method of speaking about Goethe in Goethe's own way.

My setting forth of Goethe's ideas involved the struggle, lasting for years, gradually to achieve a better understanding of him with the help of my own thoughts. When I look back upon this struggle, I have to say to myself that I owe to this in large measure the development of my spiritual experience of knowledge. This development proceeded far more slowly than would have been the case if the Goethe task had not been placed by destiny on the pathway of my life. I should then have pursued my spiritual experiences and have set these forth as they appeared before me. I should have been drawn into the spiritual world more quickly; but I should have had no inducement to immerse myself by actual striving in my own inner being.

Thus by means of the Goethe task I experienced the difference between the condition of soul in which the spiritual world manifests itself as an act of grace, so to speak, and one in which, step by step, the soul first makes its own inner self like the spirit, in order that, when the soul experiences itself as true spirit, it may then stand within the spiritual world. But it is only in *this way* of standing-within that man realizes how intimately the human spirit and the spirituality of the world may come into union, one with the other, in the human soul.

During the time when I was working at my interpretation of Goethe, I had Goethe always beside me in spirit as an admonisher, who never ceased to call to me that he who too rashly moves forward on the spiritual path may attain to a narrowly restricted experience of the spirit, but that he passes out of the richness of life poorly provided with substance of reality.

In my relation to the Goethe task, I could observe quite clearly "how karma works in human life." Destiny is made up of two fact complexes which grow into unity in human life. The one streams outward from the striving of the soul; the other approaches the human being from the outer world. My own impulses of mind moved toward the perception of the spiritual; the outer spiritual life of the world brought the Goethe work to me. I had to reduce to a harmony within my consciousness the two streams which there came together. I occupied the last years of the first chapter of my life in justifying myself alternately in my own eyes and in the eyes of Goethe.

The task I set myself in my doctoral dissertation was inwardly experienced. It was that of bringing about an "understanding of man's consciousness with itself." For I saw that it is possible to understand what the true reality in the outer world is only when the human being has perceived this true reality within himself.

This meeting together of the genuine reality of the outer world and the genuine reality of the inner being of the soul must be achieved for the cognizing consciousness through tireless spiritual activity; for the willing and the acting consciousness, it is always present when the human being in action senses his own freedom.

That freedom exists as a matter of fact for the unprejudiced consciousness, and yet becomes a riddle for cognition, is due to the fundamental fact that man does not possess his true being, his genuine self-consciousness, as something given from the beginning, but must first achieve this through the coming of his consciousness to an understanding with itself. That which is the greatest treasure of the human being—his freedom—can be comprehended only after appropriate preparation.

My *Philosophy of Freedom* is based upon an experience which consists in the fact that man's consciousness comes to an understanding with itself. In willing, freedom is *practised;* in feeling, it is *experienced;* in thinking, it is *recognized.* Only, in order to attain this last, one must not lose the life out of thinking.

While I was working at my *Philosophy of Freedom,* it was my constant endeavor, in the presentation of my thoughts, to keep my inner experience fully awake right into these thoughts. This gives to thoughts the mystical character of inner vision, but makes this vision also equivalent to the external sensible beholding of the world. If one advances to such an inner experience, one no longer finds any contradiction between knowledge of nature and knowledge of spirit. It becomes clear that the second is only a metamorphosis of the first.

Since this appeared true to me, I could later print on the title page of my *Philosophy of Freedom* the motto: *Seelische Beobachtungsresultate nach naturwissenschaftlicher Methode.*[1] For, when the

---

[1] *Findings from observation of the mind according to the method of natural science.*

natural-scientific method is faithfully followed, in connection with the spiritual realm, it leads one knowingly into this realm also.

There was great significance for me at that time in my thorough-going work upon Goethe's *Märchen von der grünen Schlange und der schönen Lilie,*[1] which forms the conclusion of his *Unterhaltungen deutscher Ausgewanderter.*[2] This "riddle fairy tale" has had many interpreters. I was not at all interested in the "interpretation" of its content. I wished simply to accept this in its poetic, artistic form. I had always an antipathy against the dissipating of creative fantasy through intellectual interpretation.

I saw how this poetical composition of Goethe's had arisen out of the converse of minds between him and Schiller. When Schiller wrote his *Briefe zur Förderung der aesthetischen Erziehung des Menschen,*[3] his mind was passing through the philosophical phase of its development. The "coming of human consciousness to an understanding with itself" was a task which occupied his mind most intensely. He saw the human mind, on the one side, wholly absorbed in rational activity. He felt that the mind, when engaged in purely rational activity, is not dependent upon the bodily-sensible. Yet he found in this form of supersensible activity something unsatisfying. The mind is "in the spirit" when given over to the "logical necessity" of reason, but in this activity it is neither free nor inwardly spiritually alive. It is given over to an abstract shadow-image of the spirit, but is not weaving and holding sway in the life and existence of the spirit. On the other hand, Schiller observed that, in an opposite sort of activity, the mind is wholly given over to the bodily—to sense-perceptions and instinctive impulses. The influence from the spiritual shadow-images is then absent from the mind, but it is given over to a natural law-conformity which does not constitute its real being.

Schiller came to the conclusion that man is not the "true human being" in either of these activities. But he can bring about of himself

---

[1] *Fairy Tale of the Green Snake and the Beautiful Lily.*
[2] *Conversations of German Emigrants.*
[3] *Letters for the Advancement of the Aesthetic Education of Man.*

that which is not given to him by nature or by the rational shadows of the spiritual which come to existence without his effort. He can introduce reason into sense-activity; and he can elevate the sensible into a higher realm of consciousness so that it acts *like* the spiritual. He thus attains to a mood midway between the logical and the natural compulsion. Schiller sees man in such a mood when he is living in the artistic. The aesthetic comprehension of the world directs its look toward the sensible, but in such a way that it perceives therein the spirit. It lives in the shadow of the spirit, but in creating or enjoying it gives to the spirit a sensible form, so that it loses its shadow-existence.

Years before this struggle of Schiller's to reach a conception of the "true human being" had attracted my attention; now, when Goethe's "riddle fairy tale" had become itself a riddle for me, Schiller's struggle occurred to me again. I saw how Goethe had taken hold of Schiller's conception of the "true human being." For him no less than for his friend, this was a vital question: How does the shadowy spiritual in the mind find the sensible-corporeal, and how does the natural in the physical body work itself up to the spiritual?

The correspondence between the two friends, and all that can be learned otherwise about their converse of minds, indicate that Schiller's solution was too abstract, too one-sidedly philosophical, for Goethe. He created the charming pictures of the stream which separates two worlds; of the will-o'-the-wisps who seek the way from one world to the other; of the snake which must sacrifice itself in order to form a bridge between the two worlds; of the "beautiful lily" who can only be surmised as holding sway in the spirit on the "far side" of the stream by those who live on "this side"; and of much more. Over against Schiller's philosophical solution he placed a poetic vision in fairy tale form. He had the feeling that, if the riddle of the soul that Schiller perceived is attacked with philosophical conceptions, the human being impoverishes himself while seeking for his true being. He desired to approach the riddle in all the wealth of the soul's experience.

The Goethe fairy tale images hark back to imaginations that had often been set forth before the time of Goethe by seekers for the soul's experience of the spirit. The three kings of the fairy tale are found in some semblance in the *Chymische Hochzeit des Christian Rosenkreutz*.[1] Other forms are revivals of what had appeared earlier in pictures of the way of knowledge. In Goethe these pictures only appear in beautiful, noble, artistic form of fantasy, whereas they had until his time borne a more inartistic character.

In this fairy tale Goethe carried imaginative creation near to the point at which it passes over into the inner soul-process which is a knowing experience of the real world of spirit. I felt that it was possible to see most deeply into Goethe's nature by inwardly immersing oneself in this imaginative composition.

Not the interpretation, but surely the stimulations to soul-experience, were an important result that came to me from my work on the fairy tale. These stimulations then continued to influence my inner life, even into the formation of the Mystery Dramas which I wrote later. As to my work connected directly with Goethe, I could gain but little from the fairy tale. For it seemed to me that, in its composition, Goethe had grown in his world view beyond himself, as if impelled by the inner power of a half-unconscious life of the soul. Thus a serious difficulty arose for me. I could continue my interpretation of Goethe for the Kürschner *German National Literature* only in the style in which I had commenced this, but did not thereby satisfy myself. For I said to myself that Goethe, while writing the fairy tale, had looked across, as it were, from the boundary and had seen into the spiritual world. Nevertheless, what he wrote additionally about natural processes gave no attention to this glimpse. He could not, therefore, be interpreted on the basis of this insight.

But, even though I gained nothing for my Goethe writings from immersion in the fairy tale, yet I gained an abundance of mental stimulations from it. What came to me as content of the mind in

[1] *The Chemical Marriage of Christian Rosenkreutz*, by Johann Valentin Andreae.

connection with the fairy tale became most important material for meditation. I returned to this again and again. By this activity I prepared for myself the mood in which I entered later upon my Weimar work.

XIII

XIII

JUST at this time my outer life was thoroughly social. I was frequently with my old friends. Few as were the opportunities I had to speak of the things to which I have here referred, yet the ties of mind and heart that bound me to these friends were none the less strong. How often must I think again of the conversations, sometimes unending, which occurred at that time in a well known coffee house on Michaelerplatz in Vienna. I had occasion to think of these especially during the period following the World War, when old Austria went to pieces. For the causes of this crumbling to pieces were at that time already present everywhere. But no one was willing to recognize this. Every one had remedial ideas, each according to his own special national or cultural leanings. And if ideals which become manifest at times of the rising tide are elevating, none the less elevating in their tragic character are those born out of decadence and seeking to hold it back. Such tragic ideals were then at work in the hearts of the best Viennese and Austrians.

I frequently created an ill-humor in these idealists when I expressed a conviction which had been borne in upon me through my absorption in the period of Goethe. I said that a culmination of Occidental cultural evolution had been reached during that period. This had not been maintained. The age of the natural sciences, with its results in the lives of men and of peoples, denoted a decadence. For any further advance, I said, there was needed an entirely new impetus from the side of the spirit. There could be no further progress in

136

things spiritual by those roads which had previously been followed without a turning back. Goethe is a summit, but on this summit not a point of departure; on the contrary, an end. He develops the results of an evolution that goes as far as himself and finds in him its most complete embodiment, but which cannot be further advanced without first resorting to far more primal springs of spiritual experience than exist in this evolution. In this mood I wrote the last part of my Goethe exposition.

It was in this mood that I first became acquainted with Nietzsche's writings. *Jenseits von Gut und Böse*[1] was the first of his books that I read. I was fascinated by his way of viewing things and yet at the same time repelled. I found it hard to take a right attitude toward Nietzsche. I loved his style; I loved his audacity; but I did not love at all the way in which Nietzsche spoke of the most profound problems without immersing himself in these in spiritual experience with full consciousness of mind. But I then observed that he said many things with which I stood in the closest intimacy in my spiritual experience. And thus I felt myself close to his struggle and felt that I must find an expression for this proximity. Nietzsche seemed to me to be one of the most tragic figures of the time. And this tragedy, I believed, must result from the characteristic spiritual constitution of the natural-scientific age for human minds of more than ordinary depth. I passed my last years in Vienna with such feelings as these.

Before the close of the first phase of my life I had the opportunity to visit also Budapest and Transylvania. The friend I have previously mentioned whose family belonged to Transylvania, who had remained bound to me with rare loyalty through all these years, had introduced me to a good many of his fellow countrymen living in Vienna. Thus it happened that, in addition to my other extensive social relations, I had also this with Transylvanians. Among these were Herr and Frau Breitenstein, who became friends of mine at that time and who have remained such in the most heartfelt manner.

[1] *Beyond Good and Evil.*

For a long time they have taken a leading part in the Anthroposophical Society in Vienna. This human relation with Transylvanians led me to make a journey to Budapest. The capital of Hungary, in character so entirely unlike Vienna, made a deep impression on me. The journey there leads through a region brilliant in its wonderful natural charm, its high-spirited humanity, and the intensity of its musical life. Looking from the window of the train, one has the impression that nature herself becomes poetic in a special way, and that human beings, paying little heed to the poetic nature so familiar to them, bustle about in it accompanied by an often profoundly inward music of the heart. And when one reaches Budapest, there comes to expression a world that may be viewed with the greatest interest from the point of view of other European peoples, but which from this point of view can never be fully understood. A dark ground above which gleams a colorful play of light. This character seemed to me to be compressed into a visible unity when I stood before the Franz Deak monument. In this head of the maker of that Hungary which existed from the year 1867 till 1918 there lives a robust, proud will which lays hold courageously, which forces itself through without cunning but with elemental recklessness. I felt how true subjectively for every Hungarian was the motto I had often heard: "Outside of Hungary there is no life; and, if there is a life, it is no life."

As a child I had seen on the western borders of Hungary how Germans were made to feel this robust, proud will; now I learned to know in the midst of Hungary how this will brings the Magyar human being into a human isolation which with a certain naïveté clothes itself in a glamour obvious to itself, and is much concerned with displaying itself to the hidden eyes of nature but not to the open eyes of men.

Half a year after this visit my Transylvanian friends arranged for me to deliver a lecture at Hermannstadt. It was Christmas time. I traveled over the wide plains in the midst of which lies Arad. The melancholy poetry of Lenau sounded into my heart as I looked out over these plains where all is one expanse to which the eye can find no limit. I had to spend the night in a little border village between Hungary and Transylvania. I sat in a small inn half the night. Besides myself, there was only a group of card-players sitting round a table. In this group were all the nationalities to be found at that time in Hungary and Transylvania. The men were playing with a passion which constantly exploded at half-hour intervals, so that it came to expression in soul-clouds which rose above the table, fought one another like demons, and devoured the men completely. What differences in passionate existence were there manifested by these different national types!

I reached Hermannstadt on Christmas Day. Here I was introduced into Transylvanian Saxondom. This existed in the midst of a Rumanian and Magyar environment. A noble folk which, in the midst of a decline that it is unwilling to see, desires bravely to preserve itself. A Germanism which, as if in memory of the transfer of its life, driven centuries ago to the East, wishes to remain loyal to its origins, but which in this temper of mind shows a trait of alienation from the world, manifest everywhere in an artificial joy in life. I passed happy days among the German ministers of the Evangelical Church, among the teachers of the German schools, and among other German Transylvanians. My heart warmed to these people who, in the concern for their folk-life and in their duty to this, developed a culture of the heart which spoke first of all likewise to the heart.

This vital warmth filled my soul as I sat in a sleigh, wrapped close in heavy furs, and traveled southward with these old and newly gained friends through icy cold and over crackling snow toward the Carpathians (the Transylvanian Alps). A dark forested mountain wall when one moves toward it from the distance; a wild, precipitous, often frightful mountain landscape when one is close at hand.

The center in all that I then experienced was my friend of many years. He was always thinking up something new whereby I might learn to know thoroughly Transylvanian Saxondom. He was still

dividing his time between Vienna and Hermannstadt. At that time
he had established a weekly paper at Hermannstadt for the purpose
of fostering Transylvanian Saxondom. An undertaking this was
which arose entirely out of idealism utterly devoid of practical experience, but at which almost all representatives of Saxondom labored
together. After a few weeks it came to grief.

Such experiences as this journey came to me from destiny; through
them I was enabled to educate my apprehension of the outer world,
which has not been easy for me, whereas in the element of the spiritual I lived as in something self-evident.

It was with sad memories that I made the journey back to Vienna.
Soon afterward there came into my hands a book of whose "spiritual
richness" people in many circles were speaking: *Rembrandt als
Erzieher*.[1] In conversations about this book, which were going on
wherever one went, there was talk about the rise of an entirely new
spirit. I was forced to become aware, by reason of this very phenomenon, of the great loneliness in which I stood, with my temper of
mind, amid the cultural life of that period.

In regard to a book prized in the highest degree by all the world
my own feeling was as if some one had sat for several months in one
of the better inns and listened to what the "more outstanding" personalities at the reserved tables said by way of "witty" remarks and
had then written these down in the form of aphorisms. After this
continuous "preliminary work," he might have thrown his slips of
paper into a receptacle, shaken them together thoroughly, and then
taken them out again. After drawing out the slips, he might have
linked one to another in series and so produced a book. Of course,
this criticism is exaggerated. But my inner view of life forced me
into such a rejection of what the "spirit of the age" then praised as
a work of the highest merit. I considered *Rembrandt as Educator* a
book which moved wholly on the surface of thoughts pretending to
be clever, and which was not related in a single sentence with the
real depth of a human soul. It grieved me to know that my contem-

[1] *Rembrandt as Educator*.

poraries considered just such a book as coming from a profound personality, whereas I was forced to believe such thought-dabbling in shallow waters of the mind would drive all that is deeply human out of man's soul.

When I was fourteen years old, I had to begin tutoring; for fifteen years, up to the beginning of the second chapter of my life, that spent at Weimar, my destiny kept me engaged in this work. The unfolding of the minds of many persons, both in childhood and in youth, was in this way bound up with my own development. Through this means I was able to observe how different are the ways in which the two sexes grow into life. For, along with the giving of instruction to boys and young men, it fell to my lot to teach also a number of young girls. Indeed, for some time the mother of the boy whose instruction I had taken over because of his pathological condition was a pupil of mine in geometry, and at another time I taught this lady and her sister aesthetics.

In the family of this boy I found for a number of years a sort of home, from which I undertook for other families the activity of educator and instructor. Through the close friendship between the mother of this boy and me it came about that I shared fully in the joys and sorrows of this family. In this woman I was confronted by a uniquely beautiful human soul. She was wholly devoted to the unfolding of the destiny of her four boys. In her could be studied mother love in its great form. To cooperate with her in problems of education formed a beautiful life substance. In the musical sphere of the arts, she possessed both talent and enthusiasm. She took charge partly herself of the musical practice of her boys as long as they were still little children. She discussed intelligently with me the most various life problems, entering into everything with the deepest interest. She gave the closest attention to my scientific and other work. This was a time when I had the utmost need to discuss with her everything that intimately concerned me. When I spoke of my spiritual experiences, she listened in a peculiar way. To her intellect, the subject matter was entirely congenial, but she main-

tained a slight trait of reserve. Yet her mind absorbed everything. At
the same time she maintained in reference to man's being a certain
naturalistic view. She thought of the moral temper of soul as bound
up with the health or sickness of the bodily constitution. I mean to
say that she thought about the human being instinctively in a medical way, and this way of thinking had in her case a tendency to be
somewhat naturalistically colored. To discuss things in this direction
with her was in the highest degree stimulating. Besides, her attitude
toward all outer life was that of a woman who attended with the
strongest sense of duty to everything that fell to her lot, but who inwardly looked upon most of this external life as not belonging to
her sphere. She felt her destiny to be in many aspects something
burdensome. Yet she made no claims upon life; she accepted this
as it took form so far as it did not concern her sons. In relation to
these she felt every experience with the deepest emotions of her soul.

All this I shared vitally—the soul-life of a woman, her beautiful
devotion to her sons, the life of the family amid a wide circle of rela-
tives and acquaintances. But in this connection not everything went
smoothly. The family was Jewish. In their views they were quite free
from any sectarian or racial narrowness, but the head of the family,
to whom I was strongly attached, felt a certain sensitiveness about
any expression of a Gentile in regard to the Jews. The flame of anti-
Semitism which had sprung up at that time caused this feeling.

Now, I took an interested part in the struggle which the Germans
in Austria were then carrying on in behalf of their national existence. I was also led to occupy myself with the historical and social
position of the Jews. Especially earnest did this activity become after
the appearance of Hamerling's *Homunculus*. This eminently German poet was considered by a great part of the journalists as an anti-
Semite because of this work; indeed, he was claimed by the anti-
Semites of German nationality as one of their own. This did not
concern me at all, but I wrote a paper on the *Homunculus* in which,
as I thought, I expressed myself quite objectively in regard to the
position of Judaism. The man in whose home I was living, and who

was my friend, took this to be a special form of anti-Semitism. Not in the least did his friendly feeling for me suffer on this account, but he was affected with profound distress. When he had read the paper, he faced me, his heart torn with innermost sorrow, and said to me: "What you have written here in regard to the Jews cannot be explained in a friendly sense. This, however, is not what strikes me, but the fact that, in view of your close relation with us, you could have had the experiences which induced you to write thus only in connection with us and our friends." He was mistaken; I had formed my opinions altogether on the basis of an intellectual and historical survey; nothing personal had slipped into my judgment. He could not see the matter in this way. His reply to my explanation was: "No, the man who teaches my children is, after this paper, no 'friend of the Jews.'" He could not be induced to change his opinion. Not for a moment did he think that anything in my relation to the family ought to be altered. He considered this relation a necessity. Still less could I make this matter the occasion for a change; for I looked upon the educating of his son as a task that destiny had brought to me. But neither of us could do otherwise than to think that a tragic element had been mingled with this relation.

To all this was added the fact that many of my friends had taken on from their national struggle a tinge of anti-Semitism in their view of Judaism. They did not look sympathetically upon my holding a post in a Jewish family; and the head of this family saw in my friendly mingling with such persons only a confirmation of the impression he had received from my paper.

To the family circle in which I so intimately shared belonged the composer of *Das Goldene Kreuz,* Ignatz Brüll. A sensitive person he was, of whom I was extraordinarily fond. Ignatz Brüll was something of an alien to the world, absorbed in himself. His interests were not exclusively musical; they were directed toward many aspects of the cultural life. These interests he could apply only as a "darling of destiny" against the background of a family circle which never permitted him to be disturbed by attention to every-day affairs, but made it possible for his creative work to grow out of a certain wealth. And thus he did not grow into life but only into music. To what degree his musical creations were or were not meritorious need not be the question here. But it was charming in the best sense of the word to meet the man on the street and see him awake out of his world of tones when one addressed him. Generally he did not have his waistcoat buttons in the right button-holes. His eye expressed a gentle thoughtfulness; his walk was not steady, but expressive. One could talk with him about many things; he had a sensitive understanding for these. But one observed how the content of the conversation slipped at once for him into the realm of the musical.

In the family in which I thus lived, I became acquainted also with the distinguished physician Dr. Breuer, who was associated with Dr. Freud at the birth of psychoanalysis. Only at the beginning, however, did he share in this view, and he was probably not in agreement with Freud in his later development of it. Dr. Breuer was to me a very attractive personality. I admired the way in which he carried on his medical profession. Besides, he was a man of many interests in other fields. He spoke about Shakespeare in such a way as to stimulate one strongly. It was interesting also to hear him in his thoroughly medical way of thinking speak of Ibsen or even of Tolstoi's *Kreuzer Sonata*. When he talked with the friend I have here described, the mother of the children whom I had to teach, I often shared in this with deepest interest. Psychoanalysis was not yet born, but the problems which tended in this direction were already there. The phenomena of hypnotism had given a special coloring to medical thought. My friend had been a friend of Dr. Breuer since her youth. There I faced a fact that gave me much food for reflection. This woman thought in a certain direction more medically than the distinguished physician. They once discussed a morphine addict. Dr. Breuer was treating him. The woman once said to me: "Think what Breuer has done! He persuaded the morphine addict to promise on his word of honor that he would take no more morphine. He expected to accomplish something in this way, and he was indignant when the patient did not keep his promise. He even said: 'How can I treat a man who does not keep his promise?' Would one have believed," she said, "that so distinguished a physician could be so naive? How can one try to cure by a promise something so deeply rooted in a man's nature?" The woman may, however, not have been entirely right; the opinion of the physician regarding the therapy of suggestion may have entered then into his attempt at a cure; but no one can deny that my friend's statement indicated the extraordinary energy with which she spoke in a noteworthy manner out of the spirit that lived in the Viennese school of medicine just at the time when this was coming into flower.

This woman was in her own way significant, and she occupies the position of a significant personality in my life. She has long been dead. Among the things that made it hard for me to leave Vienna was this also, that I had to part with her.

When I reflect in retrospect upon the content of the first chapter of my life, seeking to characterize it as if from without, the feeling forces itself upon me that destiny had so guided me that I did not feel myself to be fettered by any external "profession" in my thirtieth year. I also entered the Goethe-Schiller Archives in Weimar, not to take a life position, but as a free collaborator on the edition of Goethe to be published by the Archives under a commission from the Grand Duchess Sophie. In the report which the Director of the Archives published in the twelfth volume of the Goethe Year Book, occurs this statement: "To the permanent workers, Rudolf Steiner, of Vienna, has been added since the autumn of 1890. To him has been assigned the whole field of Morphology (with the exception of the osteological part): five or probably six volumes of the Second Division, to which important material accrues from the manuscript legacy."

XIV

AGAIN for an indeterminate length of time I faced a task which had come about, not through any external cause, but through the inner processes of development of my views on life and the world. To the same cause was due the fact that the University of Rostock was the institution where I presented for my doctoral examination my dissertation on the endeavor after an "understanding of human consciousness with itself." External circumstances prevented me merely from taking the examination in Vienna. I had official credit for the work of the *Realschule,* not the *Gymnasium,* though I had completed privately the *Gymnasium* course of study while tutoring also in these studies. This fact barred me from obtaining the doctor's degree in Austria. I had grounded myself thoroughly in philosophy, but I was credited with a course of study which excluded me from everything to which the study of philosophy gives a person access.

At the close of the first phase of my life, a philosophical work had come into my hands which fascinated me extraordinarily—the *Sieben Bücher Platonismus,*[1] of Heinrich von Stein, who was then teaching philosophy at Rostock. This fact led me to submit my dissertation to the lovable old philosopher, whom I valued highly because of this book, and whom I have seen only in connection with the examination.

The personality of Heinrich von Stein is still vivid in my memory —almost as if I had lived through much with him. For the *Seven*

[1] *The Seven Books of Platonism.*

146

Books of Platonism is the expression of a sharply stamped philosophical individuality. Philosophy as thought-content is not taken in this work as something that stands on its own feet. Plato is viewed from all angles as the philosopher who sought for such a self-supporting philosophy. What he found in this direction is carefully set forth by Heinrich von Stein. In the first chapters of the book one enters vitally and wholly into the Platonic world view. Then, however, Stein passes on to the breaking into human evolution of the Christ-revelation. This actual breaking in of the spiritual life he sets forth as something higher than the elaboration of thought-content through mere philosophy.

From Plato to Christ as the fulfillment of that for which men have striven—such we may designate as the exposition of von Stein. He then traces further the influence of the world view of Platonism in the Christian evolution.

Stein is of the opinion that revelation gave content *from without* to human strivings after a world view. There I could not agree with him. I knew from experience that the human being, when he comes to an understanding with himself in a living spiritual consciousness, can possess the revelation and that this revelation can then attain to an existence in the human being in the experience of ideas. But I felt something in the book which attracted me. The real life of the spirit behind the life in ideas, even though in a form that was not my own, had set in motion an impulse toward a comprehensive exposition of the history of philosophy. Plato, the great representative of the world of ideas which waited for fulfillment through the Christ impulse—it is the setting forth of this that constitutes the content of Stein's book. In spite of my contrasting position, this book came closer to me than any of the philosophies which merely elaborate a content out of concepts and sense-experiences.

I missed in Stein also the awareness that Plato's world of ideas points back, after all, to a primal revelation of the spiritual world. This revelation (pre-Christian), which has been sympathetically set forth in Otto Willmann's *Geschichte des Idealismus*,[1] does not appear in Stein's view. He presents Platonism, not as a residue of ideas from the primal revelation, which then regains in Christianity on a higher level its lost spiritual substance; he represents the Platonic ideas as a content of concepts self-woven which then attained life through Christ.

Yet the book is one of those written with philosophical warmth, and its author a personality permeated by a deeply religious feeling who sought in philosophy an expression of the religious life. On every page of the three-volume work one is aware of the personality in the background. After I had read this book, and especially the parts dealing with the relation of Platonism to Christianity, over and over again, it was a significant experience to meet the author face to face.

A personality serene in his whole bearing, in advanced age, with mild eyes that looked as if they were made to survey kindly but penetratingly the course of development of students; speech which in every sentence carried the deliberation of the philosopher in the tone of the words—just so did Stein stand at once before me when I visited him before the examination. He said to me: 'Your dissertation is not such as is required; one can see from it that you have not produced it under the guidance of a professor; but what it contains makes it possible that I can very gladly accept it.' I had so earnestly wished to be questioned orally on something related to the *Seven Books of Platonism;* but no question bore upon this; all were drawn from the philosophy of Kant.

I have always kept the image of Heinrich von Stein deeply imprinted on my heart; and it would have given me immeasurable pleasure to have met the man again. Destiny never again brought us together. My doctoral examination is one of my pleasantest memories, because the impression of Stein's personality shines out beyond anything else pertaining to it.

[1] *History of Idealism.*

The mood in which I came to Weimar was tinged by my previous thorough-going work on Platonism. I think this mood helped me greatly in taking the right attitude toward my task at the Goethe-Schiller Archives. How did Plato live in the world of ideas, and how Goethe? This occupied my thoughts on my walk to and from the Archives; it occupied me also as I went over the manuscripts of the Goethe legacy.

This question was in the background when, at the beginning of 1891, I expressed in such words as the following my impression of Goethe's science of nature: "It is impossible for the majority of men to grasp the fact that something for whose appearance wholly subjective conditions are necessary may, nevertheless, have objective significance and character. Of this very kind is the 'archetypal plant.' It is the essential of all plants, objectively contained in them; but, if it is to attain to phenomenal existence, the human mind must freely construct it."

Or in these words: A correct understanding of Goethe's way of thinking "admits of the possibility of deciding whether it is in keeping with the conception of Goethe to identify the 'archetypal plant' or 'archetypal animal' with any physically real form which has appeared at any definite time or now appears. To this question the only possible answer is a decisive No. The archetypal plant is contained in every plant; it may be gained from the plant world by the constructive power of the mind; but no single individual form can be said to be typical." [1]

I now entered the Goethe-Schiller Archives as collaborator. This was the place where the philology of the end of the nineteenth century had taken charge of Goethe's literary estate. At the head of the Archives, as Director, was Bernhard Suphan. With him I had also, I may say, personal relations from the very first day of the Weimar phase of my life. I had frequent opportunities to be in his home.

---

[1] In the paper entitled "Über den Gewinn unserer Anschauungen von Goethes naturwissen-schaftlichen Arbeiten durch die Publikationen des Goethe-Archivs," in Volume 12 of the *Goethe-Jahrbuch*.

That Bernhard Suphan had succeeded Erich Schmidt, the first Director of the Archives, was due to his friendship with Herman Grimm.

The last descendant of Goethe, Walther von Goethe, had left the Goethe literary estate as a legacy to the Grand Duchess Sophie. She had founded the Archives in order that the legacy might be introduced appropriately into the cultural life of the time. She naturally turned to those personalities of whom she had to assume that they would know what was to be done with the Goethe literary estate.

First of all, there was Herr von Loeper. He was, so to speak, foreordained to become the intermediary between Goethe scholars and the court at Weimar, to which the control of the Goethe legacy had been entrusted. For he had attained to high rank in the Prussian cabinet, and thus stood in close relation with the Queen of Prussia, sister of the Grand Duke of Saxe-Weimar; and, besides, he was an important collaborator on the most famous edition of Goethe of that time, that of Hempel.

Loeper was a unique personality, a very congenial mixture of man of the world and singular character. As an amateur, not a professional, had he grown into "Goethe research." But he had attained to high distinction in this. In his opinions about Goethe, which appeared in such excellent form in his edition of *Faust,* he was entirely independent. What he advanced he had learned from Goethe himself. Since he had now to advise who could best administer the Goethe literary legacy, he had to turn to those with whom he had become familiar as Goethe scholars through his own work with Goethe.

The first to be considered was Herman Grimm. It was as a historian of art that Herman Grimm had become concerned with Goethe; in this capacity he had delivered lectures on Goethe at the University of Berlin, which were then published as a book. But he might well look upon himself, at the same time, as a sort of cultural descendant of Goethe. He was rooted in those circles of the German cultural life which had always been conscious of a living tradition of Goethe, and which might, in a sense, consider themselves united in a personal way with him. The wife of Herman Grimm was Gisela von Arnim, the daughter of Bettina, author of the book *Goethes Briefwechsel mit einem Kinde*.[1]

Herman Grimm's judgments about Goethe were those of an art enthusiast. Moreover, as a historian of art he had developed in scholarship only so far as this was possible while maintaining a personally colored relation to art as a connoisseur.

I think that Herman Grimm could easily come to an understanding with Loeper, with whom he was naturally on friendly terms by reason of their common interest in Goethe. I imagine that, when the two discussed Goethe, the human interest in the genius came strongly to the fore and scholarly considerations fell into the background.

This scholarly way of looking at Goethe was the vital matter for Wilhelm Scherer, professor of the history of German literature at the University of Berlin. In him both Loeper and Grimm had to recognize the official Goethe scholar. Loeper did so in a childlike, naive manner; Herman Grimm with a certain inner opposition. For him the philological point of view which characterized Scherer was uncongenial.

With these three persons rested the actual direction in the administration of the Goethe legacy. But it really slipped, nevertheless, entirely into the hands of Scherer. Loeper probably intended to do no more than to advise and to share from without as a collaborator in the task; he had his fixed social relations through his position in the cabinet of the Prussian King. Nor did Herman Grimm have any other intention. Because of his position in the cultural life, his inclination could only be to contribute points of view and right directions for the work; for the directing in details he could not take responsibility.

Quite different was the matter for Wilhelm Scherer. For him, Goethe was an important chapter in the history of German literature.

[1] *Goethe's Correspondence with a Child.*

In the Goethe Archives, new sources had come to light of immeasurable value for this chapter. Therefore, the work in the Goethe Archives must be systematically integrated into the general work of the history of literature. The plan arose for an edition of Goethe which would take a philologically correct form. Scherer took over the primary intellectual supervision; the direction of the Archives was left to his student Erich Schmidt, who then occupied the chair of the history of modern German literature in Vienna.

It was thus that the work of the Goethe Archives received its stamp. Not only this, but also everything else that took place at the Archives or by reason of it. Everything bore the character of the contemporary philological way of thinking and working.

In Wilhelm Scherer literary-historical philology strove for an imitation of contemporary natural-scientific methods. People took the prevailing ideas of the natural sciences and sought to form philological and literary-historical ideas on these as models. Whence had a poet derived something? How had this something been modified in him? These were the questions that were made fundamental to the history of the evolution of cultural life. The poetic personalities disappeared from view; instead there came forward questions as to how "material" and "motif" were developed in passing through these personalities. The climax of such a view was reached in Erich Schmidt's extended monograph on Lessing. In this, Lessing's personality is not the main thing but the extremely painstaking consideration of the motifs of *Minna von Barnhelm, Nathan,* and the like.

Scherer died young, shortly after the establishment of the Archives. His students were numerous. Erich Schmidt was called from the Goethe Archives to Scherer's position in Berlin. Herman Grimm then brought it about that not one of the numerous students of Scherer should have the direction of the Archives, but instead Bernhard Suphan.

As to his post before this time, he had been teaching in a *Gymnasium* in Berlin. At the same time he had undertaken the editing of Herder's works. Through this he seemed preordained as the person to take direction also of the edition of Goethe.

Erich Schmidt still exercised a certain influence; through this fact Scherer's spirit still continued to rule over the Goethe task. But, side by side with all this, the ideas of Herman Grimm came forward in stronger fashion, if not in the manner of the work, yet in the personal relations within the Archives.

When I came to Weimar, and entered into a closer relation with Bernhard Suphan, he was a man sorely tried in his personal life. His first and second wives, who were sisters, he had seen buried at an early age. He lived now with his two boys in Weimar, grieving over those who had left him, without any happiness in life. His sole satisfaction lay in the good will which the Grand Duchess Sophie, his profoundly honored lady, bore to him. In this respect for her, there was nothing servile: Suphan loved and admired the Grand Duchess in an entirely personal way.

In loyal attachment was Suphan devoted to Herman Grimm. He had previously been considered a member of the household of Grimm in Berlin, and had breathed with satisfaction the cultural atmosphere of that home. But there was something in him that prevented him from getting adjusted to life. It was possible to speak freely with him about the highest cultural matters, yet something tart, arising from his feelings, would easily enter into the conversation. Most of all did this mood dominate in his own mind; then he would help himself past this feeling by means of a dry humor. Thus one could not feel warm in his company. He could in a moment grasp some large idea quite sympathetically, and then, without any transition, fall at once into the petty and trivial. He always showed good will toward me. In the spiritual interests vital in my own mind he could take no part, even treating these at times from the viewpoint of his dry humor; but in the trend of my work in the Goethe Archives and in my personal life he felt the warmest interest.

I cannot deny that I was often painfully disturbed by what Suphan did, the way in which he conducted himself in the direction of the Archives and in supervising the editing of Goethe; I never made any secret of this fact. Yet, when I look back upon the years that I passed with him, my primary feeling is a strong inner interest in the fate and the personality of this sorely tried man. He suffered through life, and he suffered through himself. I saw how, with all the good aspects of his character and all his capacities, he sank more and more, as it were, into a bottomless meaningless brooding which rose up in his soul. When the Goethe-Schiller Archives were moved to the new building erected on the Ilm, Suphan said that he looked upon himself in relation to the opening of the building like one of those human victims who in primitive times were walled up before the doors of sacred structures to bless that for which they stood. He had gradually come to the fantastic conception of himself completely in the rôle of one sacrificed for the cause, with which, nevertheless, he did not feel wholly united. Like a beast of burden of the Goethe work he felt himself, unable to experience any joy in a task in which others might have shared with utmost enthusiasm. In this mood I always found him later when I met him after I had left Weimar. He ended his life by suicide in a darkened state of consciousness.

Besides Bernhard Suphan, there was engaged at the Goethe-Schiller Archives at the time of my entrance Julius Wahle. He was one of those called by Erich Schmidt. Wahle and I had become well acquainted from the time of my first sojourn at Weimar; a warm friendship developed between us. Wahle was working at the editing of Goethe's diaries. Eduard von der Hellen worked as Registrar, and also was responsible for editing Goethe's letters.

In "Goethe's Works" a great part of the whole body of Germanists in Germany participated. There was a constant coming and going of professors and instructors in philology. One was much in company with them during their longer or shorter visits even outside of hours at the Archives. It was possible to enter vitally into the circle of interests of these persons.

Besides these actual collaborators in the Goethe task, the Archives

were visited by a number of persons interested in one or another of
the rich collections of manuscripts of other German poets; for the
Archives gradually became the place for collecting the literary estates
of many poets. Other interested persons came also who were less
interested in manuscripts than simply in studying in the library contained within the rooms of the Archives. There were, moreover,
many visitors who merely wished to see the treasures there.

Everybody who worked at the Archives was happy when Loeper
appeared. He entered with sympathetic and amiable remarks. He
requested the material he needed for his work, sat down, and worked
for hours with a concentration seldom seen in any one. No matter
what was going on around him, he did not look up. If I were seeking
for a personification of amiability, I should choose Herr von Loeper.
Amiable was his Goethe research, amiable every word he uttered
to any one. Especially amiable was the stamp his whole inner life
had taken on from the fact that he seemed to be thinking almost
always of one thing only: how to bring the world to a true understanding of Goethe. I once sat beside him during a presentation of
Faust in the theater. I began to discuss the manner of the presentation, the quality of the acting. He did not hear at all what I said. But
he replied: 'Yes, these actors often use words and phrases that do not
quite agree with those of Goethe.' Still more lovable did Loeper appear to me in his absent-mindedness. When, during an intermission,
I chanced to speak of something which required a reckoning of the
duration of time, Loeper said: "Well, the hours of 100 minutes, the
minutes of 100 seconds. . . ." I looked at him and said, "Your Excel-
lency, 60 minutes, 60 seconds." He took out his watch, tested it,
laughed heartily, counted and said: "Yes, yes, 60 minutes, 60 seconds."
I often observed in him such instances of absent-mindedness. But
even over such instances of Loeper's peculiar temper of mind I could
not laugh, since they seemed to me a necessary by-product of the
earnestness of the personality, an earnestness so free from pose, so
unsentimental, I might say graceful—which had at the same time a
charming effect. He spoke in rather gushing sentences, almost with-

out modulation; but one heard through the colorless speech a firm articulation of thought.

Cultural distinction entered the Archives when Herman Grimm appeared. Ever since I had read—while still in Vienna—his book on Goethe, I felt the deepest sympathy with his type of mind. And, when I was able to meet him for the first time at the Archives, I had read almost everything that had come from his pen up to that time. Through Suphan I was soon afterward brought into much closer acquaintance with him. Then, while Suphan was absent once from Weimar, and he came for a visit to the Archives, he invited me to luncheon at his hotel. I was alone with him. It was plainly agreeable to him to see how I could enter into his way of viewing the world and life. He became communicative. He spoke to me of his idea of a *Geschichte der deutschen Phantasie*,[1] which he had in mind. I received the impression at the time that he intended to write such a book. This did not come to pass. But he explained to me beautifully how the continuous stream of historic evolution has its impulse in the creative fantasy of the folk, which, in his conception, took on the character of a living, active supersensible genius. During this luncheon I was completely engrossed in the exposition of Herman Grimm. I believed that I knew how the supersensible spirituality works through human beings. I had before me a person whose spiritual vision reached as far as the creative spirituality, but who would not lay hold upon the actual life of this spirituality, but remained in the region where the spiritual expresses its life in man in the form of fantasy.

Herman Grimm had a special gift for surveying greater or lesser epochs of the history of culture and for setting forth the period surveyed in precise, spirited epigrammatic characterization. When he described a single personality—Michelangelo, Raphael, Goethe, Homer—his presentation always appeared against the background of such a survey. How often have I read the essays in which he characterizes in his striking surveys the Greek and Roman cultures and

[1] *History of German Fantasy.*

the Middle Ages. The whole man was the revelation of a unified style. When he fashioned his beautiful sentences in oral discourse, I had the feeling: "This might appear just so in one of his essays"; and, when I read an essay of his after having become acquainted with him, I felt as if I were listening to him. He permitted himself no laxity in oral discourse, but he had the feeling that in artistic literary presentation one must remain the same person who moves about in every-day life. Herman Grimm, however, did not move about in every-day life like other men. It was inevitable for him to live a life possessed of style.

When Herman Grimm appeared in Weimar, and in the Archives, one felt that the place of the legacy was united with Goethe, so to speak, by secret spiritual threads. Not so when Erich Schmidt came. He was bound to these manuscripts preserved in the Archives, not by ideas, but by the historic-philological methods. I could never gain a human relation with Erich Schmidt. And so all the great respect shown him by those who worked at the Archives as Scherer philologists made practically no impression on me.

Those were always pleasant moments when the Grand Duke Carl Alexander appeared in the Archives. An inwardly true enthusiasm—though manifested in a distinguished bearing—for everything pertaining to Goethe was a part of the nature of this man. Because of his age, his long connection with much that was important in the cultural life of Germany, and because of his captivating amiability, he made a satisfying impression. It was a pleasing thought to know that, as the protector of Goethe's work, he was in the Archives.

The Grand Duchess Sophie, owner of the Archives, one saw there only on special festival occasions. When she had anything to say, she caused Suphan to be summoned. The collaborating visitors were taken to her to be presented. But her solicitude for the Archives was extraordinary. She herself made personally at that time all the preliminary preparations for the erection of a public edifice in which the poetic legacies might be worthily housed.

The heir of the Grand Duke, Carl August, who died before he became Grand Duke, came often to the Archives. His interest in everything going on there was not profound, but he liked to converse with us collaborators. Interesting himself in the affairs of the cultural life he viewed rather as a duty. But the interest of the heiress, Pauline, was full of warmth. I was able many times to converse with her about things pertaining to Goethe, poetry, and the like. As regards its social intercourse, the Archives were between the scientific and artistic circles and the courtly circle in Weimar. From both sides it received its social coloring. Scarcely would the door have closed after a professor when it would reopen to admit some princely personage who had come to the court for a visit. Many men of all social positions shared in what went on in the Archives. In truth, it was a stirring life, stimulating in many aspects.

Immediately beside the Archives was the Weimar Library. In this resided as chief librarian a man of childlike temperament and unlimited scholarship, Reinhold Köhler. The collaborators at the Archives often had occasion to resort there, for what they had in the Archives as literary aid in their work was here greatly augmented. Reinhold Köhler was acquainted in a uniquely comprehensive way with the myths, fairy tales, sagas; his knowledge in the field of linguistic scholarship was of the most admirable universality. He knew where to turn for the most out-of-the-way literary documents. At the same time, his modesty was most touching, and he was warmheartedly obliging. He never permitted any one else to bring the books needed from their resting places into the work-room of the library where we did our work. I came in once and asked for a book that Goethe had used in connection with his studies in botany, in order to look into it. Reinhold Köhler went to get the antique book, which had rested somewhere on the topmost shelves, unused for decades. He did not come back for a long time. Some one went to see where he was. He had fallen from the ladder on which he had to climb to get the book, and had broken his thigh. The noble and lovable person never recovered from the effect of the accident. After a lingering illness, the widely known man died. I grieved over the painful thought that the accident had occurred while he was attending to a book for me.

XV

Two lectures that I had to deliver shortly after the beginning of the Weimar chapter of my life are associated for me with important memories. One took place in Weimar, and was entitled *Die Phantasie als Kulturschöpferin;*[1] it preceded the conversation I have described with Herman Grimm about his views on the history of the evolution of fantasy.

Before I delivered this lecture, I summarized in my mind what I could say, on the basis of my spiritual experience, about the unconscious streaming of the real spiritual world into human fantasy. What lives in fantasy seemed to me to be stimulated by human sense-experiences only as regards its material substance. What is truly creative in the genuine formations molded by fantasy seemed to me to be a reflection of the spiritual world existing outside the human being. I desired to show that fantasy is the gateway through which the Beings of the spiritual world, working creatively in an indirect way through man, influence the development of human cultures.

Since I had arranged my ideas for such a lecture toward this objective, Herman Grimm's exposition made a deep impression on me. He felt no need whatever to seek for the supersensible sources of fantasy; what enters the human mind as fantasy he took as a matter of fact and proposed to observe this in the course of its evolution.

I first set forth one pole of the unfolding of fantasy—dream-life. I showed how external sense-impressions are experienced in dreams—

[1] *Fantasy as the Creatress of Culture.*

160

because of the subdued life of consciousness—not as in waking life, but transformed into symbolic pictures; how inner bodily processes are experienced in the same symbolization; how experiences rise in consciousness, not in sober memories, but in a way that indicates a powerful working of the thing experienced in the depths of the soul life.

In dreams, consciousness is subdued; it then sinks down into the sensible-physical reality, and beholds the action within the sense existence of something spiritual which, to ordinary sense-perception, remains concealed, and which even to the half-sleeping consciousness appears only as a play of colors from the bottomless depths of the sensible.

In fantasy, the mind rises just as far above the ordinary state of consciousness as it sinks below this in dream-life. The spiritual that is concealed within the sense existence does not appear, yet the spiritual does influence the human being. But he cannot grasp this in its very own form but symbolizes it unconsciously to himself by means of a soul-content which he borrows from the sense-world. Consciousness does not penetrate all the way to the vision of the spiritual world, but it experiences this in pictures which draw their material from the sense-world. In this way the genuine creations of fantasy are productions of the spiritual world, even though this world itself does not penetrate to human consciousness.

By means of this lecture I wished to show one of the ways in which the Beings of the spiritual world influence the evolution of life.

It was thus that I strove to discover means whereby I might bring to expression the world of spirit that I experienced, and yet in some way connect it with what is familiar to ordinary consciousness. I was of the opinion that it was necessary to speak of the spirit, but that the forms of expression customary in this scientific age must be respected.

The other lecture I gave in Vienna at the invitation of the Scientific Club. It dealt with the possibility of a monistic conception of the world together with the maintenance of a real knowledge of the

spiritual. There I set forth that man grasps with his senses the physical side of reality "from without" and grasps with his spiritual perception its spiritual side "from within," so that all which is experienced appears as a unitary world in which the sensible manifests
the spirit and the spirit reveals itself creatively in the sensible.

This occurred at a time when Haeckel had formulated his own
monistic philosophy through his lecture on *Monismus als Band
zwischen Religion und Wissenschaft.*[1] Haeckel, who knew of my
being in Weimar, sent me a copy of his address. I reciprocated his
courtesy by sending him the issue of the magazine in which my
lecture in Vienna was printed. Any one who reads this lecture must
see how opposed I then was to the monism advanced by Haeckel
when there was occasion for me to express what has to be said about
this monism by a person for whom the world of spirit is something
into which he sees.

But there was at that time another necessity for me to reflect about
monism in the coloring given to it by Haeckel. He seemed to me
a phenomenon of the age of natural science. Philosophers saw in
Haeckel a philosophical dilettante, who really knew nothing except
the forms of living creatures, to which he applied the ideas of Darwin
in the manner in which he had interpreted them, and who explained
boldly that nothing else must be employed for the formation of a
world view than what can be conceived by a trained Darwinian
observer of nature. Scientists saw in Haeckel a fantastic person who
drew from natural-scientific observations quite arbitrary conclusions.

While my work required that I should explain what was the inner
temper of thinking about the world and man, about nature and
the spirit, as this had been dominant a hundred years earlier in Jena,
when Goethe injected his natural-scientific ideas into this thinking,
I saw in Haeckel an illustration of what was being thought in this
direction in the contemporary period. Goethe's relation to the views
on nature belonging to his period I had to visualize inwardly in all its
details during my work. At the place in Jena from which came the

[1] *Monism as Connecting Religion and Science.*

important stimulations to Goethe to formulate his ideas on natural phenomena and living entities in nature, Haeckel was at work a century later with the pretension that he could draw from a knowledge of nature the determinative element for a world view.

In addition, it happened that at one of the first meetings of the Goethe Society in which I participated during my work in Weimar Helmholtz read a paper on *Goethes Vorahnungen kommender naturwissenschaftlicher Ideen.*[1] There my attention was called to many natural-scientific ideas of which Goethe had "premonitions" by reason of fortunate inspiration; but it was also pointed out that errors of Goethe's in this field were manifested in his theory of color.

When I turned my attention to Haeckel, I wished always to set before my mind Goethe's own judgment of the evolution of natural-scientific conceptions in the century following that which witnessed the development of his own; as I listened to Helmholtz, I had before my mind the judgment passed upon Goethe by this evolution.

I could not then do otherwise than to say to myself that, if one's *thinking* about the essential being of nature was in accordance with the prevailing temper of mind of that time, the result must be that which Haeckel thought in utter philosophical naïveté. Those who opposed him showed everywhere that they limited themselves to mere sense-perception and would avoid the further development of this perception by means of thinking.

I had at first no desire to become personally acquainted with Haeckel, about whom I was impelled to think very much. Then his sixtieth birthday came. I had occasion to share in the brilliant festival that was arranged in Jena. The human element in this festival attracted me. During the banquet, Haeckel's son, whom I had come to know in Weimar, where he was attending the school of painting, came to me and said that his father wished that I be presented to him. The son then introduced me.

Thus I became personally acquainted with Haeckel. He was a fascinating personality. A pair of eyes that looked naively into the

---

[1] *Goethe's Premonitions of Coming Scientific Ideas.*

world, so mild that it seemed as if their look would have to break if the sharpness of thought should penetrate through it. This look could endure only sense-impressions, not thoughts that are manifest in things and occurrences. Every movement of Haeckel's was directed to the purpose of admitting what the senses expressed, not to permit the ruling thoughts to manifest themselves through the senses. I understood why Haeckel liked so much to paint. He surrendered himself to physical vision. Where he ought to have begun to think, there he ceased to unfold the activity of the mind, preferring to fix by means of his brush what he had seen. Such was the very being of Haeckel. Had he unfolded this alone, something human unusually charming would have been revealed.

But in one corner of his soul something burrowed which was wilfully determined to enforce itself as definite thought-content—something originating in quite different world trends from his feeling for nature. The trend of a previous earthly life, with a coloring of fanaticism directed toward something very different from nature, craved to break forth. Religious politics came to living manifestation from the substrata of the soul and made use of ideas about nature for its self-expression.

In such contradictory fashion lived two beings in Haeckel: a man with mild, love-filled feeling for nature, and in the background something like a shadowy being with incompletely developed, narrowly limited ideas, breathing out fanaticism. When Haeckel spoke, his mildness almost wholly prevented the fanaticism from streaming forth into his words; it was as if the gentleness which he desired by nature blunted in speech a hidden demonic something. A human riddle which one could not but love when beholding it, but about which one could often pass over into anger when it expressed judgments. Thus I saw Haeckel before me when he was preparing in the 'nineties of the last century what led later to the furious spiritual battle that raged over his trend of thinking at the turn of the century.

Among the visitors to Weimar was Heinrich von Treitschke. I had the opportunity to meet him when Suphan included me among the guests to meet Treitschke at luncheon. I received a profound impression from this very controversial personality. Treitschke was completely deaf. Others conversed with him by writing what they wished to say on little slips of paper which Treitschke would hand to them. The effect of this was that, in any company where he chanced to be, his person became the central point. When something had been written down, Treitschke then talked about this without the development of a real conversation. He was present for the others in a far more real way than they were for him. This had entered into his whole attitude of mind. He spoke without having to reckon upon objections such as meet other persons when they express their ideas in a group of people. It could clearly be seen how this fact had fixed its roots in his self-consciousness. Since he could not hear any opposition to his thoughts, he was strongly impressed with the worth of what he himself thought.

The first question that Treitschke addressed to me was to ask where I came from. I wrote that I was an Austrian. Treitschke responded: "The Austrians are entirely good and gifted persons or else rascals." When he said such things as this, one became aware that the loneliness in which his mind dwelt because of his deafness drove him to such paradoxes, and found in these a satisfaction. Luncheon guests usually remained at Suphan's the whole afternoon. So it was this time when Treitschke was among them. One could see this personality unfolding. The broad-shouldered man had something in his spiritual personality also through which he made an expansive impression on his fellow men. It could not be said that Treitschke lectured, since everything he said bore a personal character. A passionate eagerness to express himself was manifest in every word. How commanding was his tone even when he was only narrating something! He wished his words to lay hold upon the emotions of the other person also. An unusual fire that sparkled from his eyes accompanied his assertions. The conversations touched at that time upon Moltke's world view as this had found expression in his memoirs. Treitschke objected to the impersonal way—suggestive of mathematical thinking—in which Moltke conceived world phenomena. He could not judge things otherwise than with a ground-tone of utterly personal sympathies and antipathies. Persons like Treitschke, who stick fast within their own personalities, can make an impression on others only when the personal element is at the same time both significant and also deeply interwoven with what they are setting forth. This was the case with Treitschke. When he spoke of something historical, he discoursed as if everything were in the present and he were personally involved with all his pleasure and all his vexation. One listened to the man with the impression of the personal in unmitigated strength; but one gained no relation to the content of what he said.

With another visitor to Weimar I came into a friendly intimacy. This was Ludwig Laistner. A fine personality he was, in harmony with himself, living in the spiritual in the most beautiful way. He was at the time literary adviser to the Cotta publishing house, and as such had to work at the Goethe Archives. I was able to spend with him almost all the leisure time we had. His chief work, *Das Rätsel der Sphinx*,[1] was then already before the world. It is a sort of history of myths. He follows his own road in the interpretation of myths. Our conversations dealt very much with the field treated in that very important book. Laistner rejected all interpretation of fairy-lore, of the mythical, which maintains the idea of the more or less consciously symbolizing fantasy. He sees in dreams, especially in nightmares, the original source of the myth-making view of nature held by the folk. The oppressive nightmare which appears to the dreamer as a tormenting questioning spirit becomes the incubus, the elf, the demonic tormentor; the whole troop of spirits arise for Ludwig Laistner out of the dreaming man. The riddling sphinx is another metamorphosed form of the simple midday-woman who appears to the sleeper in the field at midday and puts questions to him which he has to answer. All that the dream creates in the form of paradoxes, reflective and meaningful, of tormenting and joy-filled

---

[1] *The Riddle of the Sphinx.*

forms—all this Ludwig Laistner traces out in order to point to it again in the images of fairy-lore and myths. In every conversation I had the feeling: "The man could so easily find the way from the creative subconscious in the human being, which is at work in the dream-world, to the super-conscious that touches the real world of spirit." He listened to my explanations of this kind with the utmost good will; said nothing in opposition to them; but gained no inner relation to them. In this matter he, too, was hindered by the fear belonging to the conviction of that time of losing the "scientific" ground from under him the moment he should approach the spiritual as such. But Ludwig Laistner stood in a special relation to art and poetry by reason of the fact that he traced the mythical into the real experiences of dreams and not into the abstractly creative imagination. Everything creative in man thus took on, in his view, a world significance. Possessing a rare inner serenity and self-sufficiency of mind, he was also a discriminating poetical personality. His utterances in regard to every kind of thing had a certain poetic quality. Conceptions that are unpoetical he simply did not know at all. In Weimar and later during a visit in Stuttgart, where I had the pleasure of staying in his home, I spent the most delightful hours in his company. Beside him stood his wife, who entered completely into his spiritual nature. For her Ludwig Laistner was really all that bound her to the world. He lived only a short while after his sojourn in Weimar. The wife followed her deceased husband after an exceedingly brief interval; the world was empty for her when Ludwig Laistner was no longer in it. Truly, an exceptionally lovable woman, notable in the lovableness of her nature. She always knew how to be absent when she feared that she might disturb; she never failed to be present when there was anything requiring her attention. Like a mother she stood by the side of Ludwig Laistner, who, with his refined spirituality, was very delicate in body.

With Ludwig Laistner I could converse as with few other persons about the Idealism of the German philosophers Fichte, Hegel, Schelling. He had a vital sense for the reality of the essence of ideas which

lived in these philosophers. When I once spoke to him of my solicitude about the one-sidedness of the natural-scientific world view,
he said: '*Those* people simply have no sense of the significance of
the creative in the human mind. They do not know that a cosmic
content dwells in this creative element in the human being just as in
the phenomena of nature.'

In dealing with the literary and artistic, Ludwig Laistner did not
lose touch with the purely human. Very modest were his bearing and
behavior; whoever possessed an understanding for such things felt
the significant element in his personality very soon after forming
his acquaintance. The official researchers in mythology were opposed
to his view; they paid scarcely any attention to it. Thus there remained hardly noticed at all in the cultural life of the time a man
who, by reason of his inner worth, deserved a foremost place. From
his book *The Riddle of the Sphinx* the science of mythology might
have received entirely new impulses. It remained almost wholly
without influence.

Ludwig Laistner had at that time to undertake for the *Cotta'sche
Bibliothek der Weltliteratur* editions of the complete works of Schopenhauer and of selections from Jean Paul.[1] He entrusted both of
these to me. Thus I had to combine with my Weimar tasks the thorough working through of the pessimistic philosopher and the para-
doxical genius, Jean Paul. I entered upon such undertakings with the
deepest interest, because I loved to transplant myself into attitudes
of mind utterly opposed to my own. Ludwig Laistner had no external reasons in making me the editor of Schopenhauer and of Jean
Paul; the assignment was due entirely to the conversations we had
held about the two persons. Indeed, the thought of entrusting these
tasks to me came to him during a conversation.

There were living in Weimar at that time Hans Olden and Frau
Grete Olden. They gathered about them a sociable group of those
who wished to live in "the present," in contrast with all who saw—
like the continuation of a life that is past—in the Goethe Archives and

[1] German humorist, Jean Paul Richter, 1763-1865.

the Goethe Society the very center of cultural existence. Into this group I was admitted, and I look back upon all that I experienced there with warm appreciation.

However fixed one's ideas might have become in the Archives through association with the "philological method," they had to become free and fluid again when one entered the home of the Oldens, where everybody was received with interest who had the idea in his head that a new way of thinking must find its place among men, but likewise every one who in the depths of his soul found painful many an old cultural prejudice and was thinking about ideals for the future.

Hans Olden was known to the world as the author of simply plotted theatrical pieces, such as *Die Offizielle Frau*.[1] In his Weimar circle at that time he showed himself in a different light. He had a heart receptive to the highest interests manifest in the cultural life of the time. What came to expression in the plays of Ibsen, what thundered forth in the spirit of Nietzsche—about these things there were endless discussions in his home, but always stimulating.

Gabrielle Reuter, who was then writing the novel *Aus guter Familie*,[2] which soon after won a literary place for her as if by storm, was in the Olden circle, and she filled it with earnest questions of all sorts about the life of woman which were then arousing the interest of humanity.

Hans Olden could be captivating when, with his slightly sceptical way of thinking, he instantly put a stop to conversation that tended to get lost in sentimentality, but he himself could become sentimental when others fell into a happy-go-lucky mood. The wish of this circle was to develop the deepest "understanding" for everything "human"; but criticism was unsparing of anything that was displeasing in this or that human thing. Hans Olden was completely filled with the idea that the only sensible course for a person to follow was to apply himself through literature or art to the great ideals,

[1] *The Official Wife.*
[2] *Of a Good Family.*

about which there was a good deal of talk in his circle, but he was too scornful of human beings to bring his ideals to realization in his own productions. He maintained that ideals could live in a small social circle of select persons, but that any one would be "childish" who should think that he could present such ideals before a larger public. At that very time he made a beginning toward the artistic realization of wider interests with his *Kluge Käte*.[1] This play met with only moderate success in Weimar. This fact confirmed him in the view that the public must simply be given what it demands and that higher interests must be reserved for the small circle that has an understanding for them.

To a far greater degree than Hans Olden was Frau Grete Olden filled with this idea. She was the most complete sceptic in her estimation of the world's capacity for accepting the things of the mind. What she wrote was clearly inspired by a certain genius for misanthropy.

What Hans and Grete Olden offered to their circle out of such a temper of mind was enveloped in the atmosphere of an aestheticizing world-sentiment, capable of reaching up to the most serious matters, but not disdaining to escape from the most serious problems by means of a vein of light humor.

[1] *Clever Kate.*

XVI

I MUST NUMBER among the finest hours of my life those which I experienced through Gabrielle Reuter, with whom I had the privilege of becoming well acquainted by reason of this circle. She was a personality who harbored in her soul profound questions of humanity, taking hold of these with a certain radicalism of the heart and the sensibilities. In everything in the social life which seemed to her a contradiction between traditional prejudice and the primal claims of human nature, she was involved with her whole heart. She centered her attention on woman, who through life and education must bear the yoke of subjection to this traditional prejudice, and must experience in sorrow what is striving to enter into life as truth out of the depths of the soul. Radicalism of the heart, expressed in a manner serene and sagacious, suffused by artistic feeling and marked by an impressive gift for form—this was manifest as a quality of greatness in Gabrielle Reuter. Extraordinarily delightful were conversations one could have with her while she was working on her book *Of a Good Family*. As I look back into the past, I see myself standing with her at a street corner, in the blazing heat of the sun, discussing for more than an hour questions over which she was aroused. Gabrielle Reuter could converse in the most dignified way, never for a moment losing her serene bearing, about things regarding which other persons would at once become visibly excited. "Exulting to heaven, grieved even to death"—this was, indeed, her feeling within, but it remained in the mind and did not find its way into her

171

words. Gabrielle Reuter laid marked emphasis upon whatever she had to say, but she did this only in her mind and not by means of the voice. I believe that this art of keeping the articulation entirely a matter of the mind, while the audible conversation flowed evenly along, was especially characteristic of her, and that in writing she developed this unique art into her very charming style.

The admiration felt for Gabrielle Reuter in the Olden circle was something inexpressibly beautiful. Hans Olden said to me many times quite plaintively: 'This woman is great. Would that I, too,' he added, 'could rise courageously to such a height as to place before the outer world what moves me to the depth of my soul!'

This circle shared in its own way in the Weimar Goethe events. It was in a tone of irony, but never of frivolous scoffing—indeed, often aesthetic in its indignation—that the "present" here passed judgment on the "past." A whole day long would Olden sit at the typewriter after a Goethe gathering in order to write reports of what had been experienced which would give, according to his feeling, the judgment of a "man of the world" about the Goethe prophets.

Into this tone soon fell also that of another "man of the world," Otto Erich Hartleben. He seldom missed a Goethe meeting. Yet at first I could never discover why he came.

It was in the circle of journalists, theater people, and writers who gathered on the evenings of the Goethe festivals at the Hotel Chemnitius, apart from the "learned celebrities," that I became acquainted with Otto Erich Hartleben. Why he was sitting there I could at once perceive. For he was in his element when he could give expression to himself in conversations such as were there customary. There he would remain for a long while. He could not possibly go away. It was thus that I once chanced to be with him and others. The rest of us were at the Goethe meeting the next morning "as a matter of duty." Hartleben was not there. But I had already become very fond of him and felt concerned about him. So, at the close of the meeting, I looked him up in his hotel room. He was still asleep. I woke him, and told him the principal meeting of the Goethe Society was already at an end. I did not understand why he had wished to participate in the Goethe festival just in this way. But he answered in such a manner that I saw it was entirely natural to him to come to Weimar to attend a Goethe gathering in order to sleep during the program—for he had slept away the chief thing for which the others had come.

I got close to Otto Erich Hartleben in a peculiar fashion. At one of the evening gatherings to which I have referred, a conversation arose about Schopenhauer. Many words of admiration and of disapproval had been uttered about the philosopher. Hartleben had for a long while been silent. Then he entered into the tumultuous revelations of the conversation, saying: "People are stirred by him, but he means nothing for life." Meanwhile he was looking at me, questioningly, with a childishly helpless expression; he wished me to say something, for he had heard that I was then occupied with Schopenhauer. I said: "Schopenhauer I must consider a narrow-minded genius." Hartleben's eyes sparkled; he became restless; he emptied his glass and ordered another. In this moment he had locked me up in his heart; his friendship for me was fixed. "Narrow-minded genius!"—that suited him. I might just as well have used the expression about some other personality, and it would have been the same thing for him. It interested him deeply to think that even a genius could be considered narrow-minded.

For me the Goethe gatherings were strenuous. For most persons in Weimar during these meetings were either in one circle or in the other, according to their interests—either in that of the discoursing and dining philologists or in that of the Olden or Hartleben coloring. I had to take part in both. My interests impelled me in both directions. This was possible, since the sessions of one came during the day and of the other in the evening. But I was not privileged to live after the manner of Otto Erich. I could not sleep during the day sessions. I loved the many-sidedness of life, and was really just as happy at midday in the Archives circle with Suphan, who never became acquainted with Hartleben—since this was not proper for him—as I was in the evening with Hartleben and his like-minded companions.

The philosophical leanings of a succession of men confronted me during my Weimar days. For, in the case of each one with whom it was possible to converse about questions of the world and of life, such conversations came about in the direct contacts of that time. And many persons interested in such discussions passed through Weimar.

I spent this time during that period of life when the mind tends to turn strongly to the outer life; when it must find a firm bond of union with that life. To me the philosophies there coming to expression were a fragment of the outer world, and I was forced to realize that, even until then, I had really lived but little in touch with an outer world. When I withdrew from animated intercourse, I became aware again and again, just at that time, that until then the only world with which I was familiar had been the spiritual world, which I saw in inner vision. With that world I could easily enter into union. So my thinking often took the direction of saying to myself how hard had been for me the way through the senses to the outer world during all my childhood and youth. It was always difficult for me to fix in memory such external data, for instance, as must be assimilated in the field of science. I had to see a natural object again and again in order to know what it was called, in what scientific class of objects it was listed, and the like. I might even say that the sense-world was for me somewhat shadowy, or like a picture. It passed before my mind in pictures, whereas my bond of union with the spiritual bore always the genuine character of reality.

All this I experienced most of all at the beginning of the 'nineties in Weimar. I was then giving the final touches to my *Philosophy of Freedom*. I wrote down—such was my feeling—the thoughts imparted to me by the spiritual world up to my thirtieth year. All that had come to me from the outer world was only in the nature of a stimulus.

This I experienced especially when, in vital intercourse with persons in Weimar, I discussed problems pertaining to world views. I had to enter into these persons, into their ways of thinking and emotional inclinations; they by no means entered into what I had inwardly experienced and was still experiencing. I entered with vital intensity into what others perceived and thought, but I could not cause my own inner spiritual reality to flow across into this world I thus experienced. As to my own being, I had always to remain behind, within myself. Indeed, my world was separated, as if by a thin partition, from all the outer world.

In my own soul I lived in a world that bordered on the outer world, but it was always necessary for me to step across a boundary if I wished to have anything to do with the outer world. I was in the most vivid social intercourse, but in every instance I had to pass from my world, as if through a door, in order to engage in this intercourse. This made it seem to me as if, each time that I entered into the outer world, I was making a visit. Yet this did not hinder me from devoting myself with the most vital interest to the one whom I was then visiting; indeed, I felt entirely at home while on such a visit.

Thus it was with persons and also with world views. I liked to be with Suphan; I liked to be with Hartleben. Suphan never called on Hartleben; Hartleben never called on Suphan. Neither could enter into the characteristic ways of thinking and feeling of the other. With Suphan and equally with Hartleben I was immediately as if at home. But neither Suphan nor Hartleben ever really came to me. Even when they came to me, they really remained with themselves. In my spiritual world I could experience no visit.

There were present before my mind the most varied world views— the natural-scientific, the Idealistic, and many shades of each. I felt the impulse to enter into these, to move about in them; but into my spiritual world they cast no light. To me they were phenomena confronting me, not realities in which I could truly have lived.

This was the state of my mind when life brought me into immediate contact with such world views as those of Haeckel and Nietzsche.

I realized their relative justification. With my constitution of mind, I could never so deal with them as to say: "This is right; that is wrong." In that case I should have felt what was living in them as something alien to me. But I found one no more alien than the other; for I felt at home only in the spiritual world that I beheld, and I could feel "as if at home" in *every* other.

When I describe the matter thus, it may seem as if everything were to me fundamentally a matter of indifference. But such was by no means the case. As to this I had an entirely different feeling. I was conscious of a full participation in the other because I did not alienate myself from it by immediately introducing my own point of view into judgment and feeling.

I had, for instance, innumerable conversations with Otto Harnack, the gifted author of *Goethe in der Epoche seiner Vollendung*,[1] who often came at that time to Weimar because he was working at Goethe's art studies. This man, who later became involved in a terrible tragedy, I was fond of. I could be wholly Otto Harnack while I was talking with him. I accepted his thoughts, entered into them as a visitor—in the sense I have indicated—and yet as if at home. It did not even occur to me to invite him to visit me. He could live only with himself. He was so enmeshed in his own thoughts that he felt everything as alien to him which was not his own. He would have been able to listen to talk about my world only in such a way that he would have treated it as the Kantian "thing-in-itself" which lies "beyond consciousness." I felt spiritually obligated to deal with his world as being such that I was not to take a Kantian attitude toward it but must carry my consciousness across into it.

I lived thus not without spiritual perils and difficulties. Whoever rejects everything that does not accord with his way of thinking will not be imposed upon by the relative correctness of various world views. He can experience without reserve the fascination of what is thought out in a certain direction. Indeed, this fascination of intellectualism is now a part of the life of very many persons. They make

[1] *Goethe in the Epoch of His Complete Development.*

short work of anything thought out in a way unlike their own. But one who possesses a world of direct perception, such as the spiritual world *must be, sees* the justification of the most varied "standpoints"; and he must be constantly on guard in his inner being not to be too strongly drawn to one or the other of these.

But one becomes conscious of the "essential being of the outer world" if one can yield oneself to it in love and yet must always turn back to the inner world of the spirit. One learns also in this process really to live in the spiritual.

The various intellectual "standpoints" disapprove one another; spiritual vision sees in them simply "standpoints." Seen from each of these, the world has a different appearance. It is as if a house were photographed from various sides. The pictures are different; the house is the same. If one walks around the actual house, one gets a comprehensive impression. If one stands really within the spiritual world, one makes allowance for the "correctness" of a standpoint. One looks upon a photographic representation from one standpoint as something justifiable. One then asks about the justification and significance of the standpoint.

It was in this way, for example, that I had to approach Nietzsche and likewise Haeckel. Nietzsche, I felt, photographs the world from one standpoint to which a profound human personality was driven in the second half of the nineteenth century if he had to live upon the spiritual substance of that age alone; if the vision of the spiritual world would not break through into his consciousness, and yet his will in the subconscious strove with unusual force toward the spiritual. Such was the picture of Nietzsche that arose in my mind; it showed me the personality that did not behold the spirit but in whom the spirit unconsciously battled against the unspiritual views of the time.

XVII

THERE WAS ESTABLISHED in Germany at this time a branch of the Ethical Culture Society which had originated in America. It seems obvious that in a materialistic age an effort in the direction of a deepening of ethical life ought only to be approved. But this effort arose from a fundamental conception which aroused in me the profoundest doubts.

The leaders of this movement said to themselves that we are today in the midst of many opposing conceptions of the world and of life both in the sphere of knowledge and of the religious and social feelings. In the area of these conceptions men cannot be brought to understand one another. It is detrimental when the moral feelings that human beings ought to have toward one another are drawn into the area of these opposing views. What will be the outcome if those who feel differently in matters religious and social, or who differ from one another in the area of knowledge, shall express their diversity also in such a way as to determine thereby their moral behavior toward those who think and feel differently? The basic principles must be sought, therefore, of purely human ethics independent of every world view, which every one can recognize no matter how he may think in relation to the various domains of existence.

This ethical movement made upon me a profound impression. It touched upon what I considered my most important views. For I saw before me the deep abyss which the way of thinking of the most recent times had created between processes in nature and the moral-spiritual world content.

Men have come to hold a conception of nature which undertakes to represent the evolution of the world as being without moral-spiritual content. They think hypothetically of a purely material primordial state of the world. They seek for the laws under which there could have been evolved out of this primordial state the living, the ensouled, the spirit-permeated, in the form characteristic of the present age. If this way of thinking is maintained consistently—so I then said to myself—the spiritual-moral cannot be conceived otherwise than as the result of the work of nature. One then has the facts of nature, indifferent to the spiritual-moral, which in their process of evolution bring forth the moral as a by-product and which, in their moral indifference, eventually likewise bury it.

I could see clearly, of course, that the sagacious thinkers did not draw these consistent conclusions; that they simply accepted what the facts of nature seemed to say to them, and thought as regards these matters that the world significance of the spiritual-moral should simply be allowed to rest upon its own foundation. But this fact seemed to me of little importance. What concerned me was not that people said that, in the area of natural processes, thinking must be such as has no relation to morality, and what is thus thought constitutes hypotheses, but as regards the moral each person may form his own ideas. I said to myself that whoever thinks about nature, even in the least detail, in the way then customary *cannot* ascribe to the spiritual-moral any self-existent, self-sustaining reality. If physics, chemistry, biology remain as they are—and to all they seem unassailable—the entities which are held to be realities in this realm will absorb into themselves *all* reality, and the spiritual-moral *could* not, then, be anything more than the foam arising from *this* reality.

I saw into another reality—a reality at the same time spiritual-moral and also natural. It seemed to me a weakness in the striving for knowledge not to be willing to press through to *that* reality. I was forced to say to myself in accordance with my view in harmony with the spirit that, above the natural processes and also the spiritual-moral, a veritable reality exists, which reveals itself morally, but which has likewise the power to embody itself in moral action as an occurrence attaining to a validity equal to that of an occurrence in nature. This natural occurrence seemed, from my point of view, to be indifferent to the spiritual-moral only because it had lost its original union with this, as the corpse of a man has lost its union with that element in man endowed with life and soul.

To me this was certain; for I did not merely think it: I beheld it as truth in the spiritual facts and beings of the world. In the above described "ethicists" there seemed to me to have been born men to whom such an insight appeared to be a matter of indifference. They revealed more or less unconsciously the opinion that nothing is to be achieved through strivings for a world view; let us save the principles of ethics, about which there need be no inquiry as to how they are rooted in world-reality. Undisguised despair as to all striving for a world view seemed to me manifest in this phenomenon of the age. Unconsciously frivolous seemed to me any one who maintained the view: Let all world views be left alone, in order that we may be able again to spread morality among men. I took many walks with Hans and Grete Olden through the Weimar parks, during which I expressed myself in radical fashion on the theme of this frivolity. Whoever presses forward with his power of perception as far as is possible for man, so I said, will find a World Process out of which appears before him the reality of the moral as well as of the natural. In the then recently founded *Zukunft* I wrote a trenchant article against what I called ethics uprooted from all world-reality, which could not possess any power. The article met with a distinctly unfavorable reception. How, indeed, could it be otherwise, when these "ethicists" had to seem to themselves the saviors of civilization?

To me this matter was of immeasurable importance. I wished to do battle at a critical point for the confirmation of a world view which, of itself, reveals ethics as firmly rooted along with all other reality. I was *forced* to battle, therefore, against this ethics which had no philosophical basis.

I went from Weimar to Berlin in search of opportunities to present my view through the press.

I visited Herman Grimm, whom I held in high honor. I was received with the greatest possible friendliness. But it seemed to Herman Grimm very strange that I, who was filled with zeal for my cause, should bring this zeal into his home. He listened to me rather unresponsively, as I talked to him of my view about the "ethicists." I thought I could interest him in this matter which to me seemed so vital. But I did not in the least succeed. When he heard me say, however: "I wish to do something," he replied: "Well, go to these people; I am more or less acquainted with the majority of them; they are all quite amiable persons." I felt as if cold water had been thrown over me. The man whom I so highly honored felt nothing of what I desired; he thought I would "think quite sensibly" about the matter when I should have convinced myself by a call on the "ethicists" that they were all quite congenial persons.

In others I found no greater interest than in Herman Grimm. So it was at that time for me. In all that pertained to my perceptions of the spiritual I had to settle matters alone. I lived in the spiritual world; no one in my circle of acquaintance followed me there. My intercourse consisted in excursions into the worlds of others. I loved these excursions. Moreover, my reverence for Herman Grimm was not in the least diminished. But I had a good schooling in the art of understanding in love that which made no move toward understanding what I bore in my own soul.

Such was at that time the character of my loneliness in Weimar, where I had such extensive social relations. But I did not ascribe to these persons the fact that they condemned me to such loneliness. Indeed, I perceived that, unconsciously striving in many people, was the impulse toward a world view which would penetrate to the roots of existence. I saw how a way of thinking which could move securely while dealing only with what lies immediately at hand yet weighed heavily upon their minds. "Nature is the *whole* world"—such was that way of thinking. As regards this way of thinking, men believed that they *must* find it to be correct, and they suppressed in their minds everything which seemed to say that it *could not* be found to be correct. It was in this light that much became manifest to me in my spiritual surroundings at that time. It was the time when my *Philosophy of Freedom,* the essential substance of which I had long borne within me, was receiving its final form.

As soon as it was off the press, I sent a copy to Eduard von Hartmann. He read it with close attention, for I soon received back his copy of the book with detailed marginal comments from beginning to end. Besides, he wrote me, among other things, that the book ought bear the title: *Erkenntnistheoretischer Phänomenalismus und ethischer Individualismus.*[1] He had utterly misunderstood the sources of the ideas and my objectives. He thought of the sense-world in Kantian fashion even though he modified this. He considered this world to be the effect produced by an essential reality upon the mind through the senses. This essential reality, according to his view, never enters the field of perception embraced by the mind in consciousness. According to his view, it remains beyond consciousness. Only by means of logical inferences can hypothetical conceptions be formed regarding it. The sense-world, therefore, does not constitute something objectively existent in itself, but is merely a subjective phenomenon existing in the mind only so long as this embraces the phenomenon within consciousness.

I had sought to make clear in my book that no unknown lies *behind* the sense-world, but that *within* it lies the spiritual. And as to the domain of human ideas, I sought to show that these have their existence in that spiritual world. The essential nature of the spiritual world, therefore, is hidden from human consciousness only *so long as* the mind perceives by means of the senses *alone.* When, in addition to sense-perception, ideas also are experienced, the sense-world,

[1] *Epistemological Phenomenalism and Ethical Individualism.*

in its objective essential being, is embraced within consciousness. Knowing does not consist in a mirroring of something possessing essential being, but the soul's living entrance into this reality of being. *Within* consciousness occurs that advance from the still un-real sense-world to its essential reality. Thus the sense-world is a semblance (phenomenon) only so long as consciousness has not mastered it.

In truth, therefore, the sense-world is spiritual world, and the mind is in living union with this recognized spiritual world as it extends its consciousness over it. The goal of the process of knowledge is the conscious *experience* of the spiritual world, in the visible presence of which everything is resolved into spirit.

I placed the world of spiritual reality over against phenomenalism. Eduard von Hartmann thought that I intended to remain within phenomena and abandon the thought of inferring from these any kind of objective reality. He conceived the matter as if by my way of thinking I were condemning the human mind to permanent inca-pacity to reach any kind of reality, to the necessity of moving always within a world of appearance, existing only as a representation within the mind (as a phenomenon).

Thus my endeavor to reach the spirit through the expansion of consciousness was set over against the view that "spirit" exists solely in the mental representation within the human being, and apart from this can only be conceived. This was fundamentally the view of the age to which I had to introduce my *Philosophy of Freedom.* In this way of conceiving the matter, experience of the spirit had shrunken to a mere experience of human mental representations, and from these no path could be discovered to a real (objective) world of spirit.

I desired to show that, in what is subjectively experienced, the objective spiritual shines forth and becomes true content of con-sciousness. Eduard von Hartmann opposed me with the opinion that any one who maintains this view remains fixed within the sen-sibly apparent and is not dealing at all with an objective reality.

It was inevitable, therefore, that Eduard von Hartmann had to consider as dubious also my "ethical individualism."

For upon what was this based in my *Philosophy of Freedom?* I saw at the center of the soul's life its complete union with the spiritual world. I sought so to express this fact that an imaginary difficulty which disturbs many persons might be resolved into nothing. That is, it is supposed that, in order to know, the mind—or the ego—must *differentiate* itself from what is known, and must not, therefore, merge itself with this. But this differentiation is possible also when the mind swings like a pendulum, as it were, between the state of oneness with the reality of spiritual being, on the one hand, and reflection upon itself, on the other. The mind becomes "unconscious" in sinking down into the objective spirit, but with reflection upon itself it brings the complete reality of being into consciousness.

Now, if it is possible that the personal individuality of man can become submerged in the spiritual reality of the world, it is possible to experience in this reality also the world of moral impulses. Morality receives a content revealed out of the spiritual world *within* the human individuality, and consciousness, expanded into the spiritual, presses forward to the perception of this revelation. What impels man to moral action is a revelation of the spiritual world in the experiencing of this world by the mind. This experience takes place within the personal individuality of man. If man perceives himself in moral action as in reciprocal relation with the spiritual world, he is then experiencing his *freedom.* For the spiritual world acts within the mind, not by way of compulsion, but in such a way that man must develop freely the activity which causes him to embrace the spiritual.

In pointing out that the sense-world is spiritual in its essential being, and that man, as a soul-being, by means of true knowledge of the sense-world is moving and living in a world of spirit—herein lies one objective of my *Philosophy of Freedom.* In characterizing the moral world as one which causes its being to shine forth in this world of the spirit experienced by the soul, and which thereby enables man to arrive freely at this moral world—herein lies the second objective. The moral being of man is thus sought in its completely individual unity with the ethical impulses of the spiritual world. I had the feeling that the first part of *The Philosophy of Freedom* and the second part form a spiritual organism, a genuine unity. Eduard von Hartmann was forced, however, to feel that they were coupled together quite arbitrarily as phenomenalism in the theory of knowledge and individualism in ethics.

The form taken by the ideas of the book was determined by my own condition of mind at that time. Through my experience of the spiritual world in direct perception, nature was revealed to me as spirit; I wished to create a natural science in keeping with the spirit. In the self-knowledge of the human soul through direct perception, the moral world enters into the mind as entirely individual experience.

In the experience of spirit lay the source of the form which I gave to the ideas in my book. It is, to begin with, the presentation of an Anthroposophy which is orientated toward nature and toward the human being as he stands within nature with his own individual moral being.

In a certain sense, *The Philosophy of Freedom* released from me and introduced into the external world what the first chapter of my life had demanded of me in the formation of ideas through the destiny that led me to experience the natural-scientific riddles of existence. The further way could now be nothing else than a struggle to arrive at idea-forms for the spiritual world itself.

The elements of knowledge that man receives from without through sense-perception were represented by me as inner Anthroposophical experience of the spirit by the human mind. The fact that I did not yet use the term *Anthroposophical* was due to the circumstance that my mind always strives first to arrive at conceptions, and scarcely at all for terminology. I was now confronted by the task of forming ideas which could express the experience by the human mind of the spiritual world itself.

An inner struggle toward the forming of such ideas comprises the content of that episode of my life which I passed through between my thirtieth and fortieth years of age. At that time destiny placed me more than at any other period in an outer life-activity which did not so correspond with my inner life that it could have served to bring this to expression.

XVIII

To this time belongs my entrance into the circles of spiritual experience in which Nietzsche lingered.

My first acquaintance with Nietzsche's writings belongs to the year 1889. Previous to that I had never read a line of his. Upon the substance of my ideas, as these found expression in *The Philosophy of Freedom,* Nietzsche's thought had not the least influence. I read what he had written with the feeling of being attracted by the style he had developed out of his relation to life. I felt his soul as a being that was impelled by reason of inheritance and education to give attention to everything which the spiritual life of his age brought forth, but always feeling within: "What has *this* spiritual life to do with me? There must be another world in which I can live; so much of the life in this world jars upon me." This feeling made him an inwardly incensed critic of his time; but a critic reduced to illness by his own criticism—who *had* to experience illness and could only dream of health, of *his* own health. At first, he sought for means to make his dream of health the substance of his own life, and thus he sought with Wagner, with Schopenhauer, with modern Positivism to dream as if he wished to make the dream in his mind into a reality. One day he discovered that he had only dreamed. Then he began with every power belonging to his spirit to seek for realities—realities that must exist "somewhere or other." He found no "path" to these realities, but only yearnings. These yearnings then became to him realities. He continued to dream, but the mighty power of his soul created out of these dreams realities of the inner man which, without the heaviness that had so long characterized the ideas of humanity, floated within him in a mood of soul joyful but repellingly affected by the "spirit of the age."

It was thus that I felt about Nietzsche. The freely floating, weightless character of his ideas fascinated me. I found that this free-floating element in him had brought to maturity many thoughts that bore a resemblance to those which had taken form in me by ways quite unlike those of Nietzsche's mind.

Thus it was possible for me to write in 1895, in the preface to my book *Nietzsche, ein Kämpfer gegen seine Zeit:*[1] "As early as 1886, in my brochure *Grundlinien einer Erkenntnistheorie der Goetheschen Weltanschauung*[2] the same sentiment is expressed"—that is, the same as appears in certain words of Nietzsche. But what attracted me particularly was that it was possible to read Nietzsche without coming upon anything which strove to make the reader an adherent of Nietzsche's. The illumination of his mind could be gladly experienced without reserve; in this experience one felt wholly free; for one felt that his words would break into laughter if the intention to win assent were ascribed to them, as in the reading of Haeckel or Spencer.

Thus, in the book mentioned above, I could explain my relation to Nietzsche by using the words that he himself had used in his book on Schopenhauer: "I belong among those readers of Nietzsche who, after having read their first page from him, know for a certainty that they will read every page and listen to every word he has ever uttered. My confidence in him was immediate. . . . I understood him as if he had written for me, to express me intelligibly, but immodestly, foolishly."

Shortly before I began the actual writing of that book, Nietzsche's sister, Elisabeth Förster-Nietzsche, appeared one day at the Goethe-Schiller Archives. She was taking the preliminary steps toward the

---

[1] *Nietzsche, a Battler against His Age.*
[2] *The Theory of Knowledge Implicit in Goethe's World-Conception.* Anthroposophic Press, New York.

establishment of Nietzsche Archives and wished to learn how the Goethe and Schiller Archives had been organized. Soon afterward there came to Weimar also the editor of Nietzsche's works, Fritz Koegel, and I made his acquaintance.

Later I got into a serious conflict with Frau Elisabeth Förster-Nietzsche. Her sprightly and amiable spirit claimed at that time my deepest sympathy. I suffered inexpressibly by reason of the conflict. A complicated situation had brought this to pass; I was compelled to defend myself against accusations. I know that it was all necessary, and that, for this reason, the happy hours I was privileged to spend in the Nietzsche Archives in Naumburg and Weimar now lie under a veil of bitter memories. Yet I am grateful to Frau Förster-Nietzsche for having taken me, during the first of the many visits I had the privilege of making to her, into the chamber of Friedrich Nietzsche. There on the lounge lay the one with benighted mind, with his beautiful forehead, artist's and thinker's forehead in one. It was early afternoon. Those eyes which, even in their dullness, yet worked with the permeating power of the soul, now merely mirrored a picture of the surroundings which could no longer find access to the mind. One stood there and Nietzsche knew it not at all. And yet it might have been supposed, from that countenance permeated by the spirit, that this was the expression of a mind which had all the forenoon long been shaping thoughts within, and which now would fain rest a while. An inner sense of shock which seized upon my soul was permitted to feel that it was transformed into understanding for the genius whose gaze was directed toward me yet failed to rest upon me. The passivity of this gaze, so long fixed, set free the comprehension in my own gaze, so that it could cause the soul force of the eye to work while it was not being met.

And so there appeared before my soul the soul of Nietzsche, as if hovering above his head, already boundless in its spiritual light, surrendered freely to spiritual worlds for which it had yearned before being benighted but had not found; but still chained to the body, which knew of the soul only so long as the world of spirit continued to be the object of yearning. Nietzsche's soul was still there, but only from without could it hold the body—that body which, so long as the soul remained within it, had offered resistance to the full unfolding of its light.

I had before this *read* the Nietzsche who had written; now I beheld the Nietzsche who bore within his body ideas drawn from widely extended spiritual regions—ideas still sparkling in their beauty even though they had lost on the way their primal illuminating powers. A soul which, from previous earth lives bore a wealth of the gold of light within it, but which could not in this life cause all its light to shine. I had admired what Nietzsche wrote; but now I saw a brightly shining form behind what I had admired.

In my thoughts I could only stammer about what I then beheld, and this stammering is the content of my book *Nietzsche, a Battler against His Age.* That the book remains no more than such a stammering conceals what is none the less true: that the image of Nietzsche inspired the book.

Frau Förster-Nietzsche then requested me to set Nietzsche's library in order. In this way I was enabled to spend several weeks in the Nietzsche Archives in Naumburg. Thus also I formed a close friendship with Fritz Koegel. It was a beautiful task that placed before my eyes the books in which Nietzsche himself had read. His spirit lived in the impressions that these volumes made upon me— a volume of Emerson's filled throughout with marginal comments showing all the signs of absorbing study; Guyau's writings bearing the same indications; books containing violent critical comments from his hand; a great number of marginal comments in which could be seen his ideas in germinal form.

A penetrating conception of Nietzsche's final creative period shone clearly before me as I read his marginal comments on Eugen Dühring's chief philosophical work. Dühring there develops the thought that the cosmos can be conceived at a single moment as a combination of elementary parts. Thus the course of the world-process would be the succession of all such possible combinations. When once these should have been exhausted, the first would have to return, and the whole series would be repeated. If such a thing represents reality, it must have occurred innumerable times in the past and must occur again innumerable times in the future. We should thus arrive at the conception of the eternal repetition of the same states of the cosmos. Dühring rejects this thought as an impossibility. Nietzsche reads this; he receives from it an impression which works further in the depth of his soul and finally takes form with him as "the return of the same," which, together with the idea of the "superman," dominates his final creative period.

I was profoundly moved—indeed, shocked—by the impression received from thus following Nietzsche in his reading. For I saw what a contrast existed between the character of Nietzsche's mind and that of his contemporaries. Dühring, the extreme Positivist, who rejects everything that is not the result of a system of reasoning directed with cold and mathematical regularity, considers "the eternal repetition of the same" as an absurdity, and sets up the idea only to show its impossibility; but Nietzsche must take this up as his own solution of the world-riddle, like an intuition arising from the depths of his own soul.

Thus Nietzsche stands in direct opposition to much which assailed him as the substance of thought and feeling of his time. These assaults he so receives that they pain him deeply, and it is in grief, in inexpressible suffering of spirit, that he gives form to the content of his own mind. This was the tragedy of his creative work.

This came to its climax while he was sketching the outlines for his last work *Wille zur Macht, eine Umwertung aller Werte.*[1] Nietzsche was so constituted as to bring up in purely spiritual fashion from the depths of his soul everything that he thought or felt. To create the world-picture from the spiritual events in which the mind itself participates—this was the trend of his thinking. But the Positivistic world view of his age, the age of natural science, swept in upon him. In this view, nothing exists but the purely material world,

---

[1] *Will to Power, a Transvaluation of All Values.*

void of spirit. The residue of a spiritual way of thinking in this view was only the left-over from ancient ways of thinking, and these no longer harmonized with this view. Nietzsche's unlimited sense for truth would expunge all this. Thus he came to think as an extreme Positivist. A world of spirit behind the material became for him a lie. But he could create only out of his own spirit—so create that true creation has meaning only when it holds before itself in idea the content of the world of spirit. This content he rejected. The natural-scientific world content had taken such a hold upon his mind that he would create *this* as if in a spiritual way. Lyrically, in Dionysiac rush of soul, his mind soars aloft in *Zarathustra*. In a wonderful manner does the spiritual weave there, but in a wonderful spiritual dream woven out of the stuff of material reality. The spirit is reduced to dust in its unfolding, because it cannot find itself but can experience as its illusionary being only that dream-reflection from the material.

In my own mind I dwelt much during these Weimar days upon the contemplation of Nietzsche's type of mind. In my own experience of spirit, this type of mind had its place. This experience of the spirit could enter lovingly into Nietzsche's struggles, into his tragedy. What mattered the Positivistic forms in which Nietzsche expressed the results of his thinking?

Others looked upon me as a "Nietzschean" merely because I could unreservedly admire even what was entirely opposed to my own way of thinking. I was fascinated by the way in which the spirit was manifest in Nietzsche; in just this aspect I felt myself close to him, for in the substance of his thought he was close to no one. He met together with human beings and with periods of time only through the common experience of the *ways* of the spirit.

For some time I was in frequent intercourse with the editor of Nietzsche's works, Fritz Koegel. We discussed in detail many things bearing upon their publication. I never had any official relation to the Nietsche Archives or the publication of his works. When Frau Förster-Nietzsche wished to offer me such a relation, this led to conflicts with Fritz Koegel which henceforth rendered it impossible for me to have any share in the Nietzsche Archives.

My association with the Nietzsche Archives constituted a very stimulating episode in my life in Weimar, and the final rupture of this relation caused me profound sorrow.

Out of the extensive activities in connection with Nietzsche, there remained with me a view of his personality—that of one whose destiny it was to share tragically in the life of the age of natural science covering the latter half of the nineteenth century, and finally to be shattered by his impact with that age. He sought in that age, but nothing could he find. As to myself, I was only confirmed by my experience with him in the conviction that all seeking for reality in the data of natural science would be vain except as one's look is directed, not within these data, but through them into the world of spirit.

It was thus that Nietzsche's creative work brought the problem of natural science before my mind in a new form. Goethe and Nietzsche stood in perspective before me. Goethe's strong sense for reality was directed toward the essential being and processes of nature. He wished to remain within nature. He restricted himself to pure perception of the plant, animal, and human forms. But, while keeping his mind moving among these forms, he came everywhere upon spirit. He found the spirit which holds sway in matter. All the way to the actual vision of spirit, living and ruling in itself, he would not go. A natural science in keeping with the spirit he developed, but he paused before arriving at the knowledge of pure spirit lest he should lose his hold upon reality.

Nietzsche proceeded from the conception of the spiritual in the mythical form. Apollo and Dionysos were spiritual forms experienced by him. The course of the history of the human spirit seemed to him to have been a history of cooperation and also of conflict between Dionysos and Apollo. But he got only as far as the mythical conception of such spiritual forms. He did not press forward to the perception of real spiritual being. Beginning with the spirit-myth, he made a path for himself to nature. In Nietzsche's thinking, Apollo was meant to represent the material, in the manner of natural science; Dionysos was to act like the forces of nature. But there Apollo's beauty was dimmed; there the world-emotion of Dionysos was paralyzed by the law-conformity of nature.

Goethe *found* the spirit in the reality of nature; Nietzsche *lost* the spirit-myth in the dream of nature in which he lived.

I stood between these two opposites. The soul experiences which had come to expression in my book *Nietzsche, a Battler against His Age* could at first make no advance; on the other hand, in the last period of my life in Weimar Goethe became once more dominant in my reflections. I wished to indicate the road by which the life of humanity found expression in world views up to the time of Goethe, in order to set forth Goethe's kind of conception as proceeding out of that life. This endeavor I made in the book *Goethes Weltanschauung*,[1] which was published in 1897.

It was my purpose in this book to bring to light how Goethe, wherever he directed his attention toward pure knowledge of nature saw flashing up everywhere the spiritual; but I did not touch upon the way in which Goethe related himself to the spirit as such. My purpose was to characterize that part of Goethe's world view which was vitally expressed in a conception of nature in keeping with the spirit.

Nietzsche's ideas of the "eternal repetition" and the "superman" remained long in my mind. For in these was reflected what must be experienced with regard to the evolution of humanity and the essential being of man by a personality kept back from grasping the spiritual world by the firmly knit ideas constituting the conception of nature characteristic of the end of the nineteenth century. Nietzsche looked upon the evolution of humanity as if everything that occurs at any moment had already occurred innumerable times in the same form and would occur innumerable times in future. The atomistic structure of the universe makes the character of the pres-

[1] *Goethe's Conception of the World*, Anthroposophic Press, New York.

ent moment seem to be a certain combination of the smallest entities; this must be followed by another, and this in turn by still another—until, when all possible combinations have been formed, the first must again appear. A human life, with all its individual details has been present innumerable times and will return with all its details innumerable times.

The repeated earth lives of humanity shone darkly in Nietzsche's subconsciousness. These lead the individual human lives through the evolution of humanity to life-stages in which overruling destiny causes the human being to move by spirit-shaping paths, not to a repetition of the same experiences, but to a manifold transition through the course of the world process. Nietzsche was fettered by the natural-scientific conception. What this conception could make of repeated earth lives—this was conjured up before his mind. And this was a matter of *life* to him. For he felt *his own life* to be a tragedy filled with the bitterest experiences, weighed down by grief. To live such a life countless times!—this was what he dwelt upon, instead of the perspective of the liberating experience which is to follow upon such a tragedy in the unfolding of future lives.

Nietzsche felt also that, in the human being who experiences himself through one earthly existence, another human being is revealed, a superman, who is able out of himself to form only fragments of his whole life in a bodily existence on earth. The natural-scientific conception caused him to view this superman, not as that which holds sway spiritually within the sense-physical, but as something which is taking form through a merely natural process of evolution. As man has evolved out of the animal, so he conceived, thus will the superman evolve out of man. The natural-scientific view snatched away from Nietzsche the spirit man in the natural man, and dazzled him with the thought of a higher natural man.

What Nietzsche had experienced in this direction was present in utmost vividness in my mind during the summer of 1896. At that time Fritz Koegel gave me his collection of Nietzsche's aphorisms dealing with the "eternal repetition" to look through. The opinions

I formed at that time about the origin of Nietzsche's thought were expressed in an article published in 1900 in the *Magazin für Literatur*. Certain statements occurring in that article fix definitely my reactions at that time to Nietzsche and to natural science. I will transcribe those thoughts of mine here, freed from the polemics in which they were clothed.

"There is no doubt that Nietzsche wrote these single aphorisms in an indefinite order. . . . I still maintain the conviction I then expressed that Nietzsche grasped this idea when reading Eugen Dühring's *Kursus der Philosophie als streng wissenschaftlicher Weltanschauung und Lebensgestaltung*,[1] and under the influence of this book. On page 84 of this work the thought is quite clearly expressed, but it is there as energetically opposed as Nietzsche defends it. This book is in Nietzsche's library. It was read very eagerly by Nietzsche, as is evident from numerous pencil marks on the margins. . . . Dühring says: 'The profounder logical basis of all conscious life demands in the strictest sense of the word an *inexhaustibleness* of forms. Is this infinity, by reason of which ever new forms will be engendered, a possibility in itself? The mere number of the material parts and force-elements would in itself preclude the infinite multiplication of combinations but for the fact that the constant medium of space and time warrants a limitlessness of variations. Moreover, out of that which can be counted, only a limited number of combinations can result; but, out of that which, according to its nature, cannot without contradiction be conceived as enumerable, it must be possible for a limitless number of states and relations to come about. This limitlessness to which we may lay claim with respect to the destiny of forms in the universe is compatible with any kind of change and even with intervals of approximation to fixity or *precise repetitions* (italics are mine), but not with the cessation of all transformation. Anyone who should cherish the conception of being which accords with the primal state of things ought to reflect

---

[1] *The Course of Philosophy as a Strictly Scientific World Conception and Shaping of Life.* Leipzig, 1875.

that evolution in time has but a single true direction, and that causality is always in line with this direction. It is easier to efface the distinctions than to maintain them, and it requires but little effort, therefore, to leap over the chasm and imagine the end as analogous with the beginning. But we ought to guard against such superficial haste; for the once given existence of the universe is not merely an unimportant episode between two states of night, but rather the sole firm and illuminated ground from which we may infer the past and forecast the future. . . .' Dühring feels also that an everlasting repetition of states holds no incentive for living. He says: 'Now, it is self-evident that the principles of an incentive for living are incompatible with the eternal repetition of the same forms. . . .' "

Nietzsche was forced by the logic of the natural-scientific conception to a conclusion from which Dühring shrank back because of mathematical considerations and the repellent prospect which this conclusion presented for human life.

To quote further from my article: ". . . if we set up the postulate that, with the material parts and force-elements, a computable number of combinations is possible, we then have the Nietzschean idea of the 'return of the same.' Nothing less than a defence of a contrary idea, taken from Dühring's view of the matter occurs in Aphorism 203 (Vol. xii in Koegel's edition, and Aphorism 22 in Horneffer's work, *Nietzsche's Lehre von der ewigen Wiederkunft*[1]): 'The amount of the all-force is definite, not something endless: we must beware of such prodigality in conceptions! Accordingly, the number of stages, modifications, combinations, and evolutions of this force, though vast and practically immeasurable, is yet at all events definite and not infinite: that is, the force is eternally the same and eternally active—even to this very moment already an infinity has passed, which means that all possible evolutions must already have occurred. Therefore, the present evolution must be a repetition, and likewise that which brought it forth and that which will arise from it, and so on both forward and backward! Everything has existed innumer-

---

[1] *Nietzsche's Theory of the Everlasting Return.*

able times in so far as the sum-total of the stages of all forces is repeated. . . .' And Nietzsche's *feeling* about this thought is precisely the opposite of that which Dühring experiences. To Nietzsche
this thought is the loftiest formula in which life can be affirmed.
Aphorism 43 (in Horneffer, 234 in Koegel's edition) reads: 'the
future history: more and more will this thought triumph—and all
who do not believe in it must, in their very nature, at last die out!
Only he remains who considers his existence capable of infinite
repetitions: among such, however, a state is possible to which no
Utopian has ever attained.' It can be proven that many of Nietzsche's
thoughts originated in a manner similar to that of the infinite repetition. Nietzsche formed the contrary idea to any idea then present
before him. At length, this same tendency led to the production
of his principal work, *Umwertung aller Werte*." [1]

It was clear to me at that time that in certain of his thoughts which
strove to reach the world of spirit, Nietzsche was a prisoner of his
conception of nature. For this reason I was strongly opposed to the
mystical interpretation of his thought of repetition. I agreed with
Peter Gast, who wrote in his edition of Nietzsche's works: "The
doctrine—to be understood in a purely mechanical sense—of ex-
haustibility and consequent repetition in cosmic molecular combinations." Nietzsche believed that he had derived a climactic thought
from the basic elements of the conception of nature. This was the
way in which he had to suffer because of his time.

Thus in my glimpse of Nietzsche's soul in 1896 there had appeared before me what had to be suffered by one who looked toward
the spirit from the conception of nature prevailing at the end of
the nineteenth century.

[1] *The Will to Power, Transvaluation of All Values.*

XIX

THE LONELINESS I then experienced as regards what I bore in silence within me as my "world view," while my thoughts were directed toward Goethe on one side and Nietzsche on the other—this loneliness was my experience also in relation to many personalities with whom I felt myself united by bonds of friendship, but who, none the less, energetically rejected my spiritual life.

The friend whom I had gained in early years after our ideas had become mutually so combative that I had to say to him: "Were that true which you think about the reality of life, I had rather be the block of wood under my feet than to be a man"—this friend still continued bound to me in love and loyalty. His warm-hearted letters from Vienna always carried me back to the place which was so dear to me, especially because of the human relations in which I was there privileged to live.

But, if this friend undertook in his letters to speak of my *spiritual life,* a gulf opened between us.

He often wrote me that I was alienating myself from the primally human, that I was "rationalizing the impulses of my soul." He had the impression that in me the life of feeling was changed into a life of mere thought, and this he sensed as a certain coldness proceeding from me. Nothing that I could bring to bear against this view of his could do any good. I could not avoid seeing, indeed, that the warmth of his friendship at times diminished because he could not free himself of the belief that I must grow cold in relation to

199

what is human since I consumed my soul-life in the region of thought.

The truth that, instead of being chilled in this life of thought, I had to take with me into this life my full humanity in order by this means to lay hold upon spiritual reality in the realm of thought—this he could never grasp.

He failed to see that the purely human persists, even when raised to the realm of the spirit; nor could he see how it is possible to *live* in the sphere of thought; it was his opinion that only *thinking* is possible there, and that one must be lost in the cold realm of abstractions.

Thus he made me out a "rationalist." In this view of his I felt there was the grossest misunderstanding of what was arrived at by my spiritual paths. All thinking which turns away from reality and spends itself in the abstract—for this I felt the utmost aversion. I was in a condition of mind in which I wished to carry thought away from the sense-world only to that stage at which thought threatens to become abstract; at that moment, I said to myself, it must lay hold upon the spirit. My friend saw that I moved in thought out of the physical world; but he failed to realize that at that very moment I stepped over into the spiritual. When I spoke, therefore, of the reality of the spiritual, this was to him quite without real existence, and he perceived in my words merely a web of abstract thoughts.

I was deeply grieved by the fact that, when I was uttering what had for me the profoundest import, my friend actually felt that I was speaking of a "nothing." Such was my relation to many persons.

What I thus confronted in life I had to see also in connection with my conception of the science of nature. I could recognize as right only that method of research in nature in which thinking is applied to the task of seeing through the objective relations among sense phenomena; but I could not admit the justification of elaborating by means of thoughts hypotheses about the domain beyond that of sense phenomena, which are then presumed to indicate a super-sensible reality—but which, in truth, constitute a mere web of abstract thoughts. At the moment when thought has completed its work in determining what is rendered clear by the sense-phenomena themselves, when rightly viewed, I did not wish to begin forming hypotheses, but to begin *seeing, experiencing,* the spiritual, which lives in its real being *within* sense-reality and not, if truly conceived, *behind* sense-perception.

What I thus held firmly as my own view in the middle of the 'nineties I later set down briefly as follows in an article published in 1900 in No. 16 of the *Magazin für Literatur:* "A scientific analysis of our activity in cognition leads . . . to the conviction that the questions we have to address to nature result from the peculiar relation in which we stand to the world. We are limited individualities, and for this reason we can become aware of the world only in fragments. Each piece, considered in itself, is a riddle; or, otherwise expressed, it is a question for our cognition. But the more details we come to know the clearer does the world become to us. One percept explains others. Questions put to us by the world which cannot be answered with the means that the world provides us—these do not exist. For Monism, therefore, there exist, in principle, no limits of knowledge. At one time this or that may not be clarified, because we are not yet in a position, either in time or space, to find the things there in question. But what is not yet found today may be found tomorrow. *Limits determined in this way are only incidental, such as will vanish with the progress of empirical knowledge and of thinking.* In such cases the forming of hypotheses legitimately comes into play. Hypotheses must not be formed about anything which by its nature is supposed to be inaccessible in principle to our knowledge. The atomic hypothesis is utterly without foundation if it is considered, not merely as an aid to abstract intellect, but as an assertion about real entities beyond the qualities accessible to sensation. A hypothesis must be merely an opinion about a group of facts which, for incidental reasons, is inaccessible to us, but which belongs in its nature to the world given to us."

I stated at that time this view about the forming of hypotheses because I wished to show that the idea of "limits of knowledge" is untenable and that of the limits of natural science a matter of necessity. At that time I did this only as regards the science of nature. But this way of forming ideas has always smoothed for me the road over which to advance further, by means of the knowledge of spirit, beyond that point where one who is dependent upon the knowledge of nature reaches the inevitable "limit."

A contentment of soul and a profound inner satisfaction were mine in Weimar by reason of the element of art brought into the city by the art school and the theater, and also the musical element associated with these.

In the teachers and students of painting in the art school was manifest what was then struggling out of the ancient traditions toward a new and direct vision of nature and life. A good many among these painters might rightly have been considered "seeking human beings." How that which the painter has as color on his palette or in his color-pot is to be applied to the surface in such a way that the creation of the artist shall bear a right relation to nature as she lives in creating and as she is visible to human eyes—this was the question constantly discussed in the most varied ways, in a manner stimulating, often pleasantly fanciful, and often also in doctrinaire style, and the artistic experience of which was manifest in numerous paintings displayed by Weimar artists in the permanent exhibitions.

My feeling for art was not then so far advanced as my relation to the experience of knowledge. Yet I sought in the stimulating intercourse with the Weimar artists for a conception also of the artistic in keeping with the spirit.

To retrospective memory, what I then experienced in my own mind seems rather chaotic—when the modern painters, who wished to capture and reproduce the mood of light and atmosphere in direct perception, took up arms against the "ancients," who "knew" from tradition how this or that was to be treated. There existed in many of them an enthusiastic striving—coming from the most primal forces of the soul—to be "true" in discovering the secret of nature.

Not thus chaotic, however, but in clearest forms, appears before my mind the life of a young painter whose way of revealing himself artistically harmonized intimately with my own development in the direction of artistic fantasy. This artist, then in the bloom of youth, was for some time in closest association with me. Him also life has borne far away from me, but I have often recalled in memory the hours we spent together.

The soul-life of this young man was all light and color. What others express in ideas he uttered by means of "colors in light." Even his intellect worked in such a way that through this he combined things and events of life as one combines colors, not as mere thoughts combine which are formed by the ordinary person about the world.

This young artist was once at a wedding festival to which I also had been invited. The usual festival speeches were being made. The pastor sought the substance of his talk in the meaning of the names of the bride and groom. I endeavored to discharge the task of speaking—which rested upon me because I was a frequent visitor at the home from which the bride came—by talking of the delightful experiences that guests were privileged to enjoy at this home. I spoke because I was expected to speak. And I was expected to give a wedding toast, such as is "becoming." So I took little pleasure in the rôle I had to play. After me, rose the young painter, who also had long been a friend of the family. From him no one expected anything, for everybody knew that such ideas as are embodied in toasts simply did not belong to him. He began somewhat as follows: "Over the reddish glimmering crest of the hill the splendor of the sun poured lovingly. Clouds breathing above the hill and in the gleam of the sun, holding glowing red cheeks to the sunlight, blending into triumphal arches of spiritual colors, escorting to earth the downward striving light. An expanse of flowers far and wide; above the air, gleaming yellow, slipping into the flowers, awaking the life in them. . . ." He continued to speak in this way for a long time. He had suddenly forgotten all the wedding merriment about him and had begun to paint "in the spirit." I do not remember why he ceased to speak thus as if painting; I suppose his coat-tail was pulled by some one who was very fond of him but also wished equally that the guests should come to the peaceful enjoyment of the wedding roast.

The young painter's name was Otto Fröhlich. He often sat with me in my room, and we took walks and excursions together. While Otto Fröhlich was with me, he was always painting "in the spirit." In his company it was possible to forget that the world has any other content than light and color.

Such was my feeling about this young friend. I know that whatever I had to say to him was put before him clothed in colors in order that I might make myself intelligible to him.

The young painter really succeeded in so guiding his brush and so laying on the colors that his pictures became in a high degree a reflection of his own color-fantasies, exuberant with life. When he painted the trunk of a tree, what appeared on the canvas was not the delineated form of the object, but rather that which light and color reveal out of themselves when the tree-trunk gives them the opportunity for manifestation.

In my own way I was seeking for the spiritual substance of radiant color. In this I was compelled to see the secret of the essential nature of color. In Otto Fröhlich there stood before me a man who personally and instinctively bore within him as his experience what I was seeking in order that the color world might be comprehended by the human mind.

It was delightful to be able through this very search of mine to give the young friend many a stimulus. The following was an instance. I myself experienced in high degree the intensive color element presented by Nietzsche in the *Zarathustra* chapter on "the ugliest human being." This "valley of death," painted in poetry by Nietzsche, held for me much of the life-secret of colors.

I gave Otto Fröhlich the suggestion to paint poetically the picture done by Nietzsche in word colors of Zarathustra and the "ugliest human being." He did this. And now something really remarkable came to pass. The colors concentrated, glowing and very expressive, in the figure of Zarathustra. But this figure as such did not come out fully, since in Fröhlich the colors themselves could not yet unfold to the extent of creating Zarathustra. But so much the more livingly did the color variations boil up around the "green snakes" in the valley of the "ugliest human being." In this part of the picture there lived the whole Fröhlich. But now the "ugliest human being." There, line would have been needed, the painting characterization. Here Fröhlich failed. He did not yet know that in color the secret actually lives of causing the spirit to take on form out of the color, through the very handling of the color itself. So the "ugliest human being" became a reproduction of the model called by the Weimar painters "Füllsack." I do not know whether this was really the name of the man always used by the painters when they wished to deal with the characteristically ugly; but I know that "Füllsack's" ugliness was no longer merely bourgeois-philistine, but had something of genius in it. To place him, however, thus unchanged as the ugly "Füllsack" in the picture, a copy of a model, where Zarathustra's soul revealed itself in shining countenance and apparel, when the light conjured forth true color-being out of its intercourse with the green snakes—this ruined Fröhlich's painting. Thus the picture failed to become what I had hoped might come to pass through Otto Fröhlich.

Although I could not fail to recognize the sociability of my nature, yet in Weimar I never felt in overwhelming measure the impulse to betake myself where the artists, and all who felt socially bound up with them, spent the evenings.

This was in a romantic "Artists' Club" remodeled out of an old

smithy opposite the theater. There, united together in a dim colored
light, sat the teachers and students of the Academy of Painting; there
sat actors and musicians. Whoever "sought" for sociability must
feel impelled to go to this place in the evenings. And I did not so
feel impelled just for the reason that I did not seek sociability but
thankfully accepted it when circumstances brought it to me.

Thus I became acquainted with individual artists in other social
groups, but did not come to know the community of artists.

To know certain artists in Weimar at that time was in itself a gain
for one's life. For the tradition of the Court and the extraordinarily
congenial personality of the Grand Duke Carl Alexander gave to
the city an artistic standing which drew to Weimar in one relation
or another almost everything artistic which was occurring in that
period.

There, first of all, was the theater, with the good old traditions—
disinclined in its leading performers to allow a naturalistic flavor
to come into evidence. And where the modern would fain show
itself and expunge many a pedantry—which is, no doubt, always
associated with good traditions—there modernity was far removed
from what Brahm propagated on the stage and Paul Schlenther
through the press as the "modern conception." Among these "Weimar moderns" the chief of all was that wholly artistic, noble fire-
spirit, Paul Wiecke. To see such persons take in Weimar the first
steps of their artistic careers gave one an ineradicable impression,
and was a comprehensive school of life. Paul Wiecke needed the
background of a theater which, because of its traditions, annoys the
elemental artist. Very stimulating hours have I been privileged to
spend in the home of Paul Wiecke. He was on terms of intimate
friendship with my friend Julius Wahle, and because of this I came
into closer contact with him. It was often delightful to hear Wiecke
bluster and storm about almost everything that he had to endure
when he must go through the rehearsals for a new performance, and
then, with this in mind, to see him play the rôle into which he had
thus blustered and stormed, which, however, through his noble en-

deavor after style and his beautiful fire of enthusiasm afforded a rare enjoyment.

Richard Strauss was then making his beginning in Weimar. He was second conductor, along with Lassen. The first compositions of Richard Strauss were performed in Weimar. The musical searching of this personality revealed itself like a piece of the very spiritual life of Weimar. Such a joyful unreserved acceptance of something which, in the very act of being accepted, became an exciting problem of art was really possible only in the Weimar of that time. Round about, the peace of tradition—sustained and dignified; into this rushes Richard Strauss with his *Zarathustra Symphony,* or even his music for the *Eulenspiegel.* Everything awakes out of tradition, sustainedness, dignity; but it wakes up in such a way that the assent is lovable, the dissent harmless—and the artist can find in the most beautiful way the relationship to his creation.

How many hours long we sat at the first performance of the Richard Strauss music drama *Guntram,* in which the lovable and humanly so superior Heinrich Zeller played the leading rôle and almost sang himself out of voice!

Indeed, this profoundly congenial man, Heinrich Zeller—he, too, needed Weimar in order to become what he did become. He had the most beautiful elemental gift of song. He needed for his unfolding an environment which, with utmost patience, permitted that such a gift should in developing experiment over and over again. Thus the development of Heinrich Zeller is to be numbered among the humanly most beautiful things that can be experienced. Besides, Zeller was such a lovable personality that one must count hours that could be spent with him among the most delightful possible.

Thus it came about that, although I did not often think of going in the evening to the Artists' Club, yet, if Heinrich Zeller met me and said I must go with him, I always yielded gladly to this invitation.

Conditions in Weimar had also their drawbacks. What is traditional and peace-loving often holds the artist back as if in a sort of

mustiness. Heinrich Zeller became very little known outside of Weimar. What was at first suited to enable him to spread his wings later
crippled those wings. And so it was also with my dear friend Otto
Fröhlich. He needed, like Zeller, the artistic soil of Weimar, but the
subdued spiritual atmosphere absorbed him also too much into its
artistic comfort.

One felt this artistic comfort in the penetration of Ibsen's spirit
and that of other moderns. There one shared in everything—the
battle waged by the actors, for example, to find the style for *Nora*.
Such a searching as could there be observed occurs only where,
through the propagation of the old stage traditions, difficulties are
confronted in the effort to present what is derived from poets who
have taken the point of departure, not like Schiller from the stage,
but like Ibsen from life.

But it was possible to share also in the reflection of this modern-
ism from the "artistic comfort" of the theatrical public. A middle
way had to be found, after all, between the obligations created by
the two circumstances: First, that one was a resident in "classical
Weimar," and, on the other hand, that Weimar had been made
great by its constant understanding for the new.

It is with great happiness that I remember the productions of
Wagner's music dramas at which I was present in Weimar. The stage
manager, von Bronsart, developed a specially understanding devotion to this type of theatrical productions. Heinrich Zeller's voice
then reached its most exquisite value. A remarkable power as a
singer was Frau Agnes Stavenhagen, wife of the pianist Bernhard
Stavenhagen, who was also for a long time conductor at the theater.
Frequent music festivals brought the representative artists of the
time and their works to Weimar. Mahler was seen there, for instance,
as conductor at a music festival, when he was just getting his start.
Ineradicable was the impression of the way in which he used the
baton—not demanding music in the flood of forms, but giving it
poignancy as the experience of a supersensible element hidden between the forms.

What here comes before my mind from these Weimar events—
seemingly quite unrelated to me—is really deeply united with my
life. For these were events and conditions which I experienced as
being in the deepest sense related to me. Often afterward, when I
have encountered a person or the work of a person, with whom I
have shared experiences at his beginning in Weimar, I have recalled
with gratitude this Weimar period through which so much could
become intelligible because so much had gathered there from elsewhere to pass through its germinal stage. Thus I then experienced
in Weimar the artistic striving in such a way that I had my own
opinion about most of it, often little in agreement with opinions of
others. But, at the same time, I was just as intensely interested in
everything felt by others as in my own feelings. Here also there came
about within me a twofold life of the mind.

This was genuine discipline of the mind, brought to me by life
in the course of destiny, in order that I might pass beyond the "either
or" of abstract intellectual judgment. This kind of judgment erects
barriers separating the soul from the spiritual world. In this world
there are not beings and occurrences requiring such an "either or."
In the presence of the supersensible, it is necessary to be many-sided.
It is necessary not only to learn theoretically, but to take everything
to dwell in the innermost quickening of the soul's life, to look upon
everything from the most manifold points of view. Such "standpoints" as Materialism, Realism, Idealism, Spiritualism, as these
have been elaborated in the physical world by personalities with
abstract ways of thinking into comprehensive theories, in order that
they may signify something for things in themselves—these "standpoints" lose all interest for one who knows the supersensible. He
knows, for example, that Materialism cannot be anything else but
the aspect of the world from that point where it is manifest in material phenomena.

It is a practical training in this direction when one is in the midst
of an existence which brings the life whose waves beat outside one's
own life so inwardly close that it becomes as close as one's own judg-

ments and feelings. But for me this was true of much in Weimar. It seems to me that at the close of the century this condition ceased to be true there. Until then the spirit of Goethe and Schiller still rested upon everything. And the lovable old Grand Duke, who moved about with such distinction in Weimar and its parks, had as a boy seen Goethe. He certainly felt very strongly his "Your Highness," but he always showed that he felt himself a second time ennobled through the work that Goethe had done for Weimar.

It was the spirit of Goethe which worked so powerfully from all directions in Weimar that for me a certain aspect of the participation in what occurred there became the practical disciplining of the mind in the right presentation of the spiritual worlds.

XX

THE HOSPITABLE WELCOME I met in the home of the Registrar at the Goethe-Schiller Archives, Eduard von der Hellen, was of the most delightful character. This personality stood in a peculiar relation to the other collaborators at the Archives. He had an extraordinary reputation among the professional philologists because of his remarkably successful initial work on *Goethes Anteil an Lavaters physiognomischen Fragmenten*.[1] Von der Hellen had in this work produced something which was taken at full value by every contemporary philologist. Only the author himself did not hold this opinion. He looked upon the work as a methodical achievement which "could be learned," whereas his own many-sided endeavor was to fill his mind with inner spiritual content.

When there were no visitors, we sat for long spells together in the old room of the Archives collaborators, while this was still in the castle: von der Hellen, who was working at the editing of Goethe's letters; Julius Wahle, occupied with the journals; and I, with the natural-scientific writings. But the very cravings of von der Hellen's mental life gave rise at intervals in the midst of the work to conversations touching upon the most manifold aspects of public life, cultural or other. In this connection, however, those interests associated with Goethe always received their due. The entries written by Goethe in his journals, passages in his letters revealing a standpoint so elevated

---

[1] *Goethe's Share in Lavater's "Physiognomic Fragments."*

211

and such comprehensive vision, could give rise to reflections which led into the very depth of existence and the breadth of life.

Eduard von der Hellen was so kind as to introduce me into his family, in order further to develop the relations growing out of these meetings in the Archives, often so stimulating. A still further extension of the delightful sociability came about by reason of the fact that von der Hellen's family likewise mingled in such circles as have already been described as grouped about Olden, Gabrielle Reuter, and others.

Especially has the profoundly congenial personality of Frau von der Hellen always remained fixed in my memory. Hers was a nature wholly artistic. One of those persons she was who, but for other duties intervening in her life, possessed the capacity for achieving something beautiful in art. Such was her destiny that, so far as I am aware, the artistic side of this woman came to expression only in early beginnings. But every word that one could exchange with her about art was a satisfaction. She showed a basic quality of reserve, as it were; always cautious in judgment, and yet profoundly congenial in a purely human way. I seldom went away after such a conversation without carrying with me in long-continued reflection what Frau von der Hellen had touched upon rather than spoken.

Very lovable also were the father of Frau von der Hellen and his second daughter—the father a lieutenant-general who had fought through the war of the 'seventies as a major. In this group of persons the finest aspects of German spirituality came to life: that spirituality which flowed into all circles of the social life out of those religious, aesthetic, or popular-scientific impulses which constituted for so long the actual spiritual nature of the German.

Eduard von der Hellen's interests for some time brought me into touch with the political life of the time. Discontent with things philological drove von der Hellen into the lively political affairs of Weimar. There a broader perspective of life seemed to open for him. And my friendly personal interest in him led me also—although without active participation in politics—to become interested in the movements in public life.

Much that has demonstrated its impossibility in our present-day life, or else, in terrible metamorphoses, has given rise to absurd social forms, was to be seen at that time in its genesis, associated with all the hopes of a working class taught by eloquent and forceful leaders to believe that a new time must come for humanity in the form of the social order. More thoughtful and altogether radical elements among the workers were enforcing their views. To observe them was all the more impressive since what there appeared was like a boiling up of the social life in its lower depths. Yet in the upper levels there lived that which, as a worthy conservatism, could have come into existence only in connection with a court thinking with distinction and working energetically and impressively for everything human. In the atmosphere thus prevailing there sprang up a reactionary party which considered itself obviously indispensable, and in addition the so-called National-Liberalism.

The feeling of Eduard von der Hellen at the time—so he must be understood—was that he might so adjust himself to all this as to bring about for himself a rôle of fruitful leadership taking the direction out of this chaos. And it was natural to share in the experience through which he passed in this aspect. He discussed among his friends every detail of a brochure he was preparing. One inevitably felt as deep an interest as that of Eduard von der Hellen in the prevailing conceptions—accompanied at that time by feelings quite unlike those of the present—of the materialistic interpretation of history, the class struggle, "surplus value." It was impossible to refrain from attending the numerous gatherings at which he appeared as speaker. In contrast with the theoretically formulated Marxian program, he proposed to set up another growing out of good will toward social progress on the part of all friends of the working people in every party. He was thinking of a kind of revival of the middle parties with the incorporation into their platforms of those impulses which would enable them to solve the social problem.

The effort proved futile. I can say only that I could not have experienced the public life of that period so intensely as I did had I not shared in this struggle of von der Hellen's.

Yet public life affected me from another direction also, though far less intensely. Indeed, it became evident that I developed considerable resistance—which was not true in relation to von der Hellen —in the very proximity of anything political. Dr. Heinrich Fränkel lived in Weimar at that time, a liberal politician, an adherent of Eugen Richter and also active in politics in the same spirit. We became acquainted—a brief acquaintance brought to an end by reason of a "misunderstanding," but to which I often look back with pleasure. For the man was, in his way, extraordinarily lovable, had a strong political will, and was led to the belief that it must be possible, with good will and rational insight, to inspire people in behalf of a truly progressive path in public affairs. His life became a succession of disillusionments. Unluckily, I myself had to be the occasion of one of these for him. Just at the time that I knew him, he was working at a brochure of which he was planning a mass distribution in maximum degree. What concerned him was the desire to oppose the result of an alliance of big industry and agriculture, then already beginning to take shape in Germany, which, according to his view, would be certain to bring devastating results in the train of its later development. His brochure bore the title *Kaiser, werde hart!* [1]

He thought he could convince the entourage of the Kaiser of what he believed to be harmful. The man accomplished not the least by this effort. He saw that the party to which he belonged and for which he labored could not bring to birth the forces needed to lay a basis for the policies thought out by him.

This led him one day to develop an enthusiasm for reviving the *Deutsche Wochenschrift,* which I had edited for a short time a few years earlier in Vienna. By means of this he wished to set up a political current which would have enabled him to move forward from the "liberalism" of that time to a more independent national-liberal

[1] *Kaiser, Be Stern.*

activity. It occurred to him that I could do something together with him in this direction. That was impossible; even for the mere revival of the *Deutsche Wochenschrift* I could do nothing. The way in which I so informed him led to misunderstandings which in a short time put an end to the friendship.

But out of this friendship grew something else. The man had a very dear wife and a dear sister-in-law, and he had introduced me into his family. This in turn brought me in touch with another family. And here something came about which seems like a copy of the remarkable relation which destiny had previously brought to me in Vienna. I was intimately associated with a family there, but in such a way that the head of the family remained always unseen, and yet he came so close to me in soul and spirit that, after his death, I delivered the address at his funeral as if he had been my best friend. The whole spiritual being of this man was present to my mind in full reality by means of his family.

And now I entered into almost the same relation with the head of the family into which I was brought in a round-about way by the liberal politician. The head of this family had died a short while before. The widow's life was filled with pious thoughts about her dead husband. It came about that I left the apartment in Weimar where I had lived till then and took up residence with this family. There was the library of the dead man. A person interested spiritually in many ways, but living just like that one in Vienna, averse to contact with human beings; living like that one in his own world of spirit; considered to be a "singular character" as the other had been.

I felt this man, like that one, though I could not meet him in the physical life, striding into my destiny "from behind the veils of existence." In Vienna a beautiful relation came about between the family of the "unknown" thus known and myself; and in Weimar an even more significant relation between the second thus "known" and his family and myself.

When I must now speak of the two "unknown known," I am

aware that what I have to say will be called by most persons "wild fantastics." For this has to do with the way in which I was able to draw near to the two human souls in that sphere of the world in which they were after they had passed through the portal of death.

Everyone has the right to exclude from the range of subjects that interest him all statements about this realm; but to characterize such statements as mere fantastics is something quite different. When this is done, I must emphasize the fact that I have always sought in such branches of science as mathematics and analytical mechanics for the sources of that temper of mind which qualifies one to assert something spiritual. When, therefore, I assert what here follows, I cannot justly be accused of mere frivolous talk without cognitive responsibility.

The powers of spiritual vision which I then bore within me made it possible for me to enter into a close union with these two souls after their earthly death. They were unlike other dead persons. After earthly death, these at first pass through a life which, in content, is closely related to the earthly life, and only gradually comes to resemble that life which is experienced in the purely spiritual world where human existence continues till the next earthly life.

The two "unknown known" had been fundamentally acquainted with the thinking of this materialistic age. They had elaborated conceptually the natural-scientific way of thinking. The second, whom Weimar brought to me, was indeed well acquainted with Billroth and similar natural-scientific thinkers. On the other hand, during their earthly lives both of them had remained aloof from a spiritual conception of the world. Any spiritual conception that they might have encountered at that time would have been rejected by them, since they were forced to believe, according to the habits of thought of that time, that "natural-scientific thinking" was demanded by the facts.

But this union with the materialism of the time remained wholly in the domain of ideas of the two persons. They did not share in the habits of life which logically followed from the materialism of their thinking, and which were predominant in the case of all other persons. They became "singular characters in the eyes of the world"; lived in more primitive ways than were customary or would have been the lot of persons of their means. Thus they did not carry over into the spiritual world what a union with the materialistic "will-values" would have given to their individualities, but only that which had been planted in them by the materalistic "thought-values." Naturally this worked itself out for these souls mostly in the subconscious. And now I could see how these materialistic thought-values are not something that alienates man after death from the world of the divine-spiritual, but that this alienation comes about only through materialistic will-values. Both the soul that had come close to me in Vienna and also the one I came to know spiritually in Weimar were, after death, gloriously shining spiritual forms whose soul content was filled with images of those spiritual beings who are at the foundation of the world. The only result of their acquaintance with those ideas by means of which they more accurately thought through the element of matter during the preceding earthly life was that, after death also, they were able to develop a relation with the world supported by judgment. This would not have been the case if the ideas in question had remained unknown to them.

In these two souls there had entered upon my predestined path beings through whom the significance of the natural-scientific way of thinking was revealed to me directly from the spiritual world. I could see that this way of thinking need not, in itself, lead away from a view in keeping with the spirit. In the case of these two personalities this had happened during their earthly life because they there found no opportunity to elevate the natural-scientific way of thinking into the domain where spiritual experience begins. After death they achieved this in the most complete manner. I saw that this elevation of thinking can be achieved also during the earthly life if courage and force are brought to bear upon the task. I saw also, through sharing in the experience of significant events in the spiritual world, that humanity had *of necessity* evolved to the scientific way of thinking. Earlier ways of thinking could unite humanity with the spirit of the supersensible world; they could lead man, if he entered at all into self-knowledge (the foundation of *all* knowledge), to know himself as a copy, or even a member, of the divine spiritual world; but those earlier ways of thinking could not bring him to the point where he could feel himself to be a self-sufficient, self-enclosed spiritual being. The advance had to be made, therefore, to the grasping of a world of ideas not kindled by the spirit but awakened by matter—ideas which are, indeed, spiritual but not derived from the spirit.

Such a world of ideas cannot be called forth in man in the spiritual world where he lives after death and, respectively, before a new birth, but only in the earthly existence, because only there does he stand face to face with material forms of being.

Thus I could realize in connection with these two human souls what is gained for the whole of man's life, including the spiritual life after death, by reason of his being interwoven with the natural-scientific way of thinking. In the case of others, however, who had adopted during the earthly life the consequences of the merely natural-scientific way of thinking for the will, I could see that these estranged themselves from the spiritual world; that they had, so to speak, arrived at a totality of life in which man is less man in his full humanity with the natural-scientific way of thinking than without it.

Both these souls had been "singular persons in the eyes of the world," because they did not wish to lose their humanity during the earthly life. They had accepted the natural-scientific way of thinking in its full scope because they wished to reach that spiritual stage of humanity which cannot be achieved without this.

It might well have been impossible for me to arrive at these perceptions in connection with the two souls if I had encountered them within the earthly existence as physical personalities. In order to perceive the two individualities in the spiritual world, in which they were to reveal to me their being, and through this also many other things, I needed that sensitiveness of the soul's vision in relation to them which is easily lost when experiences of the physical world conceal what is to be experienced purely spiritually, or at least interfere with this.

I was forced, therefore, to perceive even then that the way in which both souls entered into my earthly life was something ordained by destiny for my path to knowledge.

But nothing whatever of a spiritistic character can be associated with this way of relating oneself to souls in the spiritual world. Nothing could ever count with me in relation to the spiritual world except true spiritual perception which I later discussed publicly in my Anthroposophical writings. Moreover, the Viennese family in all its members and also that in Weimar were far too sane for communion with the dead by means of mediums.

Wherever such subjects have been under discussion, I have given attention also to such a mode of seeking on the part of human souls as is manifest in spiritism. Modern spiritism is a devious path toward the spirit followed by such souls as would seek in an external way— almost experimental—even for the spirit, because they cannot any longer sense the reality, truth, genuineness of a way in keeping with the spirit. Precisely the kind of person who gives attention to spiritism in a wholly objective way, with no desire to investigate anything by means of it, can see through to correct conceptions of the purpose and the errors of spiritism. My own research has moved always by a different path from that of spiritism in any of its forms. Indeed, there were opportunities in Weimar for interesting intercourse with spiritists, for an intense interest existed for some time among artists in this way of seeking to relate oneself with the spiritual.

But from my intercourse with the two souls—he of Weimar was named Eunicke—an access of strength came to me for the writing of my *Philosophy of Freedom*. What I endeavored to do in that book was this: First, the book is the product of my course of philosophical thinking during the 'eighties. In the second place, it is the product also of my concrete experience in general of vision into the spiritual world. But, in the third place, it was reinforced by my participation in the spiritual experiences of these two souls. In them I had before me the advance which man owes to the natural-scientific world view. But I had in them also the fear which noble souls feel of entering vitally into the will-element in this world view. These souls shrank back from the moral effects of such a world view.

Now, I sought in my *Philosophy of Freedom* for that force which leads from the ethically neutral world of ideas in natural science into the world of moral impulses. I sought to show how the human being who knows himself as a self-enclosed being of a spiritual kind, because he lives in ideas that are no longer streaming from the spirit, but are stimulated in connection with material being, can develop out of his own being intuitions also for the moral. In this way the moral shines forth in the individuality, now made free, as individual impulsion toward the moral, just as ideas arise from the perception of nature.

The two souls had not advanced to this moral intuition. Hence they shrank back (unconsciously) from life, because life could not have been lived otherwise than in accordance with natural-scientific ideas not yet further extended.

I spoke at that time of "moral fantasy" as the source of the moral in the individual human being. I was far from any intention of referring to this source as something not wholly real. On the contrary, I wished to point to fantasy as the force which, in all spheres, contributes to the breaking through of the spiritual world in the individual human being. Of course, if real experience of the spiritual is to be attained, it is necessary that the forces of knowledge which are in keeping with the spirit must come into existence—imagination, inspiration, and intuition. But, to the human being conscious of himself as an individual, the first ray of spiritual revelation comes by means of fantasy; and we observe, indeed, through Goethe the way in which fantasy remains aloof from everything fantastic, and becomes a picture of the spiritually real.

In the family left behind by the Weimar "unknown known," I lived during much the greater part of the time that I spent in Weimar. I had a part of the house for myself; Frau Anna Eunicke, with whom I was soon on terms of close friendship, watched over all my needs in the most unselfish way. She attached great value to the fact that I stood beside her in her heavy responsibility for the education of the children. She had been left after Eunicke's death a widow with four daughters and a son.

The children I saw only when there was some occasion for me to do so. This occurred frequently, since I was looked upon just as if I belonged to the family. My meals, however, except the morning coffee and supper, I took elsewhere.

In this place where I had formed so delightful a family connection it was truly not I alone who felt at home. When the younger visitors from Berlin attending the meetings of the Goethe Society who had formed intimate ties with me wished for once to be quite "cozy" together, they came to me at the Eunicke home. I have every reason to assume from the way in which they acted that they felt very much at ease there.

Otto Erich Hartleben also was happy to be there whenever he was in Weimar. The *Goethe Breviary* he published was put together there by the two of us in the space of a few days.

Of my own larger works, *The Philosophy of Freedom* and *Nietzsche, a Battler against His Age* there came into existence.

I think also that numbers of Weimar friends spent many a happy hour—or several hours—with me in the Eunicke home.

In this connection I think most of all of the man to whom I was bound in genuine love and friendship, Dr. August Fresenius, from a certain time on a permanent collaborator in the Archives. Before that he had been editor of the *Deutsche Literaturzeitung*. His editorial work was universally considered a standard of excellence. I disapproved of much in philology—especially as it was then practised by the adherents of Scherer. August Fresenius disarmed me again and again by the way in which *he* was a philologist. And he never for a moment made any secret of the fact that he wished to be a philologist, and *only* a true philologist. But with him philology was really the love of the word, which filled the whole man with living force; the word was to him that human revelation in which all the laws of the universe are mirrored. Whoever wishes to see into the mysteries of words must possess an insight into all the mysteries of existence. The philologist, therefore, must do nothing less than to pursue a universal knowledge. The true philological method, rightly applied, can proceed from something quite simple until it casts a powerful illumination upon extensive and important spheres of life.

Fresenius showed this fact at that time in an example which took a strong hold on my interest. We had discussed the matter a great deal before he published it in a brief but weighty article in the *Goethe Year Book*.

Until this discovery by Fresenius, every one who had occupied himself with the interpretation of Goethe's *Faust* had misunderstood a statement made by Goethe five days before his death to Wilhelm von Humboldt. Goethe made this statement: "Es sind über sechzig Jahre, dass die Konzeption des Faust bei mir, jugendlich *von vornherein* klar, die weitere Reihenfolge hingegen weniger ausführlich vorlag." [1] The commentators had understood *von vornherein* to mean that *from the beginning* Goethe had had an idea, a plan, of the entire *Faust* drama into which he then more or less worked in the details. Even my dear friend and teacher, Karl Julius Schröer, was of this opinion.

Consider the matter: If this were correct, we should have in Goethe's *Faust* a work which the poet had conceived in main outline as a young man. We should have to assume that it was possible for such a temper of mind as Goethe's so to work out of a general idea that the process of elaboration could go on for sixty years and yet the idea remain fixed. That this was not so was proved irrefutably by

[1] "For more than sixty years the conception of Faust has been present in my mind—*the earlier parts* clear in my youth, the latter parts less fully developed."

the discovery of Fresenius. He demonstrated that Goethe never used the expression *von vornherein* in the way attributed to him by the commentators. He said, for example, that he had read a book "von vornherein, das weitere nicht mehr." [1] He used the expression *von vornherein* only in a *spatial* sense. It was thus shown that all *Faust* commentators were wrong, and that Goethe had said nothing about a plan of the Faust as existing *von vornherein*—from the first—but only that the first parts were clear to him as a young man, and that here and there he had developed something of the rest.

Thus an important light was cast upon the whole psychology of Goethe by the correct application of the philological method.

At the time I only marveled that something which ought to have been most far-reaching in its influence upon the conception of the spirit of Goethe really produced very little impression, after it was published in the *Goethe Year Book,* among those who ought to have been chiefly interested in it.

But other things than mere philology were the topics of conversation with August Fresenius. All that aroused people at that time, everything interesting to us that happened in Weimar or elsewhere, became the subjects of long conversations between us; for we spent much time together. Occasionally we grew excited in talks about certain things; but these all ended in complete harmony, for we were mutually convinced of the earnestness with which our respective views were held. So much the more distressing must it be to me to reflect upon the fact that even my friendship with August Fresenius sustained a rupture in connection with the misunderstandings which occurred in relation to the Nietzsche Archives and with Frau Dr. Förster-Nietzsche. My friends could form no conception of what had really happened. I could give them none that satisfied them. For the simple truth is that nothing at all had happened. Everything rested upon illusions caused by misunderstandings which had become fixed at the Nietzsche Archives. What I was able to say is contained in my

[1] "As to the first part but not the rest."

articles published later in the *Magazin für Literatur*. I regretted the misunderstanding deeply, for the friendship with August Fresenius was firmly rooted in my heart.

Another friendship to which I have often to look back is that which I formed with Franz Ferdinand Heitmüller, who had likewise, but later than Wahle, von der Hellen, and I, become a collaborator at the Archives.

Heitmüller was an example of a gentleman with the sensibilities of an artist. He made all decisions through his artistic sense. Intellectualism was remote from him. Something artistic entered through him into the whole tone of our conversation in the Archives. He had already published stories marked by a sensitivity of feeling. He was by no means a bad philologist, and did no worse than others in what he had to produce as philologist for the Archives. But he always maintained a sort of inner opposition to what was produced in the Archives—especially to the way in which this work was conceived. Through him it came about that, for a long time, we felt very deeply the fact that Weimar had once been the place of the most vigorous and distinguished spiritual productivity, and that people were now content with taking care of the things once produced, "fixing the readings" with literal orthodoxy, and at best interpreting the productions. Heitmüller published anonymously what he had to say about this in S. Fischer's *Neue Deutsche Rundschau* in the form of a short story, *Die versunkene Vineta*.[1] How people then tried to discover who had made of the once culturally flourishing Weimar a submerged city!

Heitmüller lived in Weimar with his mother, a wonderfully lovable woman. She became a friend of Frau Anna Eunicke, and enjoyed coming to her home. Thus I then had the pleasure of frequently seeing the two Heitmüllers also in the home in which I lived.

One friend I have to recall who came into my circle rather early during my stay in Weimar, and with whom I was associated in in-

[1] *Vineta Submerged.*

timate friendship until I left—indeed, even after I had left Weimar, when I came and went on visits. This was the painter Joseph Rolletscheck. He was a German from Bohemia, and had been attracted to Weimar by the art school. A personality he was who made an altogether lovable impression, to whom it was a pleasure to lay open one's heart. Rolletscheck was sentimental and at the same time slightly cynical; he was a pessimist on one side and inclined on the other side to value life so little that it did not seem to him worth while to lay enough stress upon things to give rise to pessimism. When he was present, the talk had to bear much upon the injustices of life; and he could storm endlessly over the injustice that the world had done to poor Schiller in contrast with Goethe, favored from the beginning by destiny.

Although daily contact with such persons kept up a constant and stimulating exchange of thought and feeling, yet it was not in accord with my nature to speak directly during my Weimar days about my experience of the spiritual world even to those with whom I was otherwise on terms of intimacy. I maintained the need of gaining an insight into the truth that the way into the spiritual world leads first to the experience of pure ideas. What I argued for in every possible form was as follows: Just as the human being can have in his conscious experience colors, tones, and qualities of heat, so also can he experience *pure* ideas, uninfluenced by any perception of the external, arising with a life purely their own; and that in these ideas is real and living spirit. All other experience of the spirit in man, so I then said, must arise in consciousness as a result of this experience of ideas.

The fact that I sought for the experience of the spirit first in the experience of ideas led to the misunderstanding of which I have already spoken—that even intimate friends did not see the living reality in ideas and considered me a rationalist or intellectualist.

Firmest in understanding of the living reality of the world of ideas was the attitude of a young man who came frequently to Weimar—Max Christlieb. It was rather in the beginning of my stay in

Weimar that I often saw him, a seeker after the knowledge of the spirit. He had completed his preparation for the Evangelical ministry, and was just then taking his doctoral examination, and getting ready to go to Japan to engage in some form of missionary work, as he soon afterward did.

This man comprehended—with enthusiasm, I can say—that the human being is living in the spirit when he is living in pure ideas; that, since all of nature must shine forth before knowledge in the world of pure ideas, therefore in everything material we have only appearance (illusions); that all physical being is revealed by means of ideas as spirit. It was profoundly satisfying to me to find a person who possessed an almost complete understanding of spiritual being. This was an understanding of the spiritual being within the idea. There, of course, the spirit so lives that feeling and creative spiritual individualities do not yet become separate for the conscious vision from the sea of general ideal spirit-being. Of these spirit individualities I could not yet speak to Max Christlieb; this would have been expecting too much of his fine Idealism. But genuine spirit-being—of this it was possible to speak to him. He had thoroughly studied everything that I had written up to that time. At the beginning of the 'nineties I had the impression that Max Christlieb had the gift of entering into the spiritual world through the living spirituality of the idea in the way that I must consider the most suitable. The fact that he did not later wholly maintain this direction of mind, but took a somewhat different course, need not here be discussed.

XXI

THROUGH the liberal politician of whom I have spoken, I became acquainted with the owner of a bookstore. This book business had seen better days than those it was passing through during my stay in Weimar. This was still true when the store belonged to the father of the young man whom I came to know as the owner. The important thing for me was the fact that the bookstore published a paper which carried well written articles on contemporary cultural life and on whatever was then appearing in the fields of literature, science, and art. The paper also was in a decline; its circulation had fallen off. But it afforded me the opportunity to write about much which then lay within the scope of my thinking or entered into it. Although the numerous articles and book reviews I wrote were read by very few, it was a pleasant thing to have a paper in which I could publish whatever I cared to write. In this was a stimulus which bore fruit later, when I edited the *Magazin für Literatur* and was obligated, therefore, to share intensely in thought and feeling in the contemporary cultural life.

In this way Weimar became for me a place to which my thoughts had often to turn back in later years. The narrow limits within which my life had been confined in Vienna were now expanded, and I had cultural and human experiences whose results appeared later on.

Most important of all, nevertheless, were the relations with persons which were then formed.

227

When in later years I have recalled in memory Weimar and my life there, my inner vision has often been directed to a house which had become dear to me in very special measure.

I became acquainted with the actor Neuffer while he was still engaged at the Weimar theater. I appreciated in him in the first place his earnest and austere conception of his profession. In his judgment about the art of the stage he allowed nothing of the dilettante to pass. This was satisfying for the reason that people are not always aware that dramatic art must fulfill practical artistic prerequisites in the same way as does, for instance, music.

Neuffer married the sister of the pianist and composer Bernhard Stavenhagen. I was introduced into his home. This meant at the same time a friendly welcome into the home of the parents of Frau Neuffer and Bernhard Stavenhagen. Frau Neuffer is a woman who radiates an atmosphere of cultural spirituality over everything about her. Her sentiments, deeply rooted in the soul, shone with wonderful fineness in the free and informal talk enjoyed in her home. Whatever she had to say was brought forward thoughtfully and yet gracefully. Every moment that I spent with the Neuffers I had the feeling that Frau Neuffer strives to reach truth in all relations of life in a way that is very rare.

That I was welcomed there was evidenced in the most varied incidents. I will choose one example.

One Christmas Eve Herr Neuffer came to my home, and—as I was not in—left the request that I must without fail come to his home for the ceremony of Christmas gifts. This was not easy, for in Weimar I always had to share in several such festivities. But I managed to do this. Then I found, beside the gifts for the children, a special gift for me, all nicely wrapped, the value of which can be seen only from its history.

One day I had been in the studio of a sculptor. The sculptor had wished to show me his work. Very little that I saw there interested me. Only a single bust which lay out of sight in a corner attracted my attention. It was a bust of Hegel. In the studio, which belonged to the home of an old lady very prominent in Weimar, there were to be seen all sorts of sculptural things. Sculptors always rented the room for only a short period, and each tenant would leave there some things he did not care to take with him. But there were also some things that had lain there for a long time unobserved, such as the bust of Hegel.

The interest I had conceived in this bust led to my mentioning it here and there. So this happened once in the Neuffer home, and there I probably added a casual remark to the effect that I should like to have the bust in my possession.

On the following Christmas Eve it was given to me as a present at Neuffer's. At lunch on the following day, to which I was invited, Neuffer told how he had procured the bust.

He first went to the lady to whom the studio belonged. He told her that some one had seen the bust in her studio, and that it would have a special value for him if he could procure it. The lady said that such things had been in her house for a long time past, but whether a "Hegel" was there—as to that she knew nothing. She seemed quite willing, however, to guide Neuffer around in order that he might look for it. Every place was thoroughly searched; not the most hidden corner was left uninspected. Nowhere was the Hegel bust discovered. Neuffer was quite sad, for there had been something very pleasant to him in the thought of giving me gratification by means of the Hegel bust. He was already standing at the door with the lady. The maidservant joined them. She heard the words of Neuffer: "Yes, it is a pity that we have not found the Hegel bust." "Hegel!" interjected the maid: "Is it, perhaps, that head with the tip of the nose broken off which is under my bed in the servant room?" Forthwith the final act of the expedition was carried through, and Neuffer actually succeeded in procuring the bust. Before Christmas, there was still time to supplement the defective nose.

Thus it was that I came by the Hegel bust, which is one of the few things that later accompanied me to many different places. I always liked to look again and again at this head of Hegel (by Wichmann, of the year 1826) when I was deeply immersed in the world of Hegel's ideas. And this, as a matter of fact, happened very often. This countenance, whose features are the most human expression of the purest thought, constitutes a life companion wielding a manifold influence.

Thus it was with the Neuffers. They spared no pains when they wished to give pleasure to some one by means of something that had a special relation to him. The children that came one by one into the Neuffer home had a model mother. Frau Neuffer brought them up less by what she did than by what she is—by her whole being. I had the happiness of being godfather to one of the sons. Every visit to this house was for me an occasion of inner satisfaction. I was privileged to make such visits also in later years after I had left Weimar but returned now and then to give lectures. Unfortunately, this has not been possible now for a long time. It thus happens that I have not been able to see the Neuffers during the years in which a painful destiny has broken in upon them; for this family is one of those most sorely put to the test by the World War.

A charming personality was the father of Frau Neuffer, the elder Stavenhagen. Before this time he had been engaged, indeed, in a practical occupation, but he had then retired from active life. He now lived wholly in the content of the library he had acquired for himself, and a thoroughly congenial picture to others was the way in which he lived there. Nothing of self-satisfaction or pride in learning had entered into the lovable old man, but rather something that revealed in every word the sincere craving for knowledge.

Relations in Weimar were then really of such a character that souls who felt elsewhere unsatisfied would turn up here. So it was with those who made a permanent home there, and also with those who loved to come again and again as visitors. One had the feeling about many persons that visits to Weimar were different for them from visits to other places.

I had this feeling in a very special way about the Danish poet Rudolf Schmidt. He came first for the production of his play, *Der verwandelte König.*[1] During this first visit I made his acquaintance. Later, however, he appeared on many occasions which brought visitors from elsewhere to Weimar. The fine figure of a man with those wavy locks was often among these visitors. The way in which a man "is" in Weimar had in it something attractive to him. He was a very sharply marked personality. In philosophy he was an adherent of Rasmus Nielson. Through this man, whose point of departure was Hegel, Rudolf Schmidt had the finest understanding of the German Idealistic philosophy. And, if Schmidt's opinions were thus clearly stamped on the positive side, they were no less so on the negative. Thus he became biting, satirical, utterly annihilating when he spoke of Georg Brandes. There was something artistic in the way a person revealed a whole expansive range of sentiments poured out before you in his antipathy. Upon me these revelations could make no other impression than an artistic one. For I had read much from Georg Brandes. Especially had I been interested in what he had written, in a manner full of life and wit, and surely out of a broad range of observation and knowledge, about the cultural streams of the European peoples. But what Rudolf Schmidt brought forward was subjectively honest, and because of the character of the poet himself it was really captivating.

At length I came to feel the most heartfelt affection for Rudolf Schmidt; I rejoiced on the days when he came to Weimar. It was interesting to hear him talk about his northern homeland, and to see what significant capacities had sprung up in him precisely from the fountainhead of his northern sentiment. It was no less interesting to talk with him about Goethe, Schiller, Byron. Here he spoke very differently from Georg Brandes. The latter is always in his judgments the international personality, but in Rudolf Schmidt spoke the Dane. For this very reason, however, he talked about many things and in many connections more interestingly than Georg Brandes.

During the latter part of my stay in Weimar, I became a close

[1] *The King Transformed.*

friend of Conrad Ansorge and his brother-in-law, von Crompton. Conrad Ansorge later developed brilliantly his great artistic powers. Here I need speak only of his relation to me in a fine friendship at the close of the 'nineties, and how he then impressed me.

The wives of Ansorge and von Crompton were sisters. Circumstances brought it about that our gatherings took place either at von Crompton's home or at the hotel Russischer Hof.

Ansorge was an energetically artistic man. He was active both as pianist and as composer. During the time of our Weimar acquaintance, he set to music poems of Nietzsche and of Dehmel. It was always a festival occasion when the friends who were gradually drawn into the Ansorge-Crompton circle had the privilege of hearing a new composition.

To this group belonged the Weimar editor Paul Böhler. He edited the paper *Deutschland,* which had a more independent existence side by side with the official journal, the *Weimarische Zeitung.* Many other Weimar friends besides these appeared in this circle: Fresenius, Heitmüller, Fritz Koegel, too, and others. When Otto Erich Hartleben showed himself in Weimar, he always appeared in this circle after it had been formed.

Conrad Ansorge had grown out of the Liszt circle. Indeed, I speak only the truth when I say that he avowed himself one of the pupils who adhered artistically most loyally to the master. But it was through Conrad Ansorge that what had survived from Liszt was brought to expression in the most beautiful way.

For everything musical which came from Ansorge arose out of an entirely original, individual humanness. This humanness in him might have been inspired by Liszt, but the delightful quality in it was its originality. I express these things just as I then experienced them; what my attitude toward them was later or is at present is not here under discussion.

Through Liszt, Ansorge had at an earlier period been bound to Weimar; at the time of which I am here speaking, his mind was free from this state of belonging to Weimar. The characteristic of this

Ansorge-Crompton circle was that it had a very different relation to Weimar from that of the great majority of persons of whom I have hitherto been able to say that they came into close touch with me.

Those other persons were in Weimar in the sense I have described in the preceding chapter. But the aspirations of this circle reached outward from Weimar, and so it came about that, at the time when my Weimar work was ended, and I had to think of leaving the city of Goethe, I had formed the friendship of persons for whom life in Weimar was not especially characteristic. In a certain sense one "lived oneself out of Weimar" while among these friends.

Ansorge, who felt that Weimar put fetters upon his artistic development, moved at nearly the same time as I to Berlin. Paul Böhler, although editor of the most widely read paper in Weimar, did not write in the contemporary "spirit of Weimar," but expressed many a sharp criticism, from a broader range of view, against that spirit. It was he who always raised his voice when it was necessary to put in a true light something inspired by opportunism and narrow-mindedness. And in this way it came about that, just at the time when he was a member of this circle, he lost his position.

Von Crompton impressed one as the most likable personality imaginable. In his home the circle passed the most delightful hours. Frau von Crompton was there the central figure, a spiritedly graceful person, like sunlight to those privileged to be about her.

The whole group stood, so to speak, under the banner of Nietzsche. They looked upon Nietzsche's view of life as being of the utmost importance. They surrendered themselves to the mood of soul manifest in Nietzsche, considering it as representing in a certain way the flowering of a genuine and free humanness. In both these aspects, von Crompton especially was a representative of the Nietzsche followers of the 'nineties. My own attitude toward Nietzsche did not change at all in this circle. But the fact that I was the one questioned when there was a desire to know something about Nietzsche brought it about that the relation of the others to Nietzsche was assumed to be mine also.

I must say, however, that just this circle looked up more understandingly to what Nietzsche believed he knew, and that they sought
to express in their lives the substance of the Nietzsche ideals of life
with greater understanding than was manifest in many other instances where the qualities of the "superman" and where *Beyond
Good and Evil* did not always bear the most desirable blossoms.

For me the circle was important because of a strong and enthrall-
ing energy that swept one along with it. On the other hand, however, I found there the most responsive understanding for everything that I felt it possible to introduce into this group.

The evenings, made brilliant by Ansorge's musical renditions, its
hours filled with talk about Nietzsche interesting to all, in which
far-reaching and weighty questions about the world and life formed,
so to speak, a satisfying converse, were indeed something to which
I can look back with contentment as having given a beautiful
character to the last part of my stay in Weimar.

Since everything which received a living expression in this circle
was derived from a direct and serious artistic feeling, and sought
to be permeated with a world view holding to the true human being
as its central point, there could not be any cause of dissatisfaction if
some opposition to the Weimar of that time received expression.
The tone, moreover, was essentially different from that which I
had previously experienced in the Olden circle. There much irony
found expression; Weimar *also* was looked upon as "human, all too
human" as other places would have been looked upon if one had
been in these. In the Ansorge-Crompton circle was manifest, rather,
the earnestly felt question how the evolution of German culture could
progress further if such a place as Weimar did so little to fulfill its
preordained task.

It was against the background of just this sociable intercourse that
my book *Goethe's Conception of the World* came into being,
with which I ended my work in Weimar. Some time ago, while preparing a new edition of his book, I sensed in the way in which I had
then shaped my thoughts in Weimar for the volume an echo of the

inner configuration of the friendly gatherings of the circle I have
described.

In this book there is somewhat less of the impersonal than would
have been the case had there not revibrated in my mind while I was
writing it what had over and over·resounded in this circle with
strong and avowed enthusiasm about the "nature of personality." It
is the only one of my books of which I would say just this. All of
them I can assert to have been personally experienced in the truest
sense of the word; not, however, in this way, when one's personality
so strongly enters into the experiences of the personalities about one.

But this concerns only the general manner of presentation of the
book. Goethe's world view, as revealed in relation to the domain of
nature, is there set forth as this had already been done in my writings
of the 'eighties. Only in regard to details had my view been broadened, deepened, or confirmed by the manuscripts first discovered in
the Goethe Archives.

In all that I have published in connection with Goethe what I
have striven to do has been to set forth Goethe's world view in its
substance and its trend. Through this approach it was intended to become evident that the quality in Goethe's research and thinking,
comprehensive and penetrating, led to detailed discoveries in the
separate domains of nature. I was not concerned to point out these
single discoveries as such, but to show that they were the flowers
borne by the plant of a view of nature in keeping with the spirit.

To characterize this view of nature as part of what Goethe gave to
the world—such was my purpose in writing descriptions of this
portion of Goethe's work as thinker and research scientist. But I
aimed at the same objective in arranging Goethe's papers in the two
editions in which I collaborated, that in the Kürschner *German
National Literature* and also the Weimar Sophie edition. I never considered it a task which could fall to my lot because of the entire
scope of Goethe's work to bring to light what Goethe, as botanist,
zoologist, geologist, color-theorist, had achieved in the way in which
such achievements are appraised before the forum of competent

scientists. Moreover, it seemed to me inappropriate to do anything in this direction in arranging the papers for the two editions.

Thus that part of the writings of Goethe which I edited for the Weimar edition also became nothing more than a document evidencing the world view of Goethe as revealed in his nature-research. How this world view cast its special light upon things botanical, geological, and the like was to be brought out. (It has been felt, for instance, that I ought to have arranged the geological-mineralogical writings differently, in order that "Goethe's relation to geology" might be seen from the contents of these. But it is only necessary to read what I said about the arrangement of Goethe's writings in this field in the introductions to my publications in the Kürschner *German National Literature,* and there could be no doubt that I would never have agreed to the point of view urged by these critics. In Weimar this could have been known when the editing was entrusted to me. For in the Kürschner edition everything had already appeared which established my point of view before the idea ever arose of entrusting to me a task in Weimar. The task was entrusted to me with the full knowledge of this circumstance. I do not by any means deny that what I have done in some details in working up the Weimar edition may be designated as "errors" by specialists. These may be corrected. But the matter should not be presented as if the form of the edition resulted from my ability or lack of ability, and not from my fundamental postulates. Especially should this not be done by those who admit that they possess no organ for perceiving what I have set forth in regard to Goethe. If the question concerned individual errors of fact here and there, I might point out to those who criticize me in this respect many much worse errors in papers I wrote as a high-school student. I have made it very clear in this account of the course of my life that, even in childhood, I lived in the spiritual world as that which was self-evident to me, but that I had to struggle hard in achieving everything pertaining to knowledge of the outer world. For this reason, I have been a person slow in development as to this form of knowledge in all its aspects. The results *of this fact* appear in details of my Goethe editions.

XXII

A T THE END of the Weimar period of my life, I had passed my thirty-sixth year. One year previously a profound revolution had already begun in my mind. With my departure from Weimar this became a decisive experience. It was quite independent of the change in the external circumstances of my life, even though this also was very great. The direct knowledge of what can be experienced in the spiritual world had always been to me something self-evident; the perceptual grasp upon the sense-world had caused me the greatest difficulty. It was as if I had not been able to pour the soul's inner experience deeply enough into the sense-organs to bring the mind into union with the full content of what was experienced by the senses.

This changed entirely from the beginning of my thirty-sixth year. My capacity for observing things, beings, and occurrences in the physical world took form both in the direction of accuracy and of depth of penetration. This was true as regards science and also the external life. Whereas before this time the situation had been such that large scientific combinations which must be grasped by the mind were inwardly appropriated by me without difficulty, and that sense-perception, and especially retaining this in memory, required the greatest effort on my part, everything now became quite different. An attentiveness not previously existent to the sense-perceptible now awakened in me. Details became important; I had the feeling that the sense-world had something to reveal which it alone could reveal.

I came to think that one's ideal should be to learn to know this world solely through what *it* has to say, without man's interjecting anything into this through his thinking or any other soul-content arising within him.

I became aware that I was experiencing a revolution in the life of the human being at a far later period in life than other persons. But I saw also that this fact carried with it very special consequences for the life of the mind. I learned that, because human beings pass early from the soul's weaving in the spiritual world to an experience of the physical, they attain to no *pure comprehension* of either the spiritual or the physical world. They mingle permanently in a wholly instinctive way what is said to their senses by things with what the mind experiences through the spirit, which it then uses jointly with the other in order to "conceive" things.

For me the accuracy and penetration of the powers of sense-observation meant that I was enabled to enter upon an entirely new world. Confronting the sense-world quite objectively, with the mind free of anything subjective, brought a revelation regarding which a spiritual perception had nothing to say.

But this also cast its light back upon the world of spirit. For, while the sense-world revealed its being in the very act of sense-perception, there was present for cognition the opposite pole, to render possible the right evaluation of the spiritual in its entirely distinct character, unmingled with the physical.

Especially incisive was this in its influence upon the soul because of the fact that it became manifest also in the domain of human life. My capacity for observation set itself the task of receiving quite objectively and purely by way of perception what is manifest in a human being. I was scrupulously careful to refrain from applying any criticism to what persons did, not to give way to either sympathy or antipathy in my attitude toward them; I wished simply to permit "the person as he is to work upon me."

I soon learned that such an observation of the world leads truly into the world of spirit. In observing the physical world, one goes completely outside oneself; and just by reason of this one returns with an intensified capacity for spiritual observation into the spiritual world.

Thus the spiritual world and the sense-world had at that time become manifest to me in all their contrast. But I did not feel the contrast to be something which must be brought into harmony by some sort of philosophical thoughts—perhaps to be resolved in a "monism" —but, rather, that to stand thus with one's mind wholly inside this contrast meant "having an understanding for life." Where the contrast seems to have been reduced to harmony the lifeless is holding sway—the dead. Where there is life, the unharmonized contrast *is active;* and life itself is the continuous overcoming, but also the recreating, of contrasts.

From all this there penetrated into my life of feeling a most intense absorption, not in theoretical comprehension by means of thoughts, but in the experiencing of all that the world contains in the form of riddles.

Over and over again, in order that I might through meditation attain to a right relation to the world, I held this thought before my mind: "There is the world full of riddles. Knowledge would take hold of these. But it seeks, for the most part, to produce a thought-content as the solution of a riddle. The riddles, however—so I had to say to myself—*are not solved by means of thoughts.* These bring the mind along the path toward the solutions, but they do not contain the solutions. In the real world *arises* a riddle; it is there as a phenomenon; its solution also arises *in reality.* Something appears which is being or event, and which represents the solution of the other."

So I said to myself also: "The whole world except man is a riddle, the real world-riddle; and *man himself is its solution.*"

In this way I arrived at the thought: "Man is able at every moment to say something about the world-riddle. What he says, however, can always give only so much of substance toward the solution as he has come to know of himself as man."

Thus cognizing also becomes an event within reality. Questions come to light in the world; answers come to light as realities; knowledge in man is his participation in what the beings and events in the spiritual and the physical world have to say.

All this, to be sure, is contained by implication, and in certain passages even distinctly, in the writings I published before the period I am here describing. Only, it became at this time the most intense soul experience, filling the hours in which knowledge sought in meditation to look upon the foundations of the world. And—which is the fact of chief importance—this soul experience in its intensity at that time came out of my objective absorption in pure, unclouded sense-observation. In this observation a new world was given to me; from what had until this time been manifest to cognition in my mind, I had to seek for that which was the counterpart in the mind's experience in order to strike a balance with the new.

The moment that I did not *think* the whole essential nature of the sense-world, but beheld this world through the senses, a riddle was presented to me in reality; and in man himself lies its solution.

In my whole soul-being existed a living enthusiasm for what I later called "knowledge in accord with reality." And especially was it clear to me that the human being, while possessed of such "knowledge in accord with reality," could not stand in some corner of the world while being and becoming take their course outside him. Knowledge became to me something that belongs, not to man alone, but to the being and becoming of the world. Just as the roots and trunk of a tree are not complete if they do not send their life into the flower, so are the being and becoming of the world nothing truly existing unless in their continued life they become the content of knowledge. Having reached this insight, I said on every appropriate occasion that man is not a being who *creates for himself* the content of knowledge, but that he *provides in his soul the stage on which for the first time the world experiences in part its existence and its becoming.* Were it not for knowledge, the world would remain incomplete.

In thus entering livingly in knowledge into the reality of the world, I found more and more the possibility of creating a defence of the nature of human knowledge against the view that in this knowledge man is making a copy, or some such thing, of the world. According to my idea of knowledge, he actually partakes in the creation of the world instead of merely making afterwards a copy which could be omitted from the world without thereby leaving the world incomplete.

But this led also to an ever increasing clarity for my knowledge with respect to mysticism. The participation of human experience in the cosmic processes was removed from the sphere of indeterminate mystical feeling and transferred to the light in which ideas are revealed. The sense-world, seen purely in its own nature, is at first void of idea, as the roots and the trunk of the tree are void of blossoms. But, just as the blossom is not a disappearance and eclipse of the plant's existence, but a transformation of that very existence, so is the idea-world in man, as related to the sense-world, a transformation of sense-existence, and not a darkly mystical interjection of something indefinite into the human soul-world. Clear as things physical become in their way in the light of the sun, so inwardly clear must that appear which lives in the human soul as knowledge.

What was then present in me in this orientation was an altogether clear experience of the mind. Yet in passing on to find a form of expression for this experience the difficulties were extraordinary.

It was in the last part of my Weimar stay that I wrote my book *Goethe's Conception of the World* and the introductions for the last volume I edited for Kürschner's *German National Literature*. I recall especially what I then wrote as an introduction to Goethe's *Sprüche in Prosa*,[1] and compare this with the formulation of the contents of *Goethe's Conception of the World*. If the matter is considered only superficially, this or that contradiction can be made out between the one and the other of these expositions, which I wrote at almost the same time. But, if one looks to what is *alive* beneath the surface—to that which, in the mere shaping of the formulations on the surface, would reveal itself as *perception* of the depths

[1] *Aphorisms in Prose.*

of life, of the soul, of the spirit—no contradictions will be found, but in my work of that very period a *striving* for means of expression: a striving to bring into the concepts forming a world view just what I have here described as experience of knowledge, of the relation of man to the world, of the riddle-arising and riddle-solving within the truly real.

When I wrote, about three and a half years later, my book entitled *Welt- und Lebensanschauungen im neunzehnten Jahrhundert,*[2] I had made still further progress in many things; and I could fruitfully draw upon my experience in knowledge here set forth in describing the individual world views as they have appeared in the course of history.

Any one who rejects writings because the life of the mind knowingly *strives* in these—that is, because, in the light of the exposition here given, the world-life *in its striving* unfolds itself still further on the stage of the human mind—cannot, according to my view, succeed in submerging himself with knowing mind into the truly real. This is something which just at that time became confirmed in me as vision, although it had long before been livingly present in my conceptual world.

Associated with the revolution in my soul-life were inner experiences of grave import for me. I came to know in the *inner experience of the soul* the nature of meditation and its importance for an insight into the spiritual world. Already before this time I had lived a life of meditation, but the impulse to this had come from knowing through ideas its value for a spiritual world view. Now, however, something came about within me which required meditation as a necessity of existence for the life of the soul. The soul-life at the stage then attained needed meditation just as an organism at a certain stage in its evolution needs to breathe by means of lungs.

How ordinary conceptual knowledge, which is attained in connection with sense-observation, is related to perception of the spirit-

---

[2] *Conceptions of the World and of Life in the Nineteenth Century.* (In later expanded form entitled *Rätsel der Philosophie: Riddles of Philosophy.*)

ual became for me at this period of my life, not only an experience
through ideas, as it had been, but one in which *the whole man* participated. The experience through ideas—which, however, takes up
into itself the real spiritual—is the element out of which my book
The Philosophy of Freedom was born. Experience by means of the
whole man comprises the spiritual world far more in accordance
with its *very being* than does experience through ideas. And yet this
latter is at a higher stage as compared with the conceptual grasp
upon the sense-world. In experience through ideas one grasps, *not*
the sense-world, but a spiritual world which borders, so to speak,
immediately upon this.

While all this was seeking for experience and expression in my
mind, three kinds of knowledge were inwardly manifest before me.
The first is conceptual knowledge, attained in connection with
sense-observation. This is acquired by the mind and then retained
within in proportion to the powers of memory available. Repetition
of the content to be acquired has no other significance than that
this shall be retained. The second kind of knowledge is that in
which concepts are not acquired in connection with sense-observation but are experienced inwardly, independently of the senses.
Then experience, by reason of its very nature, becomes the guarantor
of the fact that these concepts are grounded in reality. The realization that concepts bear within them the guarantee of spiritual reality is acquired with the same certitude from the nature of the
experience in this kind of knowledge as the certitude gained in connection with knowledge through the senses that we are not in the
presence of illusion but of reality.

In the case of this ideal-spiritual knowledge, it no longer suffices
merely to acquire knowledge—as in the case of knowledge through
the senses—with the result that this is then *possessed* in memory.
This process of acquisition must become a continuous process. Just
as it does not suffice for an organism to have breathed for a certain
length of time in order then to apply in further life-processes what
has been acquired through breathing, so also mere acquisition, as

in the case of sense-knowledge, does not suffice for ideal-spiritual knowledge. For this it is necessary that the soul shall remain in continual living intercourse with that world into which entrance is gained through this knowledge. This takes place by means of meditation, which—as indicated above—arises out of insight through ideas into the value of meditating. This intercourse I had sought long before my inner revolution (in my thirty-fifth year).

What now came about was meditation as a necessity for the life of the soul; and with this there was manifest to my mind the third form of knowledge. This not only led to further depths of the spiritual world, but also permitted an intimate, living communion with this world. By reason of an inner necessity, I was compelled to bring again and again to the very center of my consciousness an absolutely definite kind of conception.

It was this: If I enter with the life of the mind into conceptions resting upon the sense-world, I am then in a position to speak in direct experience of the reality of what is experienced only so long as I confront with sense-observation a thing or an occurrence. My sense assures me of the truth of what I observe so long as I am observing it.

Not so when I enter into union through ideal-spiritual knowledge with beings or occurrences of the spiritual world. Here the single act of perceiving includes the direct experience of the continuing existence of what is perceived beyond the duration of the perception. For instance, if the ego of man is experienced, as the inner being most fundamentally his own, the act of perceptual experience includes the knowledge that this ego was before the life in the body and will be after this. *What* is experienced thus in the ego is revealed by it directly, just as the rose reveals its redness in the act of direct perception.

In such meditation, practised because of the inner requirement of the spiritual life, the consciousness gradually evolves of an "inner spiritual man" who, in complete detachment from the physical organism, can live, perceive, and move within the spiritual. This self-sufficing spiritual man entered into my experience under the influence of meditation. The experience of the spiritual thereby underwent an important deepening. That sense-cognition comes about by means of the organism can be sufficiently proved by the kind of self-observation possible in the case of that knowledge. But spiritual-ideal knowledge also is still dependent upon the organism. Self-observation shows the following to be true as regards this: For sense-observation the single act of cognition is bound up with the organism. For ideal-spiritual cognition the *single act* is entirely independent of the physical organism; but the possibility that such knowledge may be developed at all by the human being requires that *in general* the life within the organism shall be existent. In the case of the third form of knowledge, the situation is this: It can come into existence through the spiritual man only when he can make himself *as free* from the physical organism as if it did not exist at all.

A consciousness of all this developed under the influence of the life of meditation I have described. I was able effectually to refute for myself the opinion that, in such meditation, one becomes subject to a form of auto-suggestion whose product is the resulting spiritual knowledge. For the very first ideal-spiritual knowledge had sufficed to convince me of the truth of spiritual experience: really, the very first, not only the knowledge *sustained* in its life by meditation, but indeed the very first of all, the life of which had merely begun. The method of establishing truth absolutely exactly in a discriminating consciousness I had already applied for the matter in question before there could be any problem of auto-suggestion. With regard to what was attained through intense effort in meditation, therefore, there could be no doubt that this was the experience of something whose reality I was in a position to test completely prior to the experience.

All this, associated with my inner revolution, came about in

connection with the finding resulting from a practicable self-observation which, like what has been described, came to have a momen-
tous significance for me.

I felt that the idea-element in the preceding life retired in a certain
aspect and the will-element took its place. If this is to be possible,
volition, during the unfolding of knowledge, must be able to abstain
from everything arbitrary and subjective. The will increased in proportion as the element of idea diminished. And the will took over
also the spiritual cognizing process, which had hitherto been
achieved almost wholly by the element of the idea. I had, indeed,
already come to know that the differentiation of the soul's life into
thinking, feeling, and willing has only limited significance. The
truth is that thinking includes a feeling and a willing; only, thinking predominates over the others. In feeling both thinking and willing are present; in willing, likewise, both thinking and feeling. It
became an experience to me now that willing took up more of thinking; thinking more of willing.

As meditation leads, on the one hand, to a knowledge of the spiritual, there follows, on the other hand, as a result of the findings from
such self-observation, the inner strengthening of the spiritual man,
independent of the organism, and the consolidation of his being in
the spiritual world, just as the physical man has his consolidation in
the physical world. Only, one becomes aware that the consolidation
of the spiritual man in the spiritual world increases immeasurably
when the physical organism does not limit this process of consolidation; whereas the consolidation of the physical organism in the
physical world yields to destruction—at death—when the spiritual
man no longer sustains *this* consolidation out of himself.

With such an experiential knowledge every form of theory of
knowledge is incompatible which represents the human process of
knowing as limited to a certain area, and which considers what is
"beyond" this area—the "primordial foundations," the "thing-in-
itself"—as unattainable by human cognition. Everything "unattain-

able," I felt, is such only "for the present"; it can continue unattainable only until man has evolved within himself that element of his being which is akin to the hitherto unknown, and which, therefore, can henceforth grow into one with this in experiential knowledge. This capacity of man to grow into every form of existence became for me something that must be recognized by the person who desires to see the position of man in relation to the world in its true light. Whoever cannot struggle through to this recognition cannot receive from knowledge something which really belongs to the world, but only a copy—of no significance to the world—of some part of the world-content. Through such a merely reproducing knowledge, however, man cannot grasp within himself a being who gives to him as a fully conscious individuality an inner experience of the truth that he stands fast in the universe.

What I wished to do was to speak of knowledge in such a way that the spiritual should be, not merely recognized, but recognized as being of such a nature that man may reach it with his perception. It seemed to me more important to hold fast to the truth that the "primordial grounds" of existence lie *inside* what is attainable by man within his totality of experience than to recognize in thought an *unknown* spiritual in some kind of "beyond" region.

For this reason my view rejected that form of thinking which considers the content of sense-experience (color, heat, tone, etc.) to be something which an unknown external world calls forth within man, by means of his sense-perception, while this external world itself can be conceived only hypothetically. The theoretical ideas which are fundamental in this trend in physical and physiological thinking seemed to my experiential knowledge in very special degree harmful. This feeling increased to the utmost intensity at the period of my life I am here describing. All that was designated in physics and physiology as "existing behind subjective sensation" caused me, if I may use such an expression, cognitional discomfort.

On the other hand, I saw in the thinking of Lyell, Darwin,

Haeckel something which, although incomplete as it issued from them, is nevertheless capable of becoming sound in the course of its evolution.

Lyell's basic principle—to explain by means of ideas resulting from present observation of the earth-process those phenomena which elude sense-observation because they belong to past ages— seemed to me fruitful in the direction indicated. To seek for understanding of the physical structure of man by tracing his forms from the animal forms, as Haeckel does in comprehensive fashion in his *Anthropogenie*,[1] appeared to me a good foundation for the further development of knowledge.

I said to myself that, if man places before himself a limit of knowledge, beyond which is supposed to lie the "thing-in-itself," he thus bars himself from any access to the spiritual world. If he relates himself to the sense-world in such a way that one thing explains another within that world (the present stage of the earth's development explaining past geological ages; animal forms explaining those of man), he may be ready to extend this intelligibility of beings and events also to the spiritual.

As to my experience also in this area, I can say: "This is something which just at that time became confirmed in me as vision, although it had long before been livingly present in my conceptual world."

[1] *The Evolution of Man.*

XXIII

With the inner revolution thus described I must bring to a close the second main division of my life. The paths of destiny now took a different bearing from what had preceded. During both my Vienna and also my Weimar period, the outer indications of destiny became manifest in such directions as fell in line with the content of my inner strivings. In all my writings there is vitally present the basic character of my world view in keeping with the spirit, even though an inner necessity required that my reflections should be less extended into the actual spiritual realm. In my work as an educator in Vienna the goals set up were solely those resulting from the insights of my own mind. In Weimar, as regards my work in connection with Goethe, the sole determinant was what I considered to be the responsibility attaching to such a piece of work. I never had to overcome difficulties in order to bring tendencies coming from the outer world into harmony with my own.

It was just from this course of my life that I was able to perceive the idea of freedom in a form appearing clearly to me, and thus to set it forth. I do not think that the great significance which this idea had in my own life has caused me for this reason to view it in a one-sided way. The idea corresponds with an objective reality, and what is actually experienced of such a reality cannot alter it in the course of a conscientious striving for knowledge, but can only render possible in greater or lesser degree an insight into it.

With this conception of the idea of freedom there was united the

249

"ethical individualism" of my world view, which has been misunderstood by so many persons. This also was transformed at the beginning of the third period of my life from an element in my conceptual world living in the mind into something which had now laid hold upon the entire man.

The physical and physiological world view of that time, to whose form of thinking I was opposed, and also the biological view—which, in spite of its incompleteness, I could look upon as a bridge leading to a spiritual conception—required of me that I should continually improve the formulation of my own conceptions in both these aspects of the world. I had to answer for myself the question: Can impulses for action reveal themselves to man from the external world? What I found was that the divine-spiritual forces which inwardly ensoul man's will have no way of access from the outer world to the inner man. A right way of thinking in physics and physiology, as well as biology, seemed to me to lead to this conclusion. A way in nature which, from without, gives rise to volition cannot be found. Therefore, neither can any divine-spiritual moral impulse penetrate by such a road from without to that place in the soul where man's own impulse of will, acting within him, comes into existence. External natural forces draw along with them only that in man which is akin to nature. Then, however, there is no expression of free will, but the continuation of the natural process into man and through him. Man has then not yet laid hold fully upon his being, but continues to cleave as an unfree agent to the natural element in his external aspect.

The problem can by no means be—so I said to myself again and again—to answer *this* question: Is man's will free or not?; it must be to answer this *very different* question: What is the character of the path in the life of the soul which leads from the unfree natural will to that which is free—that is, to that which is truly moral? And, in order to find an answer to this question, it was necessary to observe how the divine-spiritual lives *in each individual* human soul. It is from the individual soul that the moral proceeds; in the *wholly individual* being of the soul, therefore, must the moral impulse come to life.

Moral laws—as commands—which come from an external relation in which man finds himself, even though these laws had their primal origin in the spiritual world, do not become moral impulses within man by reason of the fact that he directs his will in accord with them, but only by reason of the fact that he himself, purely as an individual, experiences the spiritual and essential nature of their thought-content. Freedom has its life in human thinking, and it is not the will which is of itself free, but thinking which empowers the will.

In my *Philosophy of Freedom,* therefore, I had already found it necessary to lay all possible emphasis upon the freedom of thought in relation to the moral nature of the will.

This idea also was confirmed in very special degree through the life of meditation. The moral world-order stood out before me in ever clearer light as the one clearly realized imprint on earth of such ordered ranks of action as are to be found in the spiritual regions ranged above. It showed itself as that which only he lays hold upon in his conceptual world who is able to acknowledge the spiritual.

During just that epoch of my life which I am here describing, all these insights were linked up for me with the comprehensive truth to which I had attained that the beings and events of the world are not in truth explained when thinking is employed to "explain" them; but only when, by means of thinking, the events can be contemplated in that connection in which one explains another, in which one becomes the riddle and the other its solution, and man himself becomes the Word for the external world perceived by him.

Herein, however, was experienced the truth of the conception that, in the world and its working, that which holds sway is *the Logos, Wisdom, the Word.*

I believed that I was enabled by these conceptions to see clearly into the nature of Materialism. I perceived the harmful character of this way of thinking, not in the fact that the Materialist directs his attention to the material form of manifestation of a being, but in the way in which he conceives the material. He contemplates *matter* without becoming aware that he is really in the presence of *spirit*, which is simply manifesting itself in the form of matter. He does not know that spirit metamorphoses itself into matter in order to attain to ways of action which are possible only in this metamorphosis. Spirit must first take on the form of a material brain in order to lead in this form the life of the conceptual world, which can bestow upon man in his earthly life a freely acting self-consciousness. To be sure, in the brain spirit mounts upward out of matter, but only after the material brain has arisen out of spirit.

I had to reject the way of conceiving in physics and physiology only because this makes of matter that is not livingly experienced, but only *thought out,* the external cause of man's spiritual experience; and, moreover, matter so conceived in thought that it is impossible to trace it to the point where it is spirit. *Such matter, postulated by this way of thinking as real, is nowhere real.* The fundamental error of the materialistically minded thinkers about nature consists in their impossible idea of matter. Through this they block before themselves the way leading to spiritual existence. A material nature which stimulates in the mind only what man experiences in connection with nature makes the world an "illusion." The intensity with which these ideas entered my mind led me four years later to elaborate them in my work *Conceptions of the World and of Life in the Nineteenth Century,* in the chapter entitled *Die Welt als Illusion.*[1]

In the biological mode of thinking it is not possible in the same way to fall into ways of characterizing what is conceived—which expel it wholly from the sphere open to man's experience, leaving an illusion in its place in his mind. Here it is impossible to arrive at the explanation that a world exists outside of man of which he ex-

---

[1] *The World as Illusion.* (The entire work, in its expanded form, is entitled *Rätsel der Philosophie, Riddles of Philosophy.*) Anthroposophic Press, New York.

periences nothing, which makes an impression on him only through his senses, an impression, however, which may be utterly unlike that which creates it. If a person suppresses in the life of the soul the weightier elements of thinking, he may believe, indeed, that he has uttered something in asserting that the objective counterpart of the subjective perception of light consists of a wave-form in ether—such was then the conception—but he must be an absolute fanatic if he should propose to "explain" in this way what is perceived also in the realm of the living.

In no case—so I said to myself—does such thinking rise above ideas pertaining to nature to ideas concerning the moral order of the world. Such a conception can consider this moral order only as something which drops down into the physical world of man from a region foreign to man's knowledge.

The fact that these questions confronted my mind cannot be considered as having significance in relation to my entrance upon the third chapter of my life; for they had confronted me for a long time. But it was significant for me that the whole domain of knowledge within my mind—without any essential change in its content—attained by means of these questions to a living vibrancy in a greatly intensified degree as compared with what had hitherto been the case. In the *Logos* lives the human soul; how does the external world live in the *Logos?* This is the basic question even in my *Theory of Knowledge Implicit in Goethe's World-Conception* (of the middle of the 'eighties); such it continued to be in *Wahrheit und Wissenschaft*[1] and in *The Philosophy of Freedom.* This orientation of mind was determinative in all the ideas I was able to formulate in the endeavor to penetrate into the depths of the soul from which Goethe sought to bring light into the phenomena of the world.

What especially concerned me during the phase of my life here set forth was the fact that the ideas I was forced to oppose so strongly had laid hold with the utmost intensity upon the thinking of that

[1] *Truth and Science.*

period. People lived so completely within this trend of mind that it was impossible for them to realize at all the importance of anything which pointed in the opposite direction. I so experienced the contrast between what was to me plain truth and the opinions of my time that this experience gave the *prevailing color* to my life in general in the years near the turn of the century.

In every manifestation of the cultural life the impression made upon me was drawn from this contrast. Not that I rejected everything produced by this cultural life, but I had a sense of profound distress in the presence of much that was good, which I could cherish, for I believed that I saw the forces of destruction ranging themselves against what was good as the evolutional germs of the cultural life.

Thus from all directions I experienced this question: "How can a way be found whereby that which is inwardly beheld as true may be set forth in such forms of expression as can be understood by this age?"

Living in such an experience is as if it were imperative in one way or another to ascend the almost inaccessible peak of a mountain. Attempts are made from the most varied points of approach; time and again one is brought to a halt, forced to feel that all the struggles put forth have been in vain.

I spoke once during the 'nineties at Frankfurt am Main about Goethe's conception of nature. I said in my introduction that I would discuss only Goethe's conception of the living, since his ideas about light and colors were such that no possibility existed in contemporary physics for throwing a bridge across to these ideas.—As for myself, however, I was forced to view this impossibility as a most significant symptom of the spiritual orientation of the time.

Somewhat later I had a conversation with a physicist who was an important person in his field and who also occupied himself intensively with Goethe's conception of nature. The conversation came to its climax in his saying that Goethe's conception with respect to colors is such that physics cannot do anything whatever with it, and in my—*becoming silent.*

How much there was then which indicated that what was truth to me was of such a character that the thought of the time "could not do anything whatever with it."

XXIV

A<small>ND</small> *this* question became inner experience: *Must one become silent?*

With this state of my inner life I then faced the necessity of introducing into my outer activity an entirely new note. No longer could the forces which determined my outer destiny remain in such unity as hitherto with those inner directives which came from my experience of the world of spirit.

For a considerable time previously I had thought of presenting to the contemporary world through a periodical those spiritual impulses which I believed ought to be brought before the public of that time. I would not "become silent," but would say as much as it was possible to say.

To found such a periodical myself was something not to be thought of at that time. The necessary funds and the connections essential to the founding of a periodical were utterly lacking to me.

So I seized the opportunity available to me to acquire the editorship of the *Magazin für Literatur*.[1]

This was an old weekly. It was founded in the year of Goethe's death (1832), at first as the *Magazin für Literatur des Auslandes*.[2] It carried translations of whatever foreign productions in all aspects of the cultural life were thought by the editors worthy of being introduced into the cultural life of Germany. Later on, the weekly was

[1] *Magazine for Literature.*
[2] *Magazine for Foreign Literature.*

256

changed into the *Magazin für die Literatur des In- und Auslandes.*[1]
Now it published poetry, character sketches, criticism, from the
whole range of the cultural life. Within certain limits, it could get
along very well with this task. Its activity, thus defined, came at a
time when a sufficiently large number of persons in German-speak-
ing regions desired each week to have whatever was forthcoming in
the cultural domain presented to them in brief, lucid form. Then,
in the 'eighties and 'nineties, when the new literary objectives of
the younger generation entered into this peaceful and dignified way
of sharing in the cultural life, the Magazine also was soon swept into
this movement. It changed editors at frequent intervals and took its
color for the time being from these, who in one way or another belonged to the new movements. When I succeeded in acquiring the
editorship in 1897, it was in close relation with the aspirations of the
modern writers without having placed itself in strong opposition
to what was outside these aspirations. But, at all events, it was not
in a position to maintain itself financially solely on the basis of its
contents. For this reason, it had become, among other things, the
organ of the *Freie literarische Gesellschaft.*[2] This added a little to
the otherwise no longer extensive list of subscribers. But, in spite of
everything, the situation was such when I took over the Magazine
that all subscribers had to be included, even the less dependable
ones, in order barely to establish a condition adequate for its maintenance. I could take over the periodical only on the condition that
I included as part of my work an activity which appeared likely to
increase the circle of subscribers. This was the activity in the Free
Literary Society. I had so to arrange the content of the periodical
that the requirements of this Society should be met. Within this
Society the effort was made to find those persons who had an interest
in the productions of the younger generation. The headquarters of
the Society were in Berlin, where younger writers had founded it.
But it had branches also in many other German cities; it soon be-

[1] *Magazine for German and Foreign Literature.*
[2] *Free Literary Society.*

came apparent, however, that many of these branches led a very modest existence. It now became my task to deliver lectures in this Society, in order that the contact which was to be effected with the cultural life through the Magazine might be given also a personal expression.

I had thus a circle of readers for the Magazine into whose cultural requirements I had to find my way. In the Free Literary Society I had a group of members who expected something definite, since something quite definite had until now been offered them. In any case, they did not expect what I should have wished to give them from my innermost being. The stamp of the Free Literary Society was determined also by the fact that its intention was to form a sort of opposite of the Literary Society, in which such persons, for instance, as Spielhagen played leading rôles.

It was now a necessity, inherent in the fact that I stood within the spiritual world, that I should share truly in a wholly inner manner in these relations into which I had entered. I made every effort to imagine myself in the position of my circle of readers and of the membership of the Society, in order to discover from the type of mind of these persons the forms into which I should have to mould what I wished spiritually to present.

I cannot say that I yielded to illusions at the beginning of this activity and that these were gradually destroyed. But the very fact of working outward from the circle of readers and hearers, as it was appropriate for me to do, met with greater and greater resistance. No strong and serious trait of mind could be counted upon in the persons who had been drawn about the Magazine before I took it over. The interests of these men were only in a few instances deeply rooted. Even in the case of these few, there existed no strong underlying forces of the spirit, but rather a general desire seeking for expression in all kinds of artistic and other cultural forms.

Thus the question soon arose for me whether I was justified inwardly and before the spiritual world in working within this circle.

For, even though many persons who had to be considered were very dear to me, although I felt bound to them by ties of friendship, yet even these belonged among those persons who caused me to ask myself with respect to my inner living experience: Must one become silent?

In addition, there was still something else. As regards a great many persons who had until then come into near and friendly relation with me, I was justified in the feeling in the light of their attitude toward me that, although they did not go very far in their inner life on a path parallel with mine, yet they assumed that something existed in me which gave value in their eyes to whatever I did in the domain of knowledge and in many other relations of life. They often took this attitude toward my existence, without question, in the light of their experiences with me.

Those who had till now published the Magazine had no such feeling. They said to themselves: "In spite of many traits of a practical character in Steiner, he is nevertheless an idealist." And, since the sale of the Magazine had been made under the condition that instalment payments were to be made to the former owner in the course of the year, that this person had also the strongest practical interest in the continuance of the weekly, therefore from his point of view he could not do otherwise than to provide for himself, and for the matter in hand, another guarantee than that consisting in my own personality, about which he was unable to say what effect it would have within the circle of persons who had till now gathered about the Magazine and the Free Literary Society. To the terms of purchase, therefore, was added the requirement that Otto Erich Hartleben should be co-editor, sharing actively in the work.

In reflecting now upon this fact, I do not wish that the arrangement for my editorial position had been in any way different. For one who stands within the spiritual world must, as I have made clear in the preceding pages, learn to know fully through experience the facts of the physical world. And for me, especially by reason of my inner revolution, this had become an *obvious necessity*. Not to accept what I recognized clearly as forces of destiny would have been to me a sin against my experience of the spirit. I saw not only "facts" which then associated me for some time with Otto Erich Hartleben, but "facts woven by destiny (karma)."

Yet there grew out of this relation insurmountable difficulties.

Otto Erich Hartleben was a person absolutely dominated by the aesthetic. There was something graceful for me in every manifestation of his utterly aesthetic philosophy, even in his gestures, in spite of the really questionable milieu from which he often confronted me. Because of this attitude of mind, he felt the need, every now and then, of staying for some months at a time in Italy. And, when he returned, there was actually something Italian in what came to expression out of his nature. Besides, I felt a strong personal affection for him.

Only, it was really impossible to work jointly at what was now our common field. He did not direct his efforts in the least toward transplanting himself into the domain of ideas and interests belonging to the readers of the Magazine and the circle of the Free Literary Society, but wished in both cases to impose what his aesthetic feelings said to him. This affected me like something alien. Besides, he often insisted upon his right as a co-editor, but also often did not do so at all for a long time. Indeed, he was often absent in Italy for long periods. In this way there came to be a marked lack of consistency in the content of the Magazine. Moreover, with all his "mature aesthetic philosophy," Otto Erich Hartleben could never overcome the student in himself. I mean the questionable aspect of studentship, not, of course, what may be brought forward into later life as a beautiful force of existence out of student days.

At the time when I had to associate myself with him, an added circle of admirers had become his on account of his drama *Die Erziehung zur Ehe*.[1] This production had not come into existence at all from the graceful aesthetic element so charming in association

[1] *Education for Marriage.*

with him; it was the product of that wantonness and unrestraint which caused everything contributed by him to the Magazine, both in intellectual productions and also in decisions about it, to issue, not from the depths of his nature, but from a certain superficiality. The Hartleben of personal association was known to very few.

It came about as a matter of course that, after I removed to Berlin, where I had to edit the Magazine, I associated with the circle connected with Otto Erich Hartleben. For this was the circle which rendered it possible for me to supervise what pertained to the weekly and to the Free Literary Society in the requisite way.

This caused me, on the one hand, much suffering; for I was thereby hindered from seeking out those persons, and getting close to them, with whom delightful relations had continued from Weimar. And how I should have enjoyed also calling frequently on Eduard von Hartmann!

All this was impossible. The other side claimed me wholly. And so, at one stroke, much was taken from me of a valuable human element which I should gladly have retained. But I recognized this as a dispensation of destiny (karma). It would have been entirely possible for me, by reason of the deepest foundations of the soul I have here described, to apply my mind with complete interest to two such utterly different human groups as those associated with Weimar and those existing around the Magazine. Only, neither of these groups would have found any permanent satisfaction in a person who associated by turns with those belonging in soul and mind to polarically opposed world spheres. Besides, I should have been unavoidably forced in such intercourse to explain continually why I was devoting my labor exclusively to that service to which I was obliged to devote it by reason of what the Magazine was.

More and more it became clear to me that I could no longer place myself in such a relation with persons as I have been permitted to describe in connection with Vienna and Weimar. Writers assembled and learned in literary fashion to know one another as writers. Even with the best, even in the case of the most clearly marked characters, this element of the writer (or painter or sculptor) was so deeply imbedded in the soul that the purely human retired completely into the background.

Such was the impression I received when I sat among these persons, much as I valued them. All the deeper for this reason was the impression which I myself received of the human soul-background. Once, after I had given a lecture and O. J. Bierbaum a reading, in the Free Literary Society in Leipzig, I sat among a group in which was also Frank Wedekind. My eyes were held captive by this truly rare human form. I use the word *form* here in a purely physical sense. Such hands!—as if from a previous earthly life in which they had performed things such as only those human beings can perform who cause their spirit to stream into the most delicate branching of the fingers. Even if they may have given an impression of brutality, because energy had been consumed in work, yet my deepest interest was attracted to what streamed forth from those hands. And that expressive head—altogether like a gift of what came from the unusual note of will in the hands. He had something in his glance and the play of his features which could give itself so arbitrarily to the world, but which especially could withdraw again, like the gestures of the arms expressing what the hands felt. A spirit alien to the present time spoke from that head—a spirit that really set itself apart from human affairs of the present. Only, a spirit that could not inwardly attain to clear consciousness as to which world of the past was that to which it belonged. As a writer—I express now only what I beheld in him, not a literary judgment—Frank Wedekind was like a chemist who utterly rejects contemporary views in chemistry and practises alchemy, but even this without sharing inwardly in it, but with cynicism. Much could be learned about the working of the spirit in form by receiving into the vision of the soul the outer appearance of Frank Wedekind. In this, however, must not be employed the look of that kind of psychologist who "proposes to observe man," but the look which shows the purely human against the background of the spiritual world through an inner dispensation of destiny—which is not sought, but simply comes.

A person who notices that he is being observed by a psychologist may justly be indignant, but the passing over from the purely human relation to "seeing against the spiritual background" is also purely human, somewhat like passing from a casual to a more intimate friendship.

One of the most unusual personalities of Hartleben's Berlin circle was Paul Scheerbarth. He had written "poems" which at first seem to the reader arbitrary combinations of words and sentences. They are so grotesque that the reader feels himself for this reason drawn on to get past the first impression. Then he finds that a fantastic sense seeks out all kinds of unnoticed meanings in words in order to bring to expression a spiritual content derived from a fantasy of the mind not only without foundation but not in the least seeking for a foundation. In Paul Scheerbarth existed an inner cult of the fantastic, but one that moved in the sought-out forms of the grotesque. It is my opinion that he had the feeling that the intelligent person should express whatever he does set forth only in grotesque forms, because others misshape everything into humdrum forms. But this feeling of his did not develop even the grotesque in rounded artistic form, but in a lordly, purposely heedless mood of soul. And what becomes manifest in these grotesque forms *must* spring from the inner domain of the fantastic. There was a basic trait of mind in Paul Scheerbarth which did not seek for clarity in reference to the spiritual. What proceeds out of thoughtfulness does not pass over into the region of the spirit—so said this fantast to himself; therefore, it is not necessary to be thoughtful in order to express the spirit. But Scheerbarth made not one step from the fantastic to fantasy. Hence he wrote out of a spirit that remained fixed in the interesting but wild fantastic, a spirit in which whole worlds of the cosmos gleam and glitter as framework of the stories, caricature the realm of spirit, and embrace human experiences treated in the same way. Such is the case in *Tarub, Bagdad's berühmte Köchin*.[1]

In personal acquaintance the man did not appear in this light. A bureaucrat, somewhat elevated into the spiritual. The outer appearance, so interesting in Wedekind, was in him quite ordinary, commonplace. And this impression was still further strengthened if one entered into conversation with him in the early stages of one's acquaintance. He bore within him the most burning hatred of the Philistines, but had the gestures of the Philistines, their manner of speech, and behaved as if hatred came out of the fact that he had taken on too much from Philistine circles in his own appearance and was conscious of this and yet had the feeling that he could not overcome it. A kind of confession could be read at the bottom of his soul: "I should like to annihilate the Philistines because they have made me a Philistine."

But, beyond this outer appearance, in the inner nature of Paul Scheerbarth, independent of this, was unveiled an altogether fine spirit-man, only fixed in the grotesque-fantastic and remaining incomplete. One then shared in the experience, through his "luminous head," his "golden heart," of the manner in which he stood in the spiritual world. One saw clearly how strong a personality, penetrating in vision into the realm of the spirit, could there have come into the world if that incompleteness had, at least in some measure, been completed. But it became clear at the same time that "devotion to the fantastic" was already so strong that even a future completion during this earthly life was no longer within the realm of the possible.

In Frank Wedekind and Paul Scheerbarth stood before me personalities who, in their whole being, afforded the most significant experience to one who knew the truth of the repeated earthly lives of human beings. They were, indeed, riddles in the present earthly life. But, viewed with respect to what they had brought with them into this earthly life, the whole personality stood forth in unlimited en-

[1] *Tarub, Bagdad's Famous Cook.*

richment. But it was clearly visible also that their imperfections were due to earlier earthly lives, and that these could not be brought to complete unfoldment in the contemporary spiritual environment. One saw that what these imperfections could become required future earthly lives.

In like manner did many another personality in this group confront me. I recognized that *meeting them* was for me a dispensation of destiny (karma).

A purely human, heartfelt relation I could never gain even with that so entirely lovable Paul Scheerbarth. It was always the case that, in our converse, the littérateur in Paul Scheerbarth, as in others, invariably intervened. So my feelings for him, affectionate to be sure, were finally determined by the attention and interest I was impelled to give to his personality, in such high measure noteworthy.

There was, indeed, one personality in the group whose living presence was not that of a littérateur but of a human being in the fullest tense—W. Harlan. But he talked little, always really sitting there as a silent observer. When he did speak, however, his talk was always either in the best sense brilliant or else genuinely witty. He really wrote a great deal, but not exactly as a littérateur; rather, as a human being who had to express what weighed upon him. It was just at that time that the *Dichterbörse*[1] had come from his pen, a representation of life full of excellent humor. I was always glad when I came somewhat early to our place of meeting and found Harlan, as the first arrival, sitting there alone. One then got close to him. I exclude him, therefore, when I say that in this group I found only littérateurs and no "human beings." And I think he understood that I had to view the group in that light. Utterly different paths of life soon bore us far apart.

The persons associated with the Magazine and the Free Literary Society were evidently woven into *my* destiny. But I was in no manner whatever woven into *theirs*. They saw me appear in Berlin, became aware that I would edit the Magazine and work for the Free

[1] *Poets' Exchange.*

Literary Society, but did not understand just why I should do this. For the manner in which—to the eyes of their minds—I went about among them offered them no inducement to show deeper interest in me. Although not a single trace of theory clung to me, yet my spiritual activity appeared to their theoretical dogmatizing as something theoretical. This was something in which they, as "artistic natures," thought they need take no interest.

But I learned to know in direct perception an artistic current in its representatives. This was no longer so radical as that appearing in Berlin at the end of the 'eighties and the beginning of the 'nineties. It was also no longer such as to represent absolute naturalism as the salvation of art—as in the theatrical transformation under Otto Brahms. This current was without any such comprehensive artistic conviction. It relied rather upon what flowed together out of the wills and the capacities of individual personalities, which was, however, utterly without any unified endeavor toward style.

My place within this group came to be the cause of inner discomfort to me because of the feeling that I knew why I was there but the others did not know.

XXV

Associated with the Magazine group was a Free Dramatic Society. It did not belong so intimately with the Magazine as did the Free Literary Society, but the same persons were on the board of directors as in the other society, and I was elected a member of this board immediately after I came to Berlin.

The function of this society was that of presenting plays which, because of their special character, because they were not in keeping with the usual trend of taste, and the like, were at first not produced by the theaters. It was no light task that rested upon the directors to do justice to the many attempts of the "misunderstood."

The productions were carried out in such a way that in each case a company of actors was made up of artists who played on the most various stages. With them forenoon-performances were given in a theater rented or else lent freely by its managers. The actors proved to be very unselfish in relation to the Society, for it was unable, by reason of its limited means, to offer adequate compensation. But neither actors nor managers had any inner reason at that time to object to the production of works of an unusual kind. They simply said that before the ordinary public in evening performances, this could not be done, since it would cause financial injury to the theater; that the public is simply not ripe for the idea that the theater should serve exclusively the cause of art.

The activity associated with this Dramatic Society proved to be of a character in high degree suited to me; most of all the part hav-

ing to do with the staging of the plays. Along with Otto Erich Hartleben, I took part in the rehearsals. We felt that we were the real
stage-managers. We gave the plays their stage forms. In this very art
it becomes evident that all theorizing and dogmatizing are of no use
unless they come from a vital artistic sense which intuitively grasps
in the details the general requirements of style. The resort to general
rules must be steadfastly resisted. All that one is capable of in such
a sphere must appear in a flash from a sure sense for style in action,
in arrangements of the scenes. What is then done without any logical
reflection, but from the activated sense for style, acts as a benediction
for every artist in the cast, whereas management derived from the
intellect gives them the feeling that their inner freedom is being
interfered with.

To the experiences in this field which were then mine I had occasion afterward again and again to look back with satisfaction.

The first play we produced in this way was Maurice Maeterlinck's
L'Intruse.[1] Otto Erich Hartleben had made the translation. Maeterlinck was then considered by the aesthetes as the dramatist fitted to
bring on the stage before the eyes of the dimly sensing spectator the
invisible existing amid the grosser elements of life. What is ordinarily called incident in drama, the form of development in dialogue,
Maeterlinck employed in such a way that something to be vaguely
sensed is thus made effective as in a symbol. It was this symbolizing
that attracted many whose taste had been repelled by the previous
naturalism. All who were seeking for "spirit," but who did not wish
a form of expression in which a "world of spirit" is directly revealed,
found their satisfaction in a symbolism that spoke a language which
did not use naturalistic expression and yet entered into the spiritual
only to the extent that this was revealed in the vague blurred form
of the mystic-presentimental. The less it was possible to "tell distinctly" what lay behind the suggestive symbols, the more were
many enraptured by them.

I did not feel at ease in the presence of this spiritual glimmering.

[1] *The Intruder.*

Yet it was fascinating to work at the staging of such a play as *The Intruder*. For the representation of just such symbols by appropriate stage means required in unusual degree the managerial function guided in the way described above.

Moreover, it became my task to precede the performance with a brief introductory address. This practice, common in France, had at that time been adopted also in Germany in connection with certain plays—not, of course, in the ordinary theater, but for such undertakings as were adapted to the Dramatic Society. This did not occur, indeed, at every performance of the Society, but infrequently: when it seemed necessary to introduce the public to an artistic intention with which it was not familiar. The task of giving this brief stage address was satisfying to me for the reason that it afforded an opportunity to give effect in my speech to a mood radiated to me myself from the spirit. This gave me pleasure in a human environment which otherwise had no ear for the spirit.

This vital connection with dramatic art was, in itself, really important for me at that time. For that reason, I myself wrote the dramatic critiques for the Magazine. As to such critiques, moreover, I had my own views—which, however, were little understood. I considered it unnecessary that an individual should pass judgment upon a play or its production. Such judgments, as these were generally given, should really be reached by the public itself alone.

He who writes about a theatrical production should cause to arise before his readers, through an artistic painting in ideas, what relations in fantasy-form stand behind the play. In artistically moulded thoughts, there should arise before the reader a poetic reproduction in ideas as the living, though unconscious, germ from which the author created the play. For, to me, thoughts were never merely something by means of which reality is abstractly and intellectually expressed. I saw that an artistic activity is possible in the moulding of thoughts just as with colors, with forms, with stage devices. And such a minor thought-work of art should be created by one who writes about a theatrical production. But that such a thing should come about when a play is performed before an audience seemed to me a necessary demand of the life of art.

Whether a play is good or bad or mediocre will be evident in the tone and bearing of such a thought-work of art. For this cannot be concealed even though it is not said in the form of crass judgments. Anything that is an impossible artistic structure will be visible in the thought-art reproduction. For, although the thoughts are there set forth, yet they appear utterly unreal if the work of art has not come from true fantasy living within reality.

Such a life-imbued collaboration with living art I wished to have in the Magazine. In this way something was to have been brought into existence through which the weekly would not have seemed to be engaged merely in theoretically discussing, judging, art and the cultural life. It was to be itself a member in this cultural life, in this art.

For everything that the art of thinking can do for dramatic poetry can be done also for the art of the theater. It is possible by means of thought-fantasy to bring into existence what the art of the manager has introduced into the stage settings; in this way it is possible to follow the actor, and, not through criticism but by positive presentation, cause what is alive in him to stand forth. One then becomes, as a writer, a formative participant in the artistic life of the age, and not a judge standing in the corner, dreaded, pitied, or even despised and hated. When this is practised for all branches of art, a literary-artistic periodical is in the midst of actual life.

Such things, however, always result in the same experience. If the effort is made to bring them to the attention of persons engaged in writing, they either fail completely to enter into the matter, because the ideas are contrary to the writer's habits of thought, or else they listen and say: "Yes, that's right; but I have always done so." They fail completely to observe the distinction between what is proposed and what they themselves "have always done."

One who can go on his lone spiritual path need not be disturbed in mind by this. But whoever has to work among persons united in a cultural group will be affected to the depths of his soul by these relations. Especially is this true if the direction of his inner life is so firm, so grown together with him, that he cannot turn aside from this in anything essential.

Neither the presentation of my ideas in the Magazine nor that in lectures afforded me at that time inner satisfaction. Only, any one who reads them today and thinks that I intended to be a representative of Materialism is utterly mistaken. That I *never* wished to do.

This can clearly be seen from the articles and excerpts of lectures that I wrote. It is necessary only to set over against individual passages which seem to convey a materialistic note others in which I speak of the spirit, of the eternal. For example, in the article *Ein Wiener Dichter*.[1] Of Peter Altenberg I say there: "What most interests the person who enters deeply into the eternal world harmony seems foreign to him. . . . From the eternal ideas no light penetrates into Altenberg's eyes. . . . (Magazine, July 17, 1897.) The fact that this "eternal world harmony" cannot be meant to signify something materialistic and mechanical becomes clear in utterances such as those in the article on Rudolf Heidenhain (of November 6, 1897): "Our conception of nature is clearly striving toward the goal of explaining the life of the organism according to the same laws by which also the phenomena of inanimate nature must be explained. Mechanical, physical, chemical law is sought for in the bodies of animals and plants. The same kinds of laws that control a machine are supposed to be operative in the organism also—only in immeasurably more complicated, scarcely comprehensible form. Nothing is supposed to be added to these laws in order to render possible the phenomena we call life. . . . The mechanistic conception of the phenomena of life steadily gains ground. But it will never satisfy one who has the capacity to cast a deeper glance into nature's processes. . . . Contemporary researchers in nature are too cowardly in their thinking. Where the wisdom of their mechanistic explanations fails, they say the thing is to us inexplicable. . . .

[1] *A Vienna Poet.*

A bold thinking lifts itself to a higher mode of perceiving. It seeks to explain by higher laws that which is not of a mechanical character. All our natural-scientific thinking remains behind our natural-scientific empirical knowledge. At present the natural-scientific form of thinking is much praised. It is said that we live in a natural-scientific age. But at bottom this natural-scientific age is the poorest that history has to show. Its characteristic is to remain caught by the mere facts and the mechanical forms of explanation. Life will never be grasped by this form of thinking, because such a grasp requires a higher manner of conceiving than that which belongs to the explanation of a machine."

Is it not obvious that one who speaks thus of the explanation of "life" cannot think materialistically of the explanation of "spirit"?

But I often spoke of the fact that the "spirit issues" from the bosom of nature. What is meant here by "spirit"? Everything proceeding from human thinking, feeling, and will which begets "culture." To speak of another "spirit" would then have been quite futile. For no one would have understood me if I had said that, underneath what appears in man as spirit and underneath nature, exists something which is neither spirit nor nature, but the perfect unity of the two. This unity: creative Spirit, which in its creating brings matter into existence and is thereby at the same time matter, which manifests itself wholly as spirit—this unity is comprehended by means of an idea which lay as remote as possible from the habits of thought of that period. But it would have been necessary to speak of such an idea in order to present in a spiritual form of conception the primal state of the evolution of the earth and of man, and the spiritual-material Powers still active today in man himself, which, on the one hand, form his body and on the other cause to issue forth from themselves the livingly spiritual by means of which he creates culture. But external nature would have needed to be so expounded that in it the primal spiritual-material would have been represented as having died in the abstract laws of nature.

All this could not be given.

It was possible to form a connection only with natural-scientific empirical knowledge, not with natural-scientific thinking. In this empirical knowledge something existed which, in the presence of a true spirit-filled thinking, was capable of placing the world and man luminously before man's own mind—something out of which the spirit could be found again which had been lost from the creeds traditionally preserved and believed. The perception of spirit-nature I wished to draw from the experience of nature. I wished to speak of what is to be found on "this side" as the spiritual-natural, as the essentially divine. For in the creeds preserved by tradition this divine element had become a "Beyond," because the spirit of "this side" was not recognized, and was severed, therefore, from the perceptible world. It had become something submerged for man's consciousness in ever increasing darkness. Not the rejection of the divine-spiritual, but placing it within the world, invoking it on "this side," inhered in such sentences as the following in one of the lectures for the Free Literary Society: "I believe that natural science can give back to us the consciousness of freedom in a form more beautiful than that in which men have ever possessed this consciousness. In our soul-life laws are operative just as natural as those which send the heavenly bodies round the sun. *But these laws represent Something higher than all the rest of nature. This Something is present nowhere save in man alone. Whatever flows from this—in that is man free. He lifts himself above the rigid necessity of laws of the inorganic and organic; he heeds and follows himself alone.*" (The last sentences are italicized here for the first time;[1] they were not italicized in the Magazine. For these sentences, see the Magazine of February 12, 1898.)

[1] That is, in the German text. *Translator.*

XXVI

INDIVIDUAL assertions about Christianity which I wrote or expressed in lectures at this time appear to be contrary to interpretations I gave later. As to this the following fact must be noted. When I used the word "Christianity" at that time, I had in mind the doctrine of the Beyond which was in force in the Christian creeds. The whole content of religious experience referred to a world of spirit which was supposed not to be attainable by man in the unfolding of his spiritual powers. What religion has to say, what it has to give as moral precepts, was supposed to be derived from revelations which come to man from without. Against this idea my view of the spirit was opposed, maintaining that the world of spirit is experienced precisely as is the sense-world in what is perceptible in relation to man and to nature. My ethical individualism also was opposed to this idea, maintaining that the moral life proceeds, not from without in the form of commandments obeyed, but from the unfolding of the human soul and spirit, wherein lives the divine.

What occurred at that time in my mind in viewing Christianity was a severe test for me. The time between my departure from the Weimar task and the production of my book *Das Christentum als mystische Tatsache*[1] was occupied by this test. Such tests are the opposition provided by destiny (karma) which must be surmounted by one's spiritual development.

In the thinking which can result from the science of nature—

[1] *Christianity as Mystical Fact*, Anthroposophic Press, New York.

274

but which did not result at that time—I saw the basis upon which man might attain to insight into the world of spirit. I laid much stress, therefore, upon the knowledge of what underlies nature, which must lead to the knowledge of the spirit. For any one who does not stand in living reality within the world of spirit, as I do, such a submergence into a certain trend of thinking signifies a mere activity of thought. For one who experiences the world of spirit it signifies something essentially different. He is brought into contact with Beings in the world of spirit who desire to make such a trend of thinking the sole prevailing one. There one-sidedness in thinking does not lead merely to abstract error; there spiritually living intercourse with Beings is what in the human world constitutes error. I spoke later of Ahrimanic Beings when I desired to point in this direction. For these, it is absolute truth that the world must be a machine. They live in a world that borders directly upon the sense-world.

In my own ideas I never for one moment became a victim of this world, not even in the unconscious. For I took the utmost pains to insure that all my knowledge should be reached in a state of discriminating consciousness. So much the more conscious was also my inner struggle against the demonic Powers who wanted to cause the knowledge of nature to become, not perception of spirit, but a mechanistic-materialistic way of thinking.

He who seeks for knowledge of spirit must *experience* these worlds; for him a mere theoretical thinking about them does not suffice. At that time I had to save my spiritual perception by inner battles. These battles were the background of my outer experience.

In this time of testing I succeeded in progressing further only when in spiritual vision I brought before my mind the evolution of Christianity. This led to the knowledge which was expressed in the book *Christianity As Mystical Fact*. Before this, the Christian content to which I referred had always been that found in the existent creeds. This Nietzsche also did.

In an earlier passage in this biography,[1] I narrated a conversation about Christ which I had with the learned Cistercian who was a professor in the faculty of Catholic theology of the University of Vienna. I was in the presence of a sceptical mood. The Christianity which I had to seek I did not find anywhere in the creeds. After the time of testing had subjected me to stern battles of the soul, I had to submerge myself in Christianity and, indeed, in the world in which the spiritual speaks thereof.

In my attitude toward Christianity it can clearly be seen that in spiritual science I have sought and found absolutely nothing by the path which many ascribe to me. These persons state the matter as if I had collected together the knowledge of spirit existing in ancient traditions. I am supposed to have elaborated Gnostic and other teachings. What is achieved of the knowledge of spirit in *Christianity as Mystical Fact* is brought directly out of the world of spirit itself. Only in order to show to those who heard the lectures and to the readers of the book the harmony between what is spiritually beheld and the historic traditions did I take these traditions and insert them into the content. But nothing existing in these documents have I inserted into the content unless I had first confronted this in the spirit.

It was during the time when I made the statements about Christianity so opposed in literal content to later utterances that the true substance of Christianity began germinally to unfold within me as an inner phenomenon of knowledge. About the turn of the century, the germ unfolded more and more. Before this turn of the century came the testing of soul I have described. The unfolding of my soul rested upon the fact that I had stood in spirit before the Mystery of Golgotha in most inward, most earnest solemnity of knowledge.

[1] See page 92.

XXVII

THE THOUGHT then hovered before me that the turn of the century must bring a new spiritual light to humanity. It seemed to me that the exclusion of the spiritual from human thinking and willing had reached a climax. A change of direction in the process of human evolution seemed to me a matter of necessity.

Many were speaking in this way. But they did not see that man will seek to direct his attention to a real world of spirit as he directs it through the senses to nature. They supposed only that the subjective spiritual temper of the mind would undergo a change. That a real, new objective world could be revealed—such a thought lay beyond the range of vision of that time.

With the perceptions that came to me from my perspective of the future and from the impressions created by the world around me, I was forced to turn the eyes of my mind again and again back to the course of development of the nineteenth century.

I saw that, with the time of Goethe and Hegel, everything disappeared which knowingly receives conceptions of a spiritual world into man's way of thinking. Thenceforth knowledge was not to be "confused" by conceptions of the spiritual world. These conceptions were relegated to the domain of faith and "mystical" experience.

In Hegel I perceived the greatest thinker of the modern age. But he was just that—*only* a thinker. To him the world of spirit was *in* thinking. Even while I admired immeasurably the way in which he gave form to all thinking, yet I perceived that he had no feeling for the world of spirit which I beheld, and which is revealed *behind* thinking only when thinking becomes intensified into an experience whose body, in a certain sense, is thinking and which takes into itself as soul the Spirit of the World.

Since in Hegelianism everything spiritual has become thinking, Hegel represented for me the personality who brought the very last dim rays of the ancient spiritual light into a period in which the spirit became veiled in darkness for human cognition.

All this appeared thus before me whether I looked into the spiritual world or looked back in the physical world upon the century drawing to a close. But now there came forth in this century a figure which I could not trace all the way into the spiritual world—Max Stirner.

Hegel, wholly thought-man, who in his unfolding strove for a thinking which goes ever *deeper,* and in going deeper *extends* to farther horizons. This thinking in its deepening and broadening was expected at last to become one with the thinking of the World Spirit, which encompasses the whole world-content. And Stirner, all that man unfolds out of himself, drawing this wholly from his individual personal will—what comes to existence in humanity, only in the juxtaposition of the single personalities.

I dared not, at just that time, fall into one-sidedness. As I stood completely within Hegelianism, experiencing this in my mind as my own inner experience, so must I also wholly submerge myself inwardly in this opposite.

Against the one-sidedness of endowing the World Spirit merely with knowledge, the other one-sidedness had, indeed, to appear— the assertion of man as mere will-being.

Had the situation been such that these opposites had simply appeared in me as an experience of my own mind in its development, I would never have permitted anything of this to enter into my writings or lectures. I have always observed this rule with regard to such mental experiences. But this particular contrast—Hegel and Stirner— belonged to the century. Through this the century expressed itself.

And it is true, indeed, that philosophers are *not* to be considered primarily with respect to their influence on their time. Certainly very strong influences can be attributed to Hegel, but this is not the main thing. Philosophers show in the substance of their thinking the spirit of their age, as the thermometer shows the warmth of a locality. In the philosophers that becomes *conscious* which lives *unconsciously* in the age.

So did the nineteenth century live in its two extremes through the impulses manifest through Hegel and Stirner: impersonal thinking which most delights to indulge in a contemplation of the world in which man, with the creative powers of his inner being, has no part; and wholly personal volition with little feeling for the harmonious cooperation of human beings. To be sure, all possible "social ideals" appear, but they have no power to influence reality. This more and more takes on the form of what can come about when the wills of individuals work side by side.

Hegel desires the idea of the moral to take objective form in the associated life of men; Stirner feels that the "individual" (the single person) is misled by everything that thus gives harmonious form to the life of men.

My own consideration of Stirner was associated at that time with a friendship which had a decisive influence upon very much included in that consideration. This was my friendship with the important Stirner scholar and editor, J. H. Mackay. It was while still in Weimar that I was brought into contact by Gabrielle Reuter with this personality, at once altogether congenial to me. He had occupied himself with those chapters of my *Philosophy of Freedom* which deal with ethical individualism. He found a harmony between my expositions and his own social views.

At first, it was the personal impression I received from J. H. Mackay that filled my mind in regard to him. He bore the "world" within him. In his whole inner and outer bearing, there spoke world-experience. He had spent some time both in England and in America. All this was suffused with a boundless amiability. I conceived a great affection for the man.

When, therefore, J. H. Mackay came in 1898 to reside permanently in Berlin, a delightful friendship developed between us. This also, unfortunately, has been destroyed by life and especially by my public representation of Anthroposophy.

In this instance I must describe only quite subjectively how the work of J. H. Mackay appeared to me at that time, and still appears, and what effect it had upon me. For I am aware that he himself would speak quite differently about it.

Profoundly hateful to this man was everything in human social life which constitutes force (*Archie*). The greatest blunder, he felt, was the intervention of force in social administration. In "communistic anarchism" he saw a social idea in the highest degree reprehensible, because this proposed to bring about a better state for humanity through the employment of forceful means.

Now, it was a dubious thing for J. H. Mackay to battle against this idea, and the agitation based upon it, while choosing for his own social goal the identical name that his opponents had, only with another adjective preceding it. "Individualistic anarchism" was his name for what he himself represented—and that, too, as the very opposite of what was then called "anarchism." This naturally led the public to form nothing but distorted judgments of Mackay's ideas. He was in accord with the American B. Tucker,* who stood for the same conception. Tucker visited Mackay in Berlin, and in this way I came to know him.

Mackay is also the literary exponent of his conception of life. He wrote a novel, *Die Anarchisten*.[1] I read this after having become acquainted with the author. It is a noble work based upon faith in the individual man. It describes penetratingly and with great vividness the social condition of the poorest of the poor. But it sets forth also how, out of the world misery, those human beings will find a

---

* Benjamin R. Tucker.
[1] *The Anarchists.*

way to improvement who, being wholly devoted to the good forces in human nature, so bring these forces to their unfolding that they become socially effective without having to resort to compulsion. Mackay had the noble confidence that men could of themselves create a harmonious order of life. He considered, however, that this would be possible only after a long time, when in a spiritual way a requisite revolution should have been completed in the inner life of men. He demanded for the present, therefore, that those individuals who were far enough advanced should propagate the idea of this spiritual way. A social idea, therefore, which would employ only spiritual means.

J. H. Mackay gave expression to his view of life also in poems. Friends saw in these something didactic and theoretical, which they felt to be inartistic. I liked the poems very much.

Destiny had now given such a direction to my experience with J. H. Mackay and Stirner that here also I had to submerge myself in a thought-world which became for me a spiritual testing. My ethical individualism had been felt as a pure inner experience of the human being. It was remote from my intention when I formulated this to make it a basis for a political conception. But at this time, about 1898, the effort was made to draw my mind, with its purely ethical individualism, into a kind of abyss. The effort was made to change this conception from something belonging purely to the inner being of man into something external. The esoteric was to be diverted into the exoteric.

Then, at the beginning of the new century, when I could state my experience of the spiritual in such writings as *Die Mystik im Aufgange des neuzeitlichen Geisteslebens*[1] and *Christianity As Mystical Fact,* "ethical individualism" again stood, after the test, in its rightful place. Yet, here also, the testing took such a course that the externalizing played no part in full consciousness. It took its course just below the level of consciousness, and, because of this very prox-

---

[1] *Mysticism at the Beginning of the Modern Spiritual Life.* Translated under the title *Mystics of the Renaissance.* Anthroposophic Press, New York.

imity, it could flow into the forms of expression in which, during the last years of the past century, I spoke about things social. Certain statements of that time, however, which seem all too radical must be compared with others in order to arrive at a correct conception.

One who sees into the world of spirit always finds his own being externalized when he is to *express* opinions and conceptions. He enters the spiritual world, not in abstractions, but in living perceptions. Nature, likewise, which is, indeed, the sensible copy of the spiritual, does not set up opinions and conceptions, but places her forms and her process of becoming before the world.

A state of inner movement, which drove into billows and breakers all the forces of my soul, was at that time my inner experience.

My external private life became one of absolute satisfaction by reason of the fact that the Eunicke family moved to Berlin, and I could live with them under the best of care, after having experienced for a short time the utter misery of living in an apartment of my own. My friendship with Frau Eunicke was soon thereafter transformed into a civil marriage. Let this suffice with regard to this private matter. Of my private life I do not wish to introduce anywhere into this biography anything except what affected the course of my development; and living in the Eunicke house made it possible for me to have an undisturbed basis for a life which was both inwardly and outwardly very active. Otherwise, private relations are not something to be publicized. They do not concern the public.

The truth is that my spiritual development is independent of all private relations. I am conscious of the fact that this would have been quite the same had the shaping of my private life been entirely different.

Into all the activity of my life at that time entered now my continual anxiety about the possibility of an existence for the Magazine. In spite of all the difficulties confronting me, it would have been possible to expand the circulation of the weekly if material means had been available to me. But a periodical which, at the utmost, could afford only the most meager fees, which gave me almost no basis for my own material existence, and for which nothing could be done to make it known, could not thrive upon the limited circulation it had when I took it over.

So long as I edited the Magazine, it was a constant source of anxiety to me.

XXVIII

A<small>T THIS</small> difficult time of my life, the directors of the Berlin Workers' Training School came to me with the request that I take charge of the courses of instruction in history and practice in public speaking in the school. I was at first little interested in the Socialistic connections of the school. I saw the fine task offered me of teaching mature men and women of the working class, for few young people were among the "pupils." I explained to the directors that, if I took over the instruction, I would present history precisely according to my own views of the course of human evolution, not in the style in which this is customary according to Marxism in Social-Democratic circles. They still wished to have me as a teacher.

After I had made this reservation, it could no longer be a matter of concern to me that the school was a Social-Democratic establishment of the elder Liebknecht. For me the school consisted of men and women of the proletariat; the fact that the great majority were Social-Democrats did not at all concern me.

But I obviously had to be concerned with the mental character of the pupils. I had to speak in forms of expressions to which I had been till then quite unaccustomed. I had to familiarize myself with the forms of conception and judgment of these persons in order to be in some measure understood.

These forms of conception and judgment came from two sources. First, from life. These people knew physical labor and its results. The Spiritual Powers guiding mankind forward in history did not enter into their minds. It was for this reason that Marxism, with its "materialistic conception of history," had such an easy way with them. Marxism maintained that the impelling forces in the historic process are the economic-material forces, those produced in physical labor. The "spiritual factors" were considered merely a sort of by-product arising from the material-economic factor—a mere ideology.

Moreover, an eagerness for scientific education had long before developed among the workers. But this could be gratified only by means of the popular materialistic-scientific literature. For this literature alone hit upon the forms of conceptions and judgments known to the workers. Whatever was not materialistic was written in such a way that the workers could not possibly understand it. Thus came about the unspeakably tragic fact that, while the developing proletariat desired knowledge with the most intense craving, this craving of theirs was satisfied only by means of the grossest materialism.

It must be borne in mind that half-truths are imbedded in the economic Materialism which the workers take from Marxism, as "materialistic history," and that these half-truths are just the thing they easily understand. If, therefore, I had taught Idealistic history, to the complete ignoring of these half-truths, the workers would have sensed instinctively in these materialistic half-truths something which would have turned them against my presentation.

I took as my starting-point, therefore, a truth which could be understood by my hearers also. I pointed out that to speak of a domination by the economic forces prior to the sixteenth century, as Marx does, is nonsense; that, from the sixteenth century on, the economic element first reaches a condition which can be conceived in a Marxian way; and that the process then comes to its climax in the nineteenth century.

In this way it was possible to speak quite as a matter of fact of the ideal-spiritual impulses in connection with the earlier periods of history, and to show that in the most recent times these had grown weak in comparison with the material-economic impulses.

Through this manner of presentation, the workers arrived at con-

ceptions of capacities for knowledge, of religious, artistic, and moral
motive forces in history, and abandoned the habit of thinking these
to be mere "ideology." To resort to polemics against Materialism
would have been senseless; I had to cause Idealism to arise out of
Materialism.

In the practice in public speaking, however, little could be done in
the same direction. After I had discussed at the beginning of each
course the formal principles of lecturing and speaking, the pupils
made practice speeches. Inevitably, they then brought forward what
was familiar to them in their materialistic way.

The "leaders" of the labor unions did not at first trouble themselves
at all about the school, and so I had a perfectly free hand.

When the teaching of the natural sciences was annexed to that of
history, it became more difficult for me. There it was especially difficult to ascend to factual conceptions from the materialistic conceptions prevailing in science, especially among its popularizers. I did
this as well as I possibly could.

Now, however, my teaching activity was expanded within the
working class precisely through natural science. I was requested by
numerous trade unions to lecture on natural science. Especially was
instruction desired in regard to Haeckel's *Welträtsel*,[1] then creating
a sensation. In the positive biological third of this book I saw a precise brief compendium of the kinship among living beings. My general conviction that mankind can be led from this direction to
spirituality I held to be true of the workers also. I connected my reflections with this third of the book and said often enough that the
other two-thirds must be considered worthless, and really ought to
be cut out of the book and thrown away.

At the celebration of the Gutenberg Jubilee, I was entrusted with
the festival address before 7,000 typesetters and printers in a Berlin
circus. Thus my manner of speaking to the workers was found congenial.

With this activity, destiny had once more transplanted me into a

[1] *The Riddle of the Universe at the Close of the Nineteenth Century.*

piece of life into which I had to submerge myself. I came to see that the single souls within this working class slumbered and dreamed, and that a sort of mass-soul laid hold upon this humanity, encircling its conception, judgment, attitude of mind.

But it must not be imagined that the single souls were dead. As to this, I was able to look deeply into the souls of my pupils and of the working class in general. This sustained me in the task I set myself in this whole activity. The attitude toward Marxism was not yet what it became two decades later. Marxism was still something which they elaborated with complete deliberation as a sort of economic gospel. Later it became something with which the mass of the proletariat is, as it were, obsessed.

The proletariat consciousness consisted of feelings manifesting themselves like the effect of mass-suggestion. Many of the single souls said again and again that a time must come when the world will again develop spiritual interests, but that, for the present, the proletariat must be freed by purely economic means.

I found that my lectures wrought much good in their souls. Even what contradicted Materialism and the Marxian conception of history was accepted. Later, when the "leaders" learned of my way of working, they fought against it. In a gathering of my pupils, one of these "minor leaders" spoke. He made this statement: "We do not wish freedom in the proletarian movement; we wish rational compulsion." The intention in this was to drive me out of the school against the will of my pupils. The activity was gradually rendered so difficult for me that, soon after I began my Anthroposophical work, I dropped it.

It is my impression that, if at that time the workers' movement had been followed with interest by a greater number of unprejudiced persons, and if the proletariat had been dealt with understandingly, this movement would have developed quite differently. But the people were left to live in their own class, and others lived in theirs. The conceptions of one class of human beings held by the other were mainly theoretical. Discussion of wages occurred when strikes and the like rendered this necessary; and all kinds of welfare institutions were established. These latter were exceedingly meritorious.

But the immersing of these world-stirring questions in a spiritual sphere was wholly lacking. And yet only this could have taken from the movement its destructive forces. It was the time when the "higher classes" had lost the community feeling, when egotism spread abroad with its fierce competitive struggles—the time in which the world catastrophe of the second decade of the twentieth century was already in course of preparation. Side by side with this, the proletariat developed the community sense in its own way as the proletarian class-consciousness. It shared in the "culture" which had been developed in the "upper classes" only so far as these provided material for the justification of the proletarian class-consciousness. Gradually there ceased to be any bridge between the different classes.

Thus by reason of the Magazine I was under the necessity of submerging myself in the nature of the bourgeoisie, and through my activity among the workers in that of the proletariat. A rich field for the purpose of sharing knowingly in the motive forces of the time.

XXIX

IN THE SPIRITUAL DOMAIN, a new light upon the evolution of humanity was seeking to break through into the knowledge gained during the last third of the nineteenth century. But the spiritual sleep caused by the materialistic interpretation of these acquisitions in knowledge prevented any inkling of this, much less any awareness of it.

Thus the very time arrived which ought to have developed in a spiritual direction through its own nature, but which belied its own nature—the time which began actually to bring about the impossibility of life.

I wish to set down here certain sentences taken from articles I wrote in March 1898 for the *Dramaturgische Blätter* (which had become a supplement of the Magazine at the beginning of 1898). Referring to the "art of oral utterance," I said: "In this field more than in any other, the learner is left wholly to himself and to chance. . . . Because of the form that our public life has taken on, almost everybody nowadays has frequent need to speak in public. . . . The elevating of ordinary speech to a work of art is a rarity. . . . We lack almost wholly the feeling for the beauty of speaking, and still more for speaking that is characteristic. . . . No one devoid of all knowledge of correct singing is considered justified in writing about a singer. . . . In the case of dramatic art, the requirements are far slighter. . . . Persons who know whether a verse is properly spoken or not become steadily scarcer. . . . Artistic speaking is often regarded nowadays as mistaken idealism. . . . We could never have come to this pass had we been more aware of the possibility of the artistic cultivation of speech. . . ."

What I then had in mind could come to a form of realization only much later, within the Anthroposophical Society. Marie von Sivers (Marie Steiner), who was enthusiastic about the art of speech, first dedicated herself to genuinely artistic speaking, and then it became possible with her help to work for the elevation of this domain of culture to a true art by means of courses in speech-formation and in dramatic presentation.

I have ventured to introduce this subject here in order to show that certain ideals have striven for realization throughout my life, since many persons endeavor to find something contradictory in my development.

To this period belongs my friendship with the poet Ludwig Jacobowski, who died at an early age. He was a personality whose basic mood of soul breathed the breath of inner tragedy. It was hard for him to bear the destiny that made him a Jew. He represented a bureau which, under the guidance of a liberal Deputy, directed the Association for Defence against Anti-Semitism, and published its organ. An excessive burden of work in this connection rested upon Ludwig Jacobowski, and work of a kind which renewed every day a burning pain, for it brought home to him daily the impression of the feeling against his people which caused him so much suffering.

In addition to this he developed a fruitful activity in the field of ethnology. He collected everything obtainable as the basis for a work on the evolution of peoples from primitive times. Various papers of his based upon his rich fund of knowledge in this field are very interesting. They were written in the Materialistic spirit of the time; but, had Jacobowski lived longer, he would certainly have been open to a spiritualizing of his research.

Out of this activity radiated the poetry of Ludwig Jacobowski— not wholly original, and yet marked by deep human feeling and filled with an experience imbued with the forces of the soul. *Leuch-*

tende Tage[1] he called his lyrical poems. These, when the mood bestowed them upon him, were really something in his life-tragedy that affected him like days of spiritual sunlight. Besides, he wrote novels. In *Werther der Jude*[2] is embodied all the inner tragedy of Ludwig Jacobowski. In *Loki, Roman eines Gottes*,[3] he produced a work born of German mythology. The soulful quality that speaks from this novel is a beautiful reflection of the poet's love of the mythological element in folk-culture.

A survey of what Ludwig Jacobowski accomplished leaves one astonished at its fullness in the most diverse fields. Yet he associated with many persons and enjoyed social life. Moreover, he was then editing the monthly *Die Gesellschaft*,[4] which meant for him an enormous excessive burden of work.

He had a consuming passion for life, whose essence he craved to know in order that he might mould this into artistic form.

He founded a society, *Die Kommenden*,[5] consisting of writers, artists, scientists, and persons interested in the arts. Meetings of this society were held weekly. Poets read their poems; lectures were given in the most diverse fields of knowledge and life. The evening ended in a free and easy social gathering. Ludwig Jacobowski was the center of this ever growing circle. Everybody was attracted to the lovable personality, so full of ideas, who even developed in this association a fine and noble humor.

Away from all this he was snatched by an early death, when he had just reached thirty years. He was taken off by meningitis, caused by his unceasing exertions.

For me there remained only the duty of giving the funeral address for my friend and editing his literary estate.

A beautiful memorial was created for him by his friend Marie Stona, in the form of a book comprising literary contributions by friends of his.

[1] *Luminous Days.*
[2] *Werther, the Jew.*
[3] *Loki, Romance of a God.*
[4] *Society.*
[5] *The Coming Ones.*

Everything about Ludwig Jacobowski was lovable: his inner tragedy, his striving away from this to his "luminous days," his absorption in an intensely active life. I have always kept alive in my heart the memory of our friendship, and look back upon our brief association with a heartfelt devotion to my friend.

Another friend with whom I came to be associated at that time was Martha Asmus, a lady of a philosophical mind but strongly inclined to Materialism. This tendency was modified, however, through the fact that Martha Asmus kept intensely alive the memory of her brother Paul Asmus, who had died early, and who was a decided Idealist.

Still once again, during the last third of the nineteenth century, Paul Asmus experienced, like a philosophical hermit, the Idealism of the time of Hegel. He wrote a paper on the ego, and one on the Indo-Germanic religions—both characteristically Hegelian in style but both wholly independent in content.

This interesting personality, who had then long been dead, was brought really close to me through the sister, Martha Asmus. It seemed to me that, in him, the philosophy of the beginning of the nineteenth century, inclined toward the spirit, flamed out like a meteor toward its end.

Less intimate but, nevertheless, significant for a time were the relations which came about between the "Friedrichhageners"—Bruno Wille and Wilhelm Bölsche—and myself. Bruno Wille is the author of a work entitled *Philosophie der Befreiung durch das reine Mittel.*[1] Only the title bears a reminiscence of my *Philosophy of Freedom;* the content moves in an entirely different sphere. Bruno Wille became very widely known through his very significant *Offenbarungen des Wachholderbaumes,*[2] a philosophical book written out of the finest feeling for nature, permeated by the conviction that spirit speaks out of all material existence. Wilhelm Bölsche is known through numer-

[1] *Philosophy of Liberation through Pure Means.*
[2] *Revelations of the Juniper Tree.*

ous popular writings on the natural sciences which are greatly admired within the most extensive circles of readers.

From this side came the establishment of a Free Academy, in which I was invited to participate. I was entrusted with the teaching of history. Bruno Wille took charge of philosophy, Bölsche of natural science, and Theodor Kappstein, a liberal-minded theologian, of the science of religion.

A second foundation was the Giordano Bruno Union. In this the idea was to bring together such persons as were sympathetic toward a spiritual-monistic philosophy. Emphasis was placed upon the idea that there are not two World Principles—matter and spirit—but that Spirit, as the unitary Principle, creates the whole of existence. Bruno Wille inaugurated the Union with a very brilliant lecture based on the saying of Goethe: "Matter, never without spirit." Unfortunately, a slight misunderstanding arose between Wille and me after this lecture. My words following the lecture—that, long after Goethe had coined this beautiful aphorism, he had supplemented it in impressive fashion, in that he had seen polarity and enhancement as the concrete spiritual forms operative in the spiritual activity of existence, and that in this way the general aphorism first received its full content,—this remark of mine was interpreted as an objection against Wille's lecture, the importance of which, however, I had fully recognized.

But I brought upon myself the direct opposition of the Giordano Bruno Union when I delivered a lecture on Monism. In this I laid stress upon the fact that the crass Dualistic conception, "matter and spirit," is really a creation of the most recent times, and that only during the most recent centuries, likewise, have spirit and nature been brought into the contrast with each other which the Giordano Bruno Union would combat. I then called attention to the fact that Scholasticism is Monism, in contrast with this Dualism. Even though Scholasticism withdrew from human knowledge a part of existence, and assigned this part to "faith," yet Scholasticism presents a world system marked by a unified (Monistic) constitution, from the Godhead and the world of spirit all the way to the details of nature. I thus placed Scholasticism higher also than Kantianism.

This lecture of mine aroused the greatest excitement. It was supposed that I wished to open the road for Catholicism into the Union. Of the leading personalities, only Wolfgang Kirchbach and Martha Asmus stood by me. The rest could form no notion as to what I really meant to do with the "misunderstood Scholasticism." In any case, they were convinced that I was likely to bring the greatest confusion into the Giordano Bruno Union.

I have reason to remember this lecture, because it belongs to a time when, according to the views expressed later by many persons, I was a Materialist. At that time, however, this "Materialist" passed with many persons as the one who would conjure up again medieval Scholasticism.

In spite of all this, I was able later to deliver before the Giordano Bruno Union my basic Anthroposophical lecture, which became the point of departure for my Anthroposophical activity.

With the imparting to the public of what Anthroposophy contains as knowledge of the spiritual world, decisions are necessary which are not altogether easy.

The character of these decisions can best be understood if one glances at a certain historical fact.

In accordance with the quite differently characterized soul constitutions of an earlier humanity, there has always been a knowledge of the spiritual world up to the beginning of the modern age, approximately until the fourteenth century. This knowledge, however, was quite different from Anthroposophical knowledge which is adapted to the cognitional requirements of the present day.

After the period mentioned, humanity could at first bring forth no knowledge of the spiritual world. Mankind preserved the "ancient knowledge," which the mind had beheld in pictorial form, and which was available later also only in symbolic-pictorial form.

This "ancient knowledge" was fostered in remote times only within the "Mysteries." It was imparted to those who had first been made ripe for it, the "initiates." It was not to reach the public because there the tendency arises too easily to use it in an unworthy manner. This practice has been maintained by those later personalities who received the lore of the "ancient knowledge" and continued to foster it. They did this in the most restricted circles with persons whom they had previously prepared.

And this has continued even till the present day.

Of the persons maintaining such a demand regarding spiritual knowledge whom I have encountered, I may select one who was active in the Viennese circle of Frau Lang to which I have referred, but whom I met also in other circles with which I was associated in Vienna. This is Friedrich Eckstein, the distinguished expert in that "ancient knowledge." While I was associated with Friedrich Eckstein, he did not write much. But what he did write was filled with the spirit. No one sensed, however, from his expositions the intimate expert in ancient knowledge of the spirit. This was effective in the background of his spiritual work. Long after life had removed me from this friend also, I read in a collection of writings a very significant treatise on the Bohemian Brothers.

Friedrich Eckstein represented vigorously the conviction that esoteric spiritual knowledge should not be publicly propagated like ordinary knowledge. He was not alone in this conviction; it was and is that of almost all experts in the "ancient wisdom." To what extent this conviction of the guardians of the "ancient wisdom," strongly enforced by rule, was violated in the Theosophical Society founded by H. P. Blavatsky—of this I shall have occasion to speak later.

Friedrich Eckstein wished that what was dealt with publicly by an "initiate in the ancient knowledge" should be endued with the force that comes from this "initiation," but that the exoteric should be strictly separated from the esoteric, which should remain within the most restricted circle which understands how to value it fully.

If I was to develop a public activity on behalf of spiritual knowledge, I had to decide to break with this tradition. I found myself confronted by the requirements of the contemporary spiritual life. In the presence of these, the practice of keeping things secret, which was a matter of course in ancient times, was an impossibility. We live in the age which demands publicity wherever any kind of knowledge appears. The point of view favoring the preservation of mysteries is an anachronism. The sole and only possibility is that persons should be taught spiritual knowledge by stages, and that no one should be admitted to a stage at which the higher portions of this knowledge are to be imparted until he knows the lower. This, indeed, corresponds with the practice in lower and higher schools.

Moreover, I was under no obligation to any one to guard mysteries, for I accepted nothing out of "ancient wisdom"; what I possess of spiritual knowledge is entirely the result of my own research. Only, when an item of knowledge has come to me, I then introduce whatever of the "ancient knowledge" has already been made public from some direction or other, in order to point to the harmony between the two and, at the same time, the advance which is possible to contemporary research.

Thus, after a certain point of time, it was quite clear to me that in the public presentation of spiritual knowledge I should be doing the right thing.

XXX

THE DECISION to give public expression to the esoteric knowledge I inwardly experienced impelled me to write for the Magazine for August 28, 1899, on the occasion of the one hundred and fiftieth anniversary of Goethe's birth, an article on Goethe's fairy tale of the *Green Snake and the Beautiful Lily* under the title *Goethes geheime Offenbarung*.[1] This article was, of course, only slightly esoteric. But I could not expect more of my public than I there gave. In my own mind, the content of the fairy tale existed as something wholly esoteric, and it was out of an esoteric mood that the discussion was written.

Since the 'eighties I had been occupied with imaginations which had become associated in my mind with this fairy tale. What I saw presented in the fairy tale was Goethe's way from the observation of external nature into the interior of the human soul, as he placed this before himself, not in concepts, but in pictures. Concepts seemed to Goethe far too poor, too dead, to be capable of representing the life, the activity, of the forces of the soul.

In Schiller's letters concerning education in aesthetics, Goethe had been confronted by an endeavor to grasp this life and activity by means of concepts. Schiller sought to show how the life of man is under subjection to natural necessity through his corporeal aspect and to spiritual necessity through his reason, and he believed that the soul-nature must establish an inner equilibrium between the two.

[1] *Goethe's Hidden Revelation.*

In this equilibrium, he felt, man lives in freedom a life really worthy of the human being.

This is ingenious, but for the real life of the soul it is far too simple. The soul-life causes its forces, which are rooted in the depths, to flash forth in consciousness, but to disappear again in the very act of shining forth, after they have influenced other forces just as fleeting. These are processes which, even in arising, pass away; but abstract concepts can be linked only to that which continues for a longer or shorter time.

All this Goethe knew through feeling; he placed his picture-knowledge in the fairy tale over against Schiller's conceptual knowledge.

In experiencing this creation of Goethe's, one is in the outer court of the esoteric.

This was the time when I was invited by Countess and Count Brockdorff to deliver a lecture at one of their weekly gatherings. These meetings were attended by persons from all circles. The lectures there delivered had to do with all fields of life and knowledge. I knew nothing of all this until I was invited to deliver a lecture; nor did I know the Brockdorffs, but heard of them then for the first time. The theme proposed to me was a discussion of Nietzsche. This lecture I gave. I now observed that among the hearers were persons with a great interest in the world of spirit. Therefore, when I was invited to give a second lecture, I proposed the subject *Goethe's Hidden Revelation,* and in this lecture I became entirely esoteric in dealing with the fairy tale. It was an important experience for me to be able to speak in words coined from the world of spirit after having been forced by circumstances throughout my Berlin period up to that time only to let the spirit shine through my presentation.

The Brockdorffs were leaders of a branch of the Theosophical Society founded by Blavatsky. What I had said in connection with Goethe's fairy tale led to my being invited by the Brockdorffs to deliver lectures regularly before those members of the Theosophical Society who were associated with them. I explained, however, that

I could speak only about what I vitally experienced within myself as spiritual science.

Indeed, I could speak of nothing else. For very little of the literature coming from the Theosophical Society was known to me. I had already known Theosophists while living in Vienna, and I later became acquainted with others. These acquaintanceships led me to write in the Magazine the adverse comment dealing with the Theosophists in connection with the appearance of a publication of Franz Hartmann. What I knew otherwise of the literature was for the most part entirely uncongenial to me in method and approach; I had no possibility anywhere of connecting my expositions with this literature.

So I then gave the lectures, in which I established a connection with the mysticism of the Middle Ages. By means of the ideas of the mystics from Master Eckhart to Jacob Böhme, I found expression for the spiritual perceptions which, in reality, I had decided to set forth. I then summarized the series of lectures in the book *Mystics of the Renaissance*.

During these lectures appeared one day in the audience Marie von Sivers, who was then chosen by destiny to take into strong hands the leadership of the German section of the Theosophical Society, founded soon after the beginning of my lectures. Within this section I was then able to develop my Anthroposophical activity before a constantly increasing audience.

No one was left in uncertainty of the fact that I would bring forward in the Theosophical Society only the results of my own research through direct vision. For I stated this on all appropriate occasions. When, in the presence of Annie Besant, the German section of the Theosophical Society was founded in Berlin and I was chosen its General Secretary, I had to leave the foundation sessions because I had to give before a non-Theosophical audience one of my lectures, in which I dealt with the spiritual evolution of humanity, and to the title of which I had expressly added *"Eine Anthroposophie."* [1] Annie

[1] *An Anthroposophy.*

Besant knew also that I was then presenting in lectures under this title what I had to say about the world of spirit.

When I then went to London to attend a Theosophical Congress, one of the leading personalities said to me that the true Theosophy was to be found in my book *Mysticism*. . . . I had reason to be satisfied. For I had given only the findings of my spiritual vision, and these were accepted in the Theosophical Society. There was now no longer any reason why I should not bring forward this spiritual knowledge *in my own way* before the Theosophical public, which was then the only audience that responded without restriction to a knowledge of the spirit. I subscribed to no sectarian dogmatics; I remained a person who uttered what he believed he was able to utter entirely according to what he himself experienced as the world of spirit.

Prior to the time of the founding of the section occurred a series of lectures which I gave before a circle called *Die Kommenden* under the title *Von Buddha zu Christus*.[1] In these expositions I sought to show what a mighty advance the Mystery of Golgotha signifies in comparison with the Buddha Event, and how the evolution of humanity, as it strives toward the Christ Event, approaches its culmination.

In the same circle I spoke also of the nature of the Mysteries.

All this was accepted by my hearers. It was not felt to be contradictory of lectures I had given earlier. Only after the section was founded, and I then appeared to be stamped as a Theosophist, did any objection arise. It was really not the thing itself; it was the name, and the association with a society, that no one wished to have.

On the other hand, my non-Theosophical hearers would have been inclined to permit themselves merely to be "stimulated" by my presentations, to accept these only in a "literary" sense. My heartfelt desire—to introduce into life the impulses from the world of spirit—for this there was no understanding. This understanding, however, I could gradually find among persons interested theosophically.

[1] *From Buddha to Christ.*

Before the Brockdorff circle, where I had spoken on Nietzsche and then on *Goethe's Hidden Revelation,* I gave at this time a lecture on *Faust,* from an esoteric point of view. (It is the lecture that was later published by *Philosophisch-Anthroposophischer Verlag* with my discussion of Goethe's fairy tale.[1])

The lectures on Mysticism led to an invitation from the same Theosophical circle to speak there again the following winter. I then gave the series of lectures which I later summarized in the volume *Christianity as Mystical Fact.*

From the beginning I have let it be known that the choice of the expression "as mystical fact" in the title is important. For I did not wish to set forth merely the mystical content of Christianity. My object was to set forth the evolution from the ancient Mysteries to the Mystery of Golgotha in such a way as to show that, in this evolution, not merely earthly historical forces but spiritual supramundane influences were operative. And I wished to show that the ancient Mysteries had to do with ritual pictures of cosmic events, which then took place on the historic level in the Mystery of Golgotha as *fact* transferred from the cosmos to the earth.

This was nowhere taught in the Theosophical Society. In this view I was in direct opposition to the Theosophical dogmatics of the time, before I was invited to work in the Theosophical Society.

For this invitation followed immediately after the cycle of lectures here described about Christ.

Between the two cycles of lectures that I gave before the Theosophical Society, Marie von Sivers was in Italy, at Bologna, working on behalf of the Theosophical Society in a branch established there.

Such was the development up to the time of my first attendance at a Theosophical Congress, in London, in the year 1902. At this Congress, in which Marie von Sivers also took part, it was already a foregone conclusion that a German section of the Society was now to be

[1] *Goethes Geistesart in ihrer Offenbarung durch seinen Faust und durch das Märchen "Von der Schlange und der Lilie."* Translated under title: *Goethe's Standard of the Soul as Illustrated in Faust and in the Fairy Story of "The Green Snake and the Beautiful Lily."* Anthroposophic Press, New York.

founded, with me—shortly before then invited to become a member—as General Secretary.

The visit to London was of great interest to me. I there became acquainted with important leaders of the Theosophical Society. I had the privilege of staying at the home of Mr. Bertram Keightley, one of the leaders. We became good friends. I became acquainted with Mr. Mead, the very meritorious writer of the Theosophical Movement. The most interesting conversations imaginable took place at the home of Mr. Keightley about spiritual knowledge then existing in the Theosophical Society.

Especially intimate were these conversations with Bertram Keightley himself. H. P. Blavatsky seemed to live again in these conversations. Her whole personality, with its wealth of spiritual content, was described with utmost vividness before me and Marie von Sivers by my dear host, who had experienced so much through her.

I became more casually acquainted with Annie Besant and also Sinett, author of *Esoteric Buddhism*. Mr. Leadbeater I did not meet, but only heard him speak from the platform. He made no special impression upon me.

All these interesting things that I heard stirred me deeply, but they had no influence upon the content of my views.

The intervals left over between sessions of the Congress I sought to employ in diligent visits to the natural-scientific and artistic collections of London. I can say that many an idea about the evolution of nature and of man occurred to me in connection with the natural-scientific and historical collections.

Thus I had experienced in this visit to London an event very important for me. I went away with the most manifold impressions, which stirred my mind profoundly.

In the first number of the Magazine for 1899 appears an article by me entitled *Neujahrsbetrachtung eines Ketzers*.[1] What is meant there is a heresy, not in reference to a religious creed, but in reference to the orientation in culture which the time had taken on.

[1] *New Year Reflection of a Heretic.*

We were standing before the portals of a new century. The closing century had brought forth great attainments in the domain of external life and knowledge.

Regarding this the thought forced itself upon me: "In spite of all this and many other attainments—for example, in the realm of art— no one possessed of a deeper vision can truly rejoice over the cultural content of the time. Our highest spiritual cravings long for something which the time affords only in meager measure." Reflecting upon the emptiness of the culture of that time, I glanced back to the time of Scholasticism, in which, at least in concepts, men's minds lived with the spirit. "There is no occasion for surprise if, in the presence of such phenomena, men with deeper spiritual cravings find the proud structures of thought of the Scholastics more satisfying than the idea-substance of our own time. Otto Willmann has written a noteworthy book, his *Geschichte des Idealismus,*[1] in which he appears as the eulogist of the world view of past centuries. It must be admitted that the human mind craves that proud, comprehensive illumination through thought which human knowledge experienced in the philosophical systems of the Scholastics.". . . "Lack of courage is a characteristic of the spiritual life at the turn of the century. It casts a shadow over our joy in the attainments of the most recent past."

Regarding those persons who insisted that it was precisely "true knowledge" itself which proved the impossibility of a world view comprising a picture of the totality of existence, I had to say: "If matters were as they appear to the persons who give utterance to such ideas, it would suffice one to measure, weigh, and compare things and phenomena, and investigate them by means of the available apparatus, but never would the question be raised as to the higher *meaning* of things and phenomena."

This was the mood of soul from which must be derived an understanding of those facts which brought about my Anthroposophical activity within the Theosophical Society. When I had immersed my-

[1] *History of Idealism.*

self at that time in contemporary culture in order to find the spiritual background for the editing of the Magazine, I felt after this a great need for refreshment of soul in such reading as Willmann's *History of Idealism*. Even though there was an abyss between my perception of spirit and Willmann's moulding of ideas, yet I felt that this moulding of ideas was near to the spirit.

At the end of September 1900, I was able to transfer the Magazine to other hands.

The facts narrated above show that the intention to impart the content of the world of spirit had already become a necessity growing out of my state of soul before I gave up the Magazine; that it had no connection with the impossibility of continuing further with the Magazine.

As into the very element predestined for my mind, I entered upon an activity having its impulse in the knowledge of spirit.

But I still have the feeling even today that, but for the hindrances described, my endeavor to lead through natural-scientific knowledge to the world of spirit would also have had good prospects. I look back upon what I expressed from 1897 to 1900 as something which at one time or another had to be uttered with regard to the way of thinking of the time; and, on the other hand, I look back as upon something in which I passed through my most intense spiritual testing. I learned to know fundamentally where lie the forces of the time, striving away from the spirit, disintegrating and destructive of culture, and from this knowledge came a great access of the force that I later needed in order to work out of the spirit.

It was still before the time of my activity within the Theosophical Society, and during the final period of my editing of the Magazine, that I composed my two-volume book *Conceptions of the World and of Life in the Nineteenth Century,* which from the second edition on was extended to include a survey of the evolution of world views from the Greek period to the nineteenth century, and then appeared under the title *Riddles of Philosophy.*

The external occasion for the production of this book is to be considered wholly secondary. It grew out of the fact that Cronbach, publisher of the Magazine, planned a collection of writings which was to deal with the various fields of knowledge and of life in their evolution during the nineteenth century. He wished to include in this collection an exposition of the conceptions of the world and of life, and this he entrusted to me.

I had held in mind for a long time all the substance of this book. My reflections comparing world views had a personal point of departure in that of Goethe. The contrast I had to show between Goethe's way of thinking and that of Kant, the new philosophical beginnings at the turning point between the eighteenth and nineteenth centuries in Fichte, Schelling, Hegel—all this was to me the opening of an epoch in the evolution of world views. The ingenious books of Richard Wahle, which show the cessation of all endeavor after a world view at the end of the nineteenth century, closed this epoch. Thus the endeavor of the nineteenth century to achieve a world view took on the aspect of a totality which I held in my conception, and which I gladly seized the opportunity to set forth.

When I look back to this very book, the course of my life seems to me symptomatically expressed in it. I did not move forward, as many believe, in contradictions. If this were the case, I would gladly admit it. But it would not be the reality in my spiritual progress. I advanced in such a way as to add new spheres to what was already in my mind. And an especially stimulating discovery in the spiritual realm occurred soon after the composition of *Conceptions of the World and of Life.*

Besides, I never advanced into the spiritual realm in a mystical-emotional way, but chose always to go by way of crystal-clear concepts. Experiencing of concepts, of ideas, led me out of the realm of ideas into the spiritual-real.

The true evolution of the organic from primeval times to the present confronted my imagination for the first time after the composition of *Conceptions of the World and of Life.*

During the writing of this book, I still had in mind the natural-scientific view derived from the Darwinian mode of thinking. But this I considered only as a succession of sense-perceptible facts present in nature. Within this succession of facts were active for me spiritual impulses, as these were conceived by Goethe in his idea of metamorphosis.

Thus the natural-scientific evolutionary succession, as represented by Haeckel, never constituted for me something wherein mechanical or merely organic laws hold sway, but something wherein the spirit leads the living beings from the simple through the complex up to man. I saw in Darwinism a mode of thinking which is on the way to that of Goethe but which remains behind this.

All this was still *thought* by me in idea-content; only later did I work through to imaginative perception. This perception first brought me the knowledge that something of the nature of real being different from the simplest organisms was present within spiritual reality in primeval times—that man, as a spiritual being, is older than all other beings, and that, in order to assume his present physical form, he had to cease to be a member of the World Being which comprised him and all other organisms. Hence these latter are waste elements in human evolution; not something out of which man has come, but something that he has left behind, which he severed from himself in order to take on his physical form as the image of the spiritual form. That man is a macrocosmic being who bore within him all the rest of the terrestrial world, and who has become a microcosm by eliminating all the rest—this was for me a knowledge to which I first attained in the earliest years of the new century.

And so this knowledge could not anywhere be an active influence in the composition of *Conceptions of the World and of Life.* The second volume of this very book was so composed as to indicate that a point of departure for a deepening knowledge of the world mystery might be found in a spiritualized form of Darwinism and Haeckelism seen in the light of Goethe's world view.

When I prepared later the second edition of the book, I already possessed a knowledge of the true evolution. Although I held fast to the point of view I had assumed in the first edition as being that derived from thinking without spiritual perception, yet I found it necessary to undertake slight changes in the form of expression. These were necessary, first because the book, by undertaking a general survey of the totality of philosophy, had become an entirely different composition, and secondly because this second edition appeared after my discussion of the true evolution of the living was already before the world.

In all this the form taken by my *Riddles of Philosophy* had not only a subjective justification as the firmly held point of view of a certain period in my spiritual development, but also a justification entirely objective. This consists in the fact that thinking, even when it is spiritually experienced *as thinking,* can conceive the evolution of living beings only as this is set forth in my book; and the further step must be made by means of spiritual perception.

Thus my book represents quite objectively the pre-Anthroposophical point of view into which it is necessary to submerge oneself, and which must be experienced in this submersion, in order to rise to the higher point of view. This point of view, as a stage on the way to knowledge, comes about in the cognizing human being who seeks the spiritual world, not in a mystically blurred form, but in a form clear to the mind. In the presentation of what results from this point of view, there is thus present something which the cognizing human being needs as a preliminary stage leading to the higher.

In Haeckel I could not but see at that time the person who placed himself courageously at the thinker's point of view in natural science, while all other researchers excluded thinking and admitted only the results of sense-observation. The fact that Haeckel placed value upon *creative* thinking in getting at the bottom of reality attracted me again and again to him. And so I dedicated my book to him, in spite of the fact that its content—even in its form at that time—was not conceived at all in his sense. But Haeckel was not at all of a philosophical nature. His relation to philosophy was wholly that of a layman. For this reason I considered the attacks of the philosophers, just then beating upon him like a hail-storm, as quite undeserved. In opposition to them, I dedicated my book to Haeckel, as I had already written in opposition to them my essay *Haeckel und seine Gegner.*[1] Haeckel, in all naïveté as to philosophy, had employed thinking as a means for setting forth biological reality; philosophical attacks were directed against him belonging to an intellectual sphere quite foreign to him. I believe he never knew what the philosophers demanded of him. This was my impression from a conversation I had with him in Leipzig after the appearance of his *Riddles of the Universe,* on the occasion of the presentation of Borngräber's play *Giordano Bruno.* He then said: "People say I deny the spirit. I wish they could see how substances take form through their forces; they could then perceive 'spirit' in everything that happens in a retort. Everywhere there is spirit." Haeckel, in fact, knew nothing whatever of real spirit. The very forces of nature were to him "spirit."

Such blindness to the spirit should not have been attacked at that time with philosophically dead concepts, but it should have become clear how far the age was removed from experience of the spirit, and the effort should have been made to strike the spiritual sparks out of the foundation which the age afforded—the biological interpretation of nature.

Such was then my opinion. On that basis I wrote also my *Conceptions of the World and of Life in the Nineteenth Century.*

[1] *Haeckel and His Opponents.*

XXXI

Another collective work which set forth the cultural attainments of the nineteenth century was edited at that time by Hans Kraemer. It consisted of lengthy essays on the individual branches in the domains of knowledge, technical production, and social development.

I was invited to give a description of the literary aspect of life. Thus at that time also the evolution of the life of fantasy during the nineteenth century passed through my mind. I did not describe like a philologist, who develops such things "out of their sources." I described what I had inwardly experienced of the unfolding of the life of fantasy.

This exposition also was important for me in that I had to speak of phenomena of the spiritual life without referring to the experience of the world of spirit. The real spiritual impulses from that world which become manifest in the phenomena of imaginative literature were left unmentioned.

In this case, likewise, what confronted me was that which the soul-life has to say of a phenomenon of existence when the mind places itself at the point of view of ordinary consciousness without bringing the content of this consciousness into such activity that it ascends in experience into the world of spirit.

Still more significantly did I experience this "standing before the portal" of the world of spirit in the case of a monograph which I had to write for another work. This was not a centennial work, but a

309

collection of papers which were to characterize the various domains
of knowledge and life in so far as human "egoism" is a motor force in
the development of each of these. Arthur Dix was the editor of this
work. It was entitled *Der Egoismus,*[1] and was extremely appropriate
for the time—the turning point between the nineteenth and twentieth centuries.

The impulses of intellectualism, which had asserted themselves
in all domains of life since the fifteenth century, have their roots in
the "life of the individual soul," when these impulses are really genuine expressions of their own nature. When the human being expresses himself intellectually on the basis of the social life, this is not
a genuine intellectual expression, but an imitation.

One of the reasons why the demand for social feeling has become
so intense in this age is the fact that this feeling is not experienced
with primal inwardness in intellectualism. In these things also humanity craves most of all what it does not have.

There was allotted to me for this book the exposition of *Der
Egoismus in der Philosophie.*[2] My paper bears this title only because the general title of the book required this. The title should
really have been *Der Individualismus in der Philosophie.*[3] I sought
to give in brief form a survey of Occidental philosophy since Thales,
and to show how the goal of its evolution has been to bring the human individuality to experience the world in idea-forms, just as the
purpose of my *Philosophy of Freedom* is to set this forth with reference to knowledge and the moral life.

Again in this paper, I stand before the "portal of the world of
spirit." In the human individuality become manifest the idea-forms
which reveal the world-content. They appear in such a way that
they wait for *experience* whereby the soul may step through them
into the world of spirit. In my description I stopped at this position.
An inner world is presented which shows how far mere thinking
comes in comprehending the world.

[1] *Egoism.*
[2] *Egoism in Philosophy.*
[3] *Individualism in Philosophy.*

It is evident that I described the pre-Anthroposophical life of the mind from the most varied points of view before devoting myself to the public Anthroposophical presentation of the world of spirit. In this can be found nothing inconsistent with my coming forward in behalf of Anthroposophy; for the world picture which arises is not contradicted by Anthroposophy, but extended and carried further.

If any one begins to represent the world of spirit as a mystic, it is justifiable to say: "You are speaking of your personal experiences. What you are describing is subjective." To travel such a spiritual road was not assigned to me as my task from the spiritual world.

This task consisted in creating a foundation for Anthroposophy just as objective as that of scientific thinking when this does not stop short at the registering of sensible facts, but advances to comprehensive understanding. What I set forth in scientific-philosophical manner, what I presented in a natural-scientific way in connection with Goethe's ideas, was subject to discussion. It could be considered more or less correct or incorrect. But it strove to achieve the character of the objectively scientific in the fullest sense.

It is out of this mode of cognition, free from the emotional-mystical, that I then draw the experience of the world of spirit. Let it be noted how, in my *Mysticism* and in *Christianity as Mystical Fact,* the concept of mysticism is carried in the direction of this objective cognizing. And let it be noted especially how my *Theosophy* is developed. At every step taken in this book, spiritual perception stands in the background. Nothing is said which is not derived from spiritual perception; but, while the steps are being made, the perception is clothed at first, in the beginning of the book, in scientific ideas until, in rising to the higher realms, it must occupy itself more and more in freely picturing the spiritual world. But this picturing grows out of the natural-scientific as the blossom of a plant grows from the stems and leaves. As the plant is not seen in its entirety if it is considered only up to the blossom, so nature is not experienced in its entirety if we do not rise from the sensible to the spiritual.

So what I strove for was to set forth in Anthroposophy the objective continuation of science, not to place by the side of science something subjective. It was inevitable that precisely this effort was not at first understood. Science was supposed to end with what antedates Anthroposophy, and there was no inclination so to put life into the ideas of science as to lead to the comprehension of the spiritual. People were under the spell of the habit of thought developed during the second half of the nineteenth century. They could not muster the courage to break the fetters of mere sense-observation; they feared that they might arrive at regions where everybody asserts the validity of his own fantasy.

Such was my orientation of mind when, in 1902, Marie von Sivers and I entered upon the leadership of the German section of the Theosophical Society. Marie von Sivers was the personality who, by reason of her whole being, made it possible to keep what came about through us far removed from anything sectarian, and to give to this such a character as places it within the general spiritual and cultural life. She was deeply interested in the art of the drama and of declamation and recitation, and had carried through a training in these art forms, especially in the best institutions in Paris, which had given to her talent a beautiful perfection. When I became acquainted with her in Berlin, she was still continuing her studies in order to become familiar with the various methods of artistic speech.

Marie von Sivers and I soon became devoted friends, and on the basis of this friendship, a united work developed in the most varied cultural fields over a very extensive area. To foster in common Anthroposophy, but also the art of poetry and recitation, soon became for us the very essence of life.

Only in this unitedly fostered spiritual life could the central point be found from which Anthroposophy was carried into the world, at first within the framework of the Theosophical Society.

During our first visit to London together, Marie von Sivers had heard from Countess Wachtmeister, an intimate friend of H. P. Blavatsky, much about the latter and much about the institutions and the evolution of the Theosophical Society. She was conversant in a high degree with what was once revealed as a spiritual content to the Society and the manner in which this content had been further fostered.

When I have said that it was possible to find within the framework of the Theosophical Society those persons who were willing to listen to communications from the world of spirit, this does not mean that the persons then enrolled in the Theosophical Society were to be considered before all others as being of such a character.

Many of these, to be sure, soon proved to have a high degree of understanding for my form of spiritual knowledge. But a large part of the members were fanatical followers of individual heads of the Theosophical Society. They swore by the dogmas given out by these heads, who acted in a strongly sectarian spirit.

This way of working of the Theosophical Society repelled me by the triviality and dilettantism inherent in it. Only among the English Theosophists did I still find an inner substance derived from Blavatsky, which was then fostered by Annie Besant and others in a pertinent manner. I could never have worked in the way these Theosophists worked. But I considered what existed among them as a spiritual center with which a worthy connection could be formed if the spread of spiritual knowledge in the deepest sense was taken seriously.

Thus it was not the membership united in the Theosophical Society upon which Marie von Sivers and I counted, but those persons in general who shared with heart and mind when knowledge of the spirit in a serious sense was fostered.

Working within the existing branches of the Theosophical Society, which was necessary as a starting point, comprised only a part, therefore, of our activity. The chief thing was the arranging of public lectures in which I spoke to an audience not belonging to the Theosophical Society and which attended my lectures only because of their content.

Of persons who became acquainted in this manner with what I had to say about the world of spirit and of those who, through activity within one or another "theosophical trend," found their way to this manner, was developed within the framework of the Theosophical Society what later became the Anthroposophical Society.

Among the various charges that have been directed against me in reference to my work in the Theosophical Society—even from the side of this Society itself—this accusation also has been made: that I used this Society, which already had a standing in the world, as a springboard, so to speak, in order to render easier the way for my own spiritual knowledge.

There is not the slightest ground for such a charge. When I accepted the invitation into the Society, this was the sole institution worthy of serious consideration in which a real spiritual life existed. Had the mood, bearing, and work of the Society remained the same as they then were, the withdrawal of my friends and me need never have occurred. The Anthroposophical Society might simply have been formed officially as a special section within the Theosophical Society.

But even from 1906 on manifestations were becoming effective in the Theosophical Society which indicated in a terrible degree its deterioration.

If at an earlier period, in the time of H. P. Blavatsky, such manifestations were declared by the outer world to have already occurred, yet at the beginning of the century it was clearly true that the seriousness of spiritual work on the part of the Society constituted a compensation for whatever wrong things had taken place. Moreover, the occurrence of such things was contested.

But, from 1906 on, manifestations appeared in the Society—upon whose general guidance I had not the least influence—reminiscent of the aberrations of spiritism, which made it necessary for me to warn members again and again that the part of the Society which was under my direction had absolutely nothing to do with these things. The climax in these manifestations was reached when the assertion was made about a Hindu boy that he was the person in whom Christ would appear in a new earthly life. For the propagation of this absurdity, a special society was formed within the Theosophical Society, that of the "Star of the East." It was utterly impossible for me and my friends to include the membership of this "Star of the East" as a branch of the German section, as they desired and as Annie Besant, President of the Theosophical Society, especially intended. Since we could not do this, we were excluded in 1913 from the Theosophical Society. We were forced to found the Anthroposophical Society as an independent body.

I have in this explanation advanced far ahead of the narration of the course of my life; but this was necessary, for only these later facts can throw the right light upon the intentions which I associated with my entrance into the Society at the beginning of the century.

When I spoke for the first time at the Congress of the Theosophical Society, in London in 1902, I said that the unity which the individual sections would form should consist in the fact that each should bring to the center what it contained within itself; and I strongly emphasized that for the German section this was most of all my intention. I made it clear that this section would never conduct itself as the representative of set dogmas, but as a place for independent spiritual research, which would desire to reach mutual understandings in conferences of the whole Society about the fostering of genuine spiritual life.

XXXII

IN READING discussions of Anthroposophy which are appearing
nowadays, it is painful to have to come again and again upon
thoughts, for instance, of this kind: that the World War created in
the minds of people moods favorable to the appearance of all kinds
of "mystical" and similar spiritual trends, and then to have Anthroposophy included among these trends.

Against this stands the fact that the Anthroposophical Movement
was founded at the beginning of the century, and that nothing essential has been done within this movement since its foundation to
which the inner life of the spirit has not given rise. Two and a half
decades ago, I bore a content of spiritual impressions within me. I
gave form to these in lectures, articles, and books. What I did was
done out of spiritual impulses. In its essence every theme was drawn
from the spirit. During the war I discussed also topics suggested by
the events of the time. But this did not rest upon any intention to
take advantage of the mood of the time for the propagation of Anthroposophy. These discussions occurred because a desire existed
among people to have certain events illuminated by the knowledge
which comes from the world of spirit.

On behalf of Anthroposophy no endeavor has ever been made for
anything else than that it should take the course of development
made possible by its own inner force, bestowed upon it by the spirit.
It is as inexact as possible when Anthroposophy is represented as
having desired to gain something from the dark abysses of human

souls during the World War. That the number of persons interested in Anthroposophy increased after the war, that the Anthroposophical Society increased in its membership—these things are true; only, it should be noted that these facts have never changed anything in the prosecution of the Anthroposophical cause in the spirit in which this has been done since the beginning of the century.

The form which was to be given to Anthroposophy from the essence of the inner spirit had at first to struggle through all kinds of opposition from the Theosophists in Germany.

First of all came the problem of vindicating knowledge of the spirit before the "scientific" mode of thought of the time. That this vindication is necessary I have stated frequently in this "course of my life." I took that way of thinking which rightly passes as "scientific" in the knowledge of nature and developed this for knowledge of the spirit. Through this means, the mode of the knowledge of nature became, to be sure, something different for the observation of spirit from what it is for the observation of nature, but the character which justifies it in being looked upon as "scientific" was maintained.

For just this way of giving scientific form to knowledge of the spirit those persons who considered themselves the bearers of the Theosophical Movement at the beginning of the century had neither understanding nor interest.

These were the persons grouped about Dr. Hübbe-Schleiden. He, as a personal friend of H. P. Blavatsky, had established a theosophical society as early as the 'eighties, beginning at Elberfeld. At the founding of this society, H. P. Blavatsky herself participated. Dr. Hübbe-Schleiden then published a journal, *Die Sphinx,* in which the theosophical world view was to be given publicity. The whole movement came to an end; and, when the German section of the Theosophical Society was founded, nothing existed except a number of persons, who looked upon me, however, as a sort of trespasser in their territory. These persons awaited the "scientific" justification of theosophy by Dr. Hübbe-Schleiden. They held the opinion that, until this should occur, nothing should be done in the matter within the German territory. What I began to do appeared to them as a disturbance of their "waiting," as something utterly detrimental. Yet they did not at once withdraw; for theosophy was "their" affair, and, if anything should happen in this, they did not wish to keep aloof.

What did they understand as the "scientific character" which Dr. Hübbe-Schleiden was to vindicate, whereby theosophy would be proved? To Anthroposophy they did not respond at all.

They understood by this term the atomistic basis of natural-scientific theorizing and hypothesizing. The phenomena of nature were "explained" by conceiving the "primordial parts" of the world-substance as grouping into atoms and these into molecules. A substance existed by reason of the fact that it represented a certain structure of atoms in molecules.

This mode of thinking was considered a model. Complicated molecules were constructed, which were supposed to be the basis for spiritual action also. Chemical processes were supposed to be the results of processes within the molecular structure; for spiritual processes something similar must be found.

For me this atomic theory, with the interpretation given to it by natural science, was something quite impossible even within that science; to wish to carry this over into the spiritual seemed to me an aberration in thinking which could not even be seriously discussed.

In this field there have always been difficulties for my way of establishing Anthroposophy. Assurance has been given from certain sides for a long time that theoretical Materialism had been overcome. To those who are inclined to this view, Anthroposophy seems to be attacking windmills when it discusses Materialism in science. To me, on the contrary, it was always clear that what is here called a way of overcoming Materialism is just the way unconsciously to maintain it.

It was never a matter of importance to me that atoms are conceived either in a purely mechanical or in some other activity in connection with processes in matter. What was important to me was this fact: that reflective consideration proceeds from the atomistic —the smallest formation of the world—and seeks for a transition to the organic, to the spiritual. I saw the necessity of proceeding from the whole. Atoms, or atomic structures, can be only the *results* of spiritual action, of organic action. With the *primal phenomenon, as actually beheld,* and not with an intellectual construction, would I make my beginning, in the spirit of Goethe's view of nature. Profoundly convincing to me has always been what is contained in Goethe's words: that the factual itself is theory, and that nothing should be sought for *behind* this. But this requires that, in relation to nature, we must accept what the senses give and must employ thinking in this domain solely in order to pass from the complicated derivative phenomena (appearances), which cannot be surveyed, to the simple, the primal phenomena. It is then noticed that in nature we have to do, indeed, with colors and other sense-qualities *within* which spirit is active; but we do not arrive at an atomic world behind the sense-world. What may be valid in atomism simply belongs to the sense-world.

That in this direction progress has occurred in the understanding of nature cannot be admitted by the Anthroposophical way of thinking. What appears, for example, in the views of Mach, or what has appeared recently in this field, is the beginning, to be sure, of an abandonment of the constructing of atoms and molecules, yet it shows that this constructing has so deeply penetrated into the mode of thinking that abandoning it means to lose all reality. Mach has even yet spoken of concepts only as economical generalizations of sense-percepts; he has not spoken of something which exists within a spirit-reality. And it is the same with more recent scientists.

Hence what appears there as opposition against theoretical Materialism is no less remote from the spiritual existence in which Anthroposophy lives than was the Materialism of the last third of the

nineteenth century. What was brought forward at that time by Anthroposophy against the habits of thinking in the physical sciences
holds good today, not in lesser but in greater measure.

The presentation of these matters might seem like theorizing
interpolations into this "course of my life." To me they are not; for
what is contained in these explanations was for me a matter of *experience,* of the most intense experience, far more significant than
anything that has ever come to me from without.

Immediately upon the founding of the German section of the Theosophical Society, it seemed to me a matter of necessity to have a
periodical of our own. So Marie von Sivers and I established the
monthly *Lucifer.* The name was, naturally, in no way associated at
that time with the spiritual Power whom I later designated as Lucifer, the opposite of Ahriman. The substance of Anthroposophy
had not then been developed to such an extent that these Powers
could have been referred to. The name was intended to signify simply "Light-bearer."

Although it was my intention at first to work in harmony with
the leadership of the Theosophical Society, yet from the beginning
I had the feeling that something must originate in Anthroposophy
which evolves out of its own germ, not presented as in any way
whatever dependent in its content upon what the Theosophical
Society caused to be taught. This I could accomplish only by means
of such a publication. And what Anthroposophy is today has really
grown out of what I published in that monthly.

It is thus that the German section was established under the spon-
sorship, in a sense, of Mrs. Besant and in her presence. At that time
Mrs. Besant also delivered a lecture in Berlin on the objectives and
principles of Theosophy. Somewhat later we requested her to deliver
lectures in a number of German cities. Such lectures were delivered
in Hamburg, Berlin, Weimar, Munich, Stuttgart, Cologne. In spite
of everything, not by reason of any kind of special measures taken
by me, but as a matter of inner necessity, the Theosophical element

dried up and the Anthroposophical element unfolded in an evolution determined by inner conditions.

Marie von Sivers made all this possible through the fact that she not only made material sacrifices to the extent of her ability, but devoted her entire working powers to Anthroposophy. At first we had to work under conditions truly the most primitive. I wrote the greater part of *Lucifer*. Marie von Sivers carried on the correspondence. When an issue was ready, we ourselves attended to the wrapping, addressing, stamping, and personally carried the copies to the post office in a laundry basket.

Very soon *Lucifer* experienced an enlargement in that a certain Herr Rappaport, of Vienna, who published a journal called *Gnosis,* made the suggestion to me that this be combined with mine in a single publication. Then *Lucifer* appeared under the title *Lucifer-Gnosis*. For a time, Herr Rappaport bore a part of the expenses.

Lucifer-Gnosis made the most gratifying progress. The publication increased its circulation in a wholly satisfactory way. Numbers which had been exhausted had even to be printed a second time. Nor did it "fold up." But the spread of Anthroposophy took such a form in a relatively short time that I was called upon to deliver lectures in many cities. From the single lectures there developed in many cases cycles of lectures. At first, I tried to maintain the editorship of *Lucifer-Gnosis* along with this lecturing; but the numbers could not be issued any longer at the right time—often coming out months late. And so the strange fact came about that a periodical which was gaining new subscribers with every number could no longer be published solely because the editor was overburdened.

In the monthly magazine *Lucifer-Gnosis* I was able to bring to publication for the first time what became the foundation of Anthroposophical work. In this periodical first appeared what I had to say about the efforts that the human mind must make in order to achieve its own perceptual comprehension of knowledge of the spirit. *Wie erlangt man Erkenntnisse der höheren Welten?* [1] came

---

[1] *How Is Knowledge of the Higher Worlds Attained?* Translated under the title *Knowledge of the Higher Worlds and Its Attainment.* Anthroposophic Press, N. Y.

out in serial form from number to number. In the same way was the basis laid for Anthroposophical cosmology in serial articles entitled *Aus der Akasha-Chronik*.[1]

It was from what was here given, and not from anything borrowed from the Theosophical Society that the Anthroposophical Movement has come into being. If I gave any attention to the teachings customary in the Society, when I composed my own writings on spiritual knowledge, it was only for the purpose of dealing correctively with one thing or another which I considered erroneous in these teachings.

In this connection I must mention something which is constantly brought forward by the opposing side wrapped in a fog of misunderstandings. I should not need to say anything whatever about this for inner reasons, for it has had no influence whatever on the course of my development or on my public activities. As regards all that I have to describe here, the matter has remained a purely "private" affair. I refer to my being admitted into the "Esoteric School" existing within the Theosophical Society.

This "Esoteric School" dates back to H. P. Blavatsky. She had created for a small inner circle in the Society a place in which she communicated what she did not wish to say to the Society in general. She, like others who know the spiritual world, did not consider it possible to impart to the generality of persons certain profound teachings.

All this is bound up with the way in which H. P. Blavatsky arrived at her teachings. There has always been a tradition in regard to these teachings which go back to ancient Mystery Schools. This tradition is cherished in all kinds of societies, which take strict care to prevent any teaching from penetrating outside the societies.

But, from some direction or other, it was considered proper to impart such teachings to H. P. Blavatsky. She then combined what she had thus received with revelations which came to her in her own inner being. For she was a human personality in whom, by reason

[1] *From the Akashic Record.*

of a strange atavism, the spiritual was operative as it had once been in the leaders of the Mysteries, in a state of consciousness which—in contrast with the modern state illuminated by the consciousness-soul—was lowered to a dreamlike condition. Thus, in "the human being Blavatsky," something was renewed which in primitive times was at home in the Mysteries.

For the modern human being, there is an infallible possibility of deciding what portion of the content of spiritual perception can be imparted to wider circles. This can be done with everything which the researcher can clothe in such ideas as are appropriate to the consciousness-soul and also are prevalent, as to their character, in recognized science.

Such is not the case when the knowledge of spirit does not exist in the consciousness-soul, but in forces lying rather in the subconsciousness. These are not sufficiently independent of the forces active in the body. For this reason, the imparting of teachings thus drawn from the subconscious regions may be dangerous; for the truth is that such teachings can, in turn, be received only by the subconscious. Both teacher and learner are then moving in a region where what is wholesome for man and what is harmful must be handled with the utmost care.

All this plays no part in Anthroposophy, since this lifts all its teachings entirely above the subconscious.

The inner circle of Blavatsky survived in the "Esoteric School." I had introduced my Anthroposophical activity into the Theosophical Society. I had to be informed, therefore, as to all that occurred in the latter. For the sake of this information, and also because I myself considered a smaller circle necessary for those advanced in Anthroposophical knowledge of the spirit, I had myself admitted into the "Esoteric School." My smaller circle, however, was to have a meaning different from this school. It was to represent a higher section, a higher class, for those who had absorbed enough of the elementary knowledge of Anthroposophy. Now, I wished everywhere to link up with what was already in existence, with what history had already provided. Just as I did this in regard to the Theosophical Society, I wished to do likewise in reference to the Esoteric School. For this reason my "more restricted circle" existed at first in connection with this school. But the connection consisted solely in the arrangements and not in what I imparted from the world of spirit. Thus, during the first years, my more restricted circle appeared externally to be a section of the Esoteric School of Mrs. Besant. Inwardly, it was nothing of the sort; and, in 1907, when Mrs. Besant was with us at the Theosophical Congress in Munich, even the external connection came altogether to an end according to an agreement between Mrs. Besant and me.

That I could have learned anything special in the Esoteric School of Mrs. Besant is beyond the bounds of possibility, since from the beginning I never participated in the exercises of this school except in a few instances in which my participation was for the purpose of informing myself as to what took place there.

Indeed, no real content existed at that time in the school except what was derived from H. P. Blavatsky, and this was already in print. In addition to this printed material, Mrs. Besant gave all sorts of Indian exercises for progress in knowledge, which I, however, rejected.

Thus, until 1907 my more restricted circle was connected, as to its arrangements, with what Mrs. Besant fostered as such a circle. But to make of these facts what has been made of them by opponents is wholly unjustified. Even the absurd idea was asserted that I was introduced to spiritual knowledge solely through the Esoteric School of Mrs. Besant.

In 1903 Marie von Sivers and I again took part in the Theosophical Congress in London. Colonel Olcott, President of the Theosophical Society, was also present, having come from India. A lovable personality in whom it could still be seen how, through his energy and an extraordinary organizational capacity, he could become the associate of Blavatsky in the founding, planning, and guiding of the Theosophical Society. For, within a brief time, this Society had become, in an external sense, a large body possessing an excellent organization.

Marie von Sivers and I came closer to Mrs. Besant for a short time by reason of the fact that she resided with Mrs. Bright in London and we also were invited for our later London visits to this lovable home. Mrs. Bright and her daughter, Miss Esther Bright, were our entertainers, persons who were like an embodiment of lovableness. I look back with heartfelt happiness upon the time that I was privileged to spend in this home. The Brights were loyal friends of Mrs. Besant. Their endeavor was to knit a close tie between her and us. When it became impossible that I should stand with Mrs. Besant in certain things—of which some have already been mentioned here—this gave pain to the Brights also, who clung with bands of steel, uncritically, to the leader of the Theosophical Society.

For me Mrs. Besant was an interesting person because of certain of her characteristics. I observed that she had a certain right to speak from her own inner experience of the spiritual world. The inner approach in soul to the spiritual world she did possess. Only later was this stifled by external objectives she set for herself.

For me, a person who could speak of the spirit from the spirit was necessarily interesting. But, on the other hand, I was strongly of the opinion that in our age the insight into the spiritual world must exist within the consciousness-soul.

I saw into an ancient spiritual knowledge of humanity. It was dreamlike in character. The human being beheld in pictures through which the spiritual world was revealed. But these pictures were not developed by the will to knowledge in full clarity of mind. They appeared in the soul, given to it like dreams from the cosmos. This ancient spiritual knowledge vanished in the Middle Ages. Man came into possession of the consciousness-soul. He no longer has dream-knowledge. He summons ideas into the mind in full clarity through his will to knowledge. This capacity becomes manifest first in knowledge about the sense-world. As knowledge through the senses, it reaches its climax in natural science.

The present task of spiritual knowledge is to bring the experience of ideas, in full clarity of mind, into connection with the spiritual world by means of the will to knowledge. The cognizing human being then has a content of mind which is experienced like that of mathematics. He thinks like a mathematician. But he does not think in numbers or in geometrical figures. He thinks in pictures of the world of spirit. In contrast to the ancient waking-dream cognizing of the spirit, it is a fully conscious standing-within the spiritual world.

Within the Theosophical Society, it was impossible to gain a true relation with this cognizing of the spirit. Distrust was aroused as soon as full consciousness sought to enter into relation with the spiritual world. Full consciousness was known only for the sense-world. No true feeling existed for the development of this up to the point of experiencing the spirit. What was aimed at was really to return to the ancient dream-consciousness, with the suppression of full consciousness. And this turning back was true of Mrs. Besant also. She had scarcely any capacity for understanding the modern form of spiritual knowledge. But what she said of the world of spirit was, nevertheless, from that world. In this way she was for me an interesting personality.

Since among the other leaders of the Theosophical Society also there existed this aversion to fully conscious knowledge of the spirit, I could never feel at home in mind with respect to the spiritual in the Society. Socially, I enjoyed being in these circles; but their constitution of mind with respect to the spiritual remained alien to me.

For this reason I was also disinclined in my lectures at Congresses of the Society to speak out of my own experience of the spirit. I delivered lectures which some one could have given who had no spiritual perception of his own. This perception came to life at once in the lectures which I delivered, not within the framework of programs of the Society, but which grew out of what Marie von Sivers and I arranged from Berlin.

There arose then the Berlin, Munich, Stuttgart activity. Other places joined. The content belonging to the Theosophical Society gradually disappeared, and there came into existence that which won acceptance through the inner force living in Anthroposophy.

While carrying out the plans together with Marie von Sivers for the external activity, I elaborated the findings of my spiritual vision. On the one hand I possessed, of course, a fully developed standing-within the world of spirit; but about the year 1902, and in succeeding years also as regards many things, I had imaginations, inspirations, and intuitions. Yet these only gradually combined into what I then gave out publicly in my writings.

Through the activity developed by Marie von Sivers, there came into existence, altogether out of a small beginning, the *Philoso-phisch-Anthroposophischer Verlag*.[1] A small brochure made up out of notes of lectures I delivered before the Berlin Free Academy,[2] to which I have referred, was the first matter to be published. The necessity of getting possession of my *Philosophy of Freedom*—which could no longer be distributed by the former publisher—and of attending personally to its distribution provided a second. We bought the remaining copies and the publisher's rights for this book. All this was not easy for us, since we were without any considerable financial means.

But the work progressed just for the very reason that it could not rely upon anything external but solely upon the inner spiritual situation.

[1] Philosophical-Anthroposophical Publishing Concern.
[2] See Chapter XXIX.

XXXIII

M Y FIRST lecturing activity within the circles which had grown out of the Theosophical Movement had to be planned according to the temper of mind of these circles. Theosophical literature had been read there, and people were used to certain forms of expression for certain things. I had to hold to these if I wished to be understood.

Only with the lapse of time and the progress of the work was I able gradually to pursue my own course also in the forms of expression used.

Hence what is contained in reports of the lectures belonging to the first years of the Anthroposophical activity is assuredly a true picture inwardly and spiritually of the path by which I moved in order to propagate knowledge of the spirit stage by stage, so that from what lay close at hand the remote might be grasped; but it is necessary that this path be really considered *according to its inner nature.*

For me the years from 1901 to 1907 or 1908, approximately, were a time when I stood with all the forces of the soul under the impression of the facts and Beings of the spiritual world that were drawing near to me. Out of the experience of the spiritual world in general developed specific details of knowledge. Much is experienced in composing such a book as *Theosophy.* At every step my endeavor was to remain by all means in connection with scientific thinking. With the expansion and deepening of spiritual experience, this striving for such a connection takes on special forms. My *Theosophy* seems to slip into an entirely different tone at the moment when I pass from the description of the being of man to a setting forth of the "Soul World" and the "Spirit Land."

While describing the human being, I proceed from the findings of the science of the sense-world. I seek so to deepen anthropology that the human organism may appear in its differentiated character. It can then become evident that, in its differentiated kinds of organization, it is also connected in differentiated ways with the essential beings of soul and spirit which permeate it. Life activity is found in a form of organization; there the point of action of the etheric body becomes visible. The organs of sensation and of perception are found; there the astral body is indicated through the physical organization. Before my spiritual vision, these members of man's being were spiritually present: etheric body, astral body, ego, and so forth. In describing, I sought to link them together with what constituted the findings of physical science. Very difficult for one who wishes to remain scientific becomes the presentation of repeated earthly lives and destiny determined by these. If it is not desired at this point to speak merely from spiritual perception, it is necessary to resort to ideas which result, to be sure, from a subtle observation of the sense-world, but which people fail to grasp. For such a more subtle way of observing, the human being is seen to be different in organization and evolution from the animal world. And, if this fact of difference is observed, life itself gives rise to the idea of repeated earthly lives. But no attention is paid to this; hence such ideas seem not to have been taken from life, but to have been conceived arbitrarily or simply picked up out of more ancient world views.

I faced these difficulties in full consciousness. I battled with them. Any one who will take the trouble to review the successive editions of my *Theosophy* and see how I recast again and again the chapter on repeated earthly lives, for the very purpose of bringing the truth of this perception into relation with those ideas which are taken from

observation of the sense-world, will find what pains I took to do justice to the recognized scientific method.

Even more difficult from this point of view was the problem in
the chapters on the "Soul World" and the "Spirit Land." To one
who has read the preceding discussions only to take cognizance of
the content, the truths set forth in these chapters will seem to be
mere assertions arbitrarily uttered. But it is different for one whose
experience of ideas has received an access of strength from the reading of what is linked with the observation of the sense-world. For
him the ideas have been released from their bondage to the senses,
and have taken on an independent inner life. Now, therefore, the following process of soul can occur within him. He becomes aware of
the life of released ideas. These weave and work in his soul. He experiences them as he experiences through the senses colors, tones, sensations of warmth. And, as the world of nature is given in colors,
tones, and so forth, so is the world of spirit given to him in experienced ideas. Any one, however, who reads the first expositions in my
Theosophy without the impression of an inner experience, so that
he does not become aware of a metamorphosis of his inner experience
of ideas,—whoever, in spite of having read the preceding, goes on to
the succeeding discussions as if he should begin to read the book at
the chapter on "The Soul World"—such a person can arrive only at
a rejection of the book. To him the truths seem to be assertions set
up without proof. But an Anthroposophical book is designed to be
taken up in inner experience. Then by stages a form of understanding comes about. This may be very weak. But it can—and should—
exist. The further confirmatory deepening through exercises described in *Knowledge of the Higher Worlds and Its Attainment* is
simply a confirmatory deepening. For progress on the spiritual road
this is necessary; but a rightly composed Anthroposophical book
should be an awakener of the life of the spirit in the reader, not a
certain quantity of information imparted. The reading of it should
not be mere reading; it should be an experiencing with inner shocks,
tensions, and solutions.

I am aware how far removed is that which I have given in books from calling forth by its inner forces such an experience in the mind of the reader. But I know also that with every page my inner battle has been to reach the utmost possible in this direction. In the matter of style, I do not so describe that my subjective feelings can be detected in the sentences. In writing I subdue to a dry, mathematical style what has come out of warm and profound feeling. But only such a style can be an awakener; for the reader must cause warmth and feeling to awaken in himself. He cannot simply allow these to flow into him from the one setting forth the truth, while the clarity of his own mind remains obscured.

XXXIV

IN THE Theosophical Society artistic interests were scarcely fostered at all. From a certain point of view, this situation was at that time easily intelligible, but it could not be permitted to continue if the right spiritual attitude of mind was to be fostered. The members of such a society center all their interests at first upon the reality of the spiritual life. In the sense-world, man appears to them only in his transitory existence, severed from the spiritual. Art seems to them to have its activity within this severed existence. It seems, therefore, to be apart from the spiritual reality for which they seek.

Because this was true in the Theosophical Society, artists did not feel at home there.

To Marie von Sivers and to me, it was important to make the artistic also alive within the Society. Spiritual knowledge, as experience, gains indeed an existence in the whole human being. All the forces of the soul are stimulated. Into formative fantasy shines the light of the experience of spirit when this experience exists.

But something enters here which creates hindrances. The artist feels a certain misgiving about this shining of the spiritual world into fantasy. He desires unconsciousness regarding the sway of the spiritual world in the soul. He is entirely right if what he has in mind is the "stimulation" of fantasy by means of that element of conscious discrimination which has been dominant in the life of culture since the beginning of the consciousness epoch. This "stimulating" by the intellectual in man has a deadly effect upon art.

But just the opposite occurs when spiritual content which is actually beheld illuminates the fantasy. It is here that all the formative force in man which has ever led to art rises again to life.

Marie von Sivers was actively engaged in the art of recitation and declamation;[1] to dramatic presentation she had the finest relation.

Thus there existed a sphere of art for Anthroposophical activity in which the fruitfulness of spiritual perception for art could be tested.

The "Word" is exposed from two directions to the dangers which may arise from the evolution of the consciousness soul. It serves as means of communication in social life, and it serves for imparting what is logically and intellectually known. On both these sides, the "Word" loses its inherent value. It must fit the "sense" that it has to express. It must permit oblivion of the fact that in the tone itself, in the sound, in the modeling of sound, a reality exists. The beauty, the shining quality of the vowel, the characteristics of the consonant, are being lost from speech. The vowel becomes soulless, the consonant void of spirit. And thus speech leaves entirely the sphere in which it originates—the sphere of the spiritual. It becomes the servant of the intellectual-cognitional, and of the social life, which shuns the spiritual. It is snatched wholly out of the sphere of art.

True spiritual vision slips, as if wholly by instinct, into the "experience of the Word." It learns through intimate feeling to experience the soul-sustained resounding of the vowel and the spirit-empowered painting of the consonant. It attains to an understanding of the mystery of the evolution of speech. This mystery consists in the fact that divine spiritual Beings could once speak to the human soul by means of the Word, whereas now the Word serves only to make oneself understood in the physical world.

An enthusiasm kindled by this *insight into the spirit* is required to lead the Word again into its sphere. Marie von Sivers developed this enthusiasm. So her personality brought to the Anthroposophical Movement the possibility of fostering artistically the Word and the

---

[1] These two terms are here used to render the German term *Wortgestaltung*. Translator.

modeling in Words. As an addition to the activity of imparting truth from the spirit world, there developed the fostering of the art of recitation and declamation, which now became more and more an important part in the programs of events taking place within the Anthroposophical activity.

Recitation by Marie von Sivers on these occasions was the initial point for the infusion of the artistic element into the Anthroposophical Movement; for a direct line of development leads from these "supplementary recitations" to the dramatic performances which then took their place in Munich along with the Anthroposophical courses of lectures.

By reason of the fact that we were able to develop art along with knowledge of the spirit, we grew more and more into the truth of the modern experience of the spirit. For art grew, indeed, out of the primeval dream-picture experience of the spirit. At the time in human evolution when experience of the spirit receded, art had to seek a way for itself; it must again unite with this experience when it enters in a new form into the evolution of culture.

XXXV

THE BEGINNING of my Anthroposophical activity belongs to a time when there was a feeling of dissatisfaction among many persons with the trend in the striving for knowledge which characterized the immediately preceding period. There was a desire to find a way out of that domain of existence in which humanity had been shut up by reason of the fact that only what was comprehended by means of mechanistic ideas was allowed to pass as "trustworthy" knowledge. These endeavors of many contemporaries toward a form of spiritual knowledge affected me deeply. Biologists such as Oskar Hertwig—who began as a student of Haeckel, but had then abandoned Darwinism, because, according to his opinion, the impulses known to this view could give no explanation of the organic process of development—were to me personalities in whom was manifest the longing of the age for knowledge.

But I felt that all this longing was under a pressing burden. This pressure was the result of the belief that only what can be investigated in the world of the senses by means of measure, number, and weight can be recognized as knowledge. Courage was lacking to unfold an inwardly active thinking in order thereby to experience reality more intimately than it is experienced through the senses. Thus the only thing that occurred was that people said that, with the means hitherto used in interpreting also the higher forms of reality, such as the organic, nothing further can be done. But, when something positive should then have been reached, when what is at work in the activities of life should have been affirmed, people moved about in indeterminate ideas.

Those who were attempting to escape from the mechanistic explanation of the world lacked, for the most part, the courage to admit that any one who wished to overcome that mechanism must overcome also the habits of thinking which have led to it. Such an admission as was demanded by the time refused to appear. This is the admission: With our orientation toward the senses, we penetrate into what is mechanistic. In the second half of the nineteenth century, this orientation had become habitual. Now that the mechanistic no longer satisfies, we should not wish to penetrate into higher realms with the same orientation. The senses in man are self-unfolding, but the unfolding which the senses achieve will never enable us to perceive anything except the mechanistic. If there is a desire to know more, the deeper-lying forces of knowledge must be given, out of ourselves, a form that nature gives to the forces of the senses. The forces of knowledge for the mechanistic are awake of themselves; those for the higher forms of reality must be awakened.

This self-confession on the part of the striving for knowledge appeared to me a necessity of the time.

I felt happy when I became aware of the beginnings of this. Thus a visit to Jena remains to me a beautiful memory. I had to deliver lectures in Weimar on Anthroposophical themes, and a request came for a lecture to a smaller group in Jena. Still another very small gathering followed this lecture. There the desire was that what Theosophy had to say should be discussed. In this group was Max Scheler, who was at that time an instructor in philosophy in Jena. The discussion soon developed into a statement of what he had experienced in my lecture, and I felt at once the deeper-lying trait prevailing in his striving for knowledge. It was with inner tolerance that he met my view—the very tolerance that is necessary for one who really wishes to know.

We discussed the epistemological confirmation of spiritual cognition. We talked of the fact that the penetration into spiritual reality, on the one hand, must be susceptible of epistemological substantiation just as penetration into the sense-world must be on the other side.

Scheler's way of thinking made upon me the impression of that of a person of genius. Even till the present, I have followed his path of knowledge with deepest interest. Inner satisfaction was always afforded me when I could again meet—very seldom, unfortunately—the man who at that time became so congenial to me.

Such experiences were important for me. Every time that these occurred an inner necessity presented itself to test anew the certainty of my own way of knowledge. These constantly recurring tests develop the forces which then also lay open ever broader realms of spiritual existence.

Two results are available from my Anthroposophical work: first, my books issued for the general public; secondly, a great number of courses of lectures which were at first to be considered as privately printed and to be sold only to members of the Theosophical (later the Anthroposophical) Society. These were really reports on lectures, more or less accurate, which, for lack of time, I could not correct. It would have pleased me best if spoken words had remained spoken words. But the members wished the courses privately printed, so this came about. If I had then had time to correct the reports, the restriction "for members only" would from the beginning have been unnecessary. For more than a year now this restriction has been dropped.

At this point in this "course of my life" it is most of all necessary to say how the two things—my published works and the privately printed material—combine into what I elaborated as Anthroposophy.

Whoever wishes to trace my own inner struggle and labor to set Anthroposophy before the consciousness of the present age must do this on the basis of the writings published for general circulation. Moreover, in these writings I make my position clear with respect to everything in the nature of a striving for knowledge which exists in the present age. Here is presented that which took form for me more and more in "spiritual beholding," what became the edifice of Anthroposophy—in a form incomplete, to be sure, from many points of view.

Along with this requirement, however, of building up Anthroposophy and thereby meeting only the situation resulting from the need to impart information from the world of spirit to the contemporary cultural world in general, the other requirement now appeared—to meet fully whatever became manifest in the membership as the needs of their minds and the craving of their spirits.

Strongest of all was the inclination to hear the Gospels and the content of the Biblical writings in general placed in what had appeared as the Anthroposophical light. The desire existed to attend lecture cycles on these revelations given to mankind.

While internal lecture cycles were delivered in accordance with this requirement, something else came about in addition. Only members attended these courses. They were acquainted with the elementary communications out of Anthroposophy. It was possible to speak to them as to persons advanced in the realm of Anthroposophy. These internal lectures were conducted as they could not have been if they had been writings for the general public.

In internal groups I could rightly speak about things in a form which I should have been obliged to modify for a public presentation if from the first these things had been intended for such an audience.

Thus in the two things, the public and the private publications, something really exists which springs out of two different backgrounds. The entirely public writings are the result of what struggled and labored in me; in the privately printed material the Society itself shares in this struggle and labor. I listen to the pulsations in the soul-life of the membership, and out of my sharing in what I thus hear the form of the lecture course is determined.

Nothing has ever been said that is not in utmost degree the purest result of the developing Anthroposophy. There can be no question of any concession whatever to the preconceived opinions or sentiments of the members. Whoever reads this privately printed material can take it in the fullest sense as containing what Anthroposophy has to say. Therefore, it was possible without hesitation—when complaints became too insistent in this direction—to depart from the plan of circulating this printed matter among members alone. Only, it will be necessary to put up with the fact that erroneous matter is included in the lecture reports which I did not revise.

The right to a judgment about the content of such privately printed material can naturally be conceded only to one who knows what is taken for granted as the prerequisite basis of this judgment. And for most of this printed matter prerequisite will be *at least* the Anthroposophical knowledge of the human being, and of the cosmos, to the extent that their nature is set forth in Anthroposophy, and of what exists in the form of "Anthroposophical history" in the communications from the world of spirit.

XXXVI

A CERTAIN institution which came into existence within the Anthroposophical Society in such a way that there was never any thought of the public in connection with it does not really belong within the limits of this account. Yet it shall be described for the reason that attacks made against me have been based also upon material derived from this.

Some years after the beginning of the activity in the Theosophical Society, Marie von Sivers and I were offered by certain persons the leadership of a society of the kind that has been maintained in preservation of the ancient symbolism and ritualistic ceremonies which embody the "ancient wisdom." I never had the remotest idea of working in any way in the spirit of such a society. Everything Anthroposophical was to spring, and must spring, from its own sources of knowledge and truth. There was to be not the slightest deviation from this goal. But I had always felt a respect for what is historically given. In this resides the spirit which evolves in humanity's process of development. And so, wherever possible, I favored also the linking of the newly arising with the historically existent. I took the diploma, therefore, of the society referred to, which belonged to the stream represented by Yarker. It had the forms of Free Masonry of the so-called high degrees. But I took nothing else—really nothing whatever—from this society except the merely formal authorization, in historic succession, to initiate myself a symbolic-ritualistic activity.

340

Everything presented in content in the "ceremonies" practiced in the institution created by me was without historic dependence upon any tradition whatever. In the possession of the formally granted diploma, nothing was fostered except what results from the symbolizing of Anthroposophical knowledge; and this was done because of the craving of the members. Together with the elaboration of ideas, clothed in which the knowledge of spirit was given, there was a craving for something which speaks directly to vision, to the heart. Such requirements I wished to meet. If the offer from the society in question had not come to me, I should have undertaken to initiate a symbolic-ritualistic activity without any historical connection.

But this did not create a "secret society." Whoever entered into connection with this institution was told in the clearest possible way that he was not joining any "order," but that as participant in ceremonial rites he would experience a sort of visualization, demonstration, of spiritual knowledge. If anything took place in keeping with the forms in which the members of traditional orders were inducted or promoted to higher grades, this did not signify that such an order was being conducted, but only that the spiritual ascent in the soul's experiences was rendered visible to the senses in pictures.

That this had nothing to do with the activity in any existing order, or imparting of things which are imparted in such orders, is proved by the fact that members of the most various types of orders participated in the ceremonial rites which I instituted and found in these something altogether different from what existed in their own orders.

Once a person who had participated with us for the first time in a ceremonial came to me immediately afterward. This person had risen to a high degree in a certain order. Under the impression of the experience now shared, the wish had arisen to hand over to me the insignia of that order. For the feeling had come about in this person that, after having experienced real spiritual content, it was no longer possible to share in something which remained fixed in mere formalism. I put the matter right; for Anthroposophy must not draw any person out of the life associations in which he stands. It is to add something to these associations, but to take nothing away from them. So this person remained in that order and continued to participate further with us in the symbolic ceremonies.

It is only too easily comprehensible that, when such an institution as the one described here becomes known, misunderstandings arise. To many persons, indeed, the externality of belonging to something seems more important than the content that is given to them. And so even many of the participants spoke of the matter as if they belonged to an "order." They did not understand how to make the distinction that things were demonstrated among us without connection with an order which otherwise were given only in connection with an order.

In just this domain also we broke with the ancient traditions. Our work was carried on as work must be carried on if research in spiritual content is pursued in an original way according to the requirements of the fully conscious soul experience.

The fact that the desire arose later to select as a starting point for all kinds of slanders certain attestations signed by Marie von Sivers and me in linking up with the historic Yarker institution means that, in order to concoct such slanders, people treated the absurd with the grimace of the serious. Our signatures were given to certain "formulas." The customary thing was maintained. And, while we were giving these signatures, I said as clearly as possible: 'This is all a formality, and the institution which I shall bring about will take over nothing from the Yarker institution.'

It is obviously easy to make the observation afterwards that it would have been much more "sensible" not to link up with institutions which could later be used by slanderers. But I would remark with all modesty that, at the period of my life here under consideration, I was still one of those who assume uprightness, and not crooked ways, in the people with whom they have to do. Moreover, spiritual perception did not alter at all this faith in human beings.

This perception must not be misused for the purpose of investigating the inner intentions of one's fellow men when this investigation is not desired by the person in question himself. In other cases, the investigation of the inner nature of other souls is a thing forbidden to the knower of the spirit, just as the unauthorized opening of a letter is something forbidden. Thus one confronts those with whom one has to do in the same way as does a person who has no knowledge of the spirit. There is just this distinction—either to assume that others are straightforward in their intentions until the opposite has been experienced, or else to be distrustful toward the entire world. A social cooperation of human beings is impossible in the latter mood, for such cooperation can be based only upon trust and not upon distrust.

This institution, which gave in a cult-symbolism what is spirit-content, was a blessing to many who participated in the Anthroposophical Society. Since in this, as in every sphere of Anthroposophical work, everything was excluded which lies beyond the borders of clear consciousness, there could be no thought of unjustified magic, or suggestive influences and the like. But the members obtained that which spoke, on the one hand, to their comprehension of ideas also in such a way that the heart could participate in direct perception. For many this was something which, in turn, guided them also in the better formation of their ideas. With the beginning of the war,[1] it ceased to be possible to continue the fostering of such institutions. In spite of the fact that nothing in the nature of a secret society existed in this institution, it would have been taken for such. And so this symbolic-ritualistic division of the Anthroposophical Movement came to an end in the middle of 1914.

The fact that persons who had taken part in this institution—absolutely unobjectionable to any one who looked upon it with good will and a sense for truth—became slanderous accusers is an instance of abnormalities in human conduct which arise when persons who are not inwardly genuine become active in movements whose con-

[1] The First World War. Translator.

tent is genuinely spiritual. They expect things in keeping with their trivial soul-life; and, since they naturally do not find such things, they turn against the very institution to which they had previously turned—though with unconscious insincerity.

Such a society as the Anthroposophical could not be formed otherwise than according to the soul-needs of its members. It could not lay down an abstract program declaring that in the Anthroposophical Society this and that are done, but its work must have its source in reality. But the soul-needs of its members constitute just this reality. Anthroposophy, as content of life, was formed out of its own sources. It had appeared before the contemporary world as a spiritual creation. Many persons who were drawn to it by an inner attraction endeavored to cooperate with others. Thus it came about that the Society was a formation consisting of persons some of whom sought primarily the religious element of life, others rather the scientific, and others the artistic. And what was sought had to be made accessible for the seeker.

Because of the very fact of this working out from the reality of the soul-needs of the members, the privately printed material must be considered differently from that given to the public from the beginning. The content of this printed matter was intended as oral communications, not to be printed. The subjects discussed were determined by sensing the soul-needs of the members as these appeared with the passage of time.

What is contained in the published writings corresponds with the requirements of Anthroposophy as such; in the way in which the privately printed material evolved, the configuration of soul of the whole Society has cooperated in the sense indicated.

XXXVII

WHILE Anthroposophical knowledge was brought into the Society in the way that can be discerned, in part, from the privately printed material, Marie von Sivers and I fostered through our united efforts the artistic element especially, which was preordained, indeed, by destiny to become a life-giving element in the Anthroposophical Movement.

On the one hand, there was the element of recitation, tending toward the art of the drama and comprising the subject matter of work to be done if the Anthroposophical Movement was to receive the right content.

On the other hand, I had the opportunity, during journeys that had to be made in the service of the Society, to enter more deeply into the evolution of architecture, sculpture, and painting.

In various passages of this biography I have spoken of the importance of art to a person who lives in experience within the spiritual world.

But, up to the time of my Anthroposophical work, I had been able to study most of the works of art in the evolution of humanity only in reproductions. Of the originals, only those in Vienna, Berlin, and a few other places in Germany had been accessible to me.

As journeys were now made in the interest of Anthroposophy, together with Marie von Sivers, I came face to face with the treasures of the museums throughout the broadest expanses of Europe. In this way, from the beginning of the century—that is, during the

fifth decade of my life—I pursued advanced training in art appreciation, and together with this experienced a view of the spiritual evolution of humanity. Everywhere by my side was Marie von Sivers,
who, while entering with her fine understanding and taste into all
that I was privileged to experience in the conception of art and culture, herself shared and supplemented all this in a beautiful way.
She understood how these experiences flowed into all that gave mobility to the ideas of Anthroposophy; for all the impressions of art
which became an experience of my mind permeated what I had to
make effective in lectures.

In the actual seeing of the masterpieces of art the world appeared
before our minds out of which a different configuration of soul still
speaks from the more ancient times to the new age. We were able to
immerse our minds in the spirituality of art which still speaks out
of Cimabue. But through the viewing of art we could also plunge
into the mighty spiritual battle which Thomas Aquinas waged
against Arabianism, during the height of Scholasticism.

Of special importance for me was the observation of the evolution of the art of architecture. While I silently viewed the formation
of styles, there germinated in my mind what I was able later to
mould into the forms of the Goetheanum.

Standing before Leonardo's *Last Supper* in Milan and before the
creations of Raphael and Michelangelo in Rome, and the conversations with Marie von Sivers in connection with these observations,
must, I think, be felt with gratitude toward the disposition of destiny
precisely at that time when at a mature age they first appeared before
my soul.

But I should have to write a volume of no small scope if I should
wish to describe even briefly what I experienced in the manner indicated.

When spiritual vision forms the background, one sees indeed very
deeply into the evolution of humanity through the gaze which becomes lost in reflection in the *School of Athens* or the *Disputa*.

While advancing in observation from Cimabue through Giotto all the way to Raphael, we are in the presence of the gradual dimming of humanity's ancient spiritual vision down to the modern, more naturalistic perception. What had been revealed to me through spiritual perception as the law of human evolution appeared in clear manifestation before my mind in the development of art.

Always, indeed, I had the greatest satisfaction when I could see how the Anthroposophical Movement received ever renewed life through this continual immersion in the artistic. To embrace in ideas the realities of being in the spiritual world, and to express these in the form of ideas, requires mobility in the activity of ideation. Filling the mind with the artistic gives this mobility.

Moreover, it was decidedly necessary to guard the Society against the invasion of all those inner untruths associated with false sentimentality. Indeed, a spiritual movement is always exposed to these inroads. If informative lectures are imbued with life by means of those mobile ideas derived from living in the artistic, the inner untruthfulness derived from sentimentality which exists in the hearers will then be expelled. The artistic, although it is sustained by sentiment and feeling, but which strives toward luminous clarity in the formation and the reception, can provide the most effective counterpoise against false sentimentality.

And here I feel that it has been an especially fortunate destiny for the Anthroposophical Movement that I received in Marie von Sivers a fellow-worker bestowed by destiny who understood fully from the very depths of her nature how to cultivate this artistic, emotionally sustained, but unsentimental element.

A continuous counter activity was needed against this inwardly untrue sentimental element, for it penetrates again and again into a spiritual movement. It can by no means be simply repulsed or ignored. For persons who at first yield themselves to this element are in many cases none the less seekers in the utmost depths of their souls. But it is at first hard for them to gain a firm relation to the content imparted from the spiritual world. They seek unconsciously in sentimentality a form of stupor. They wish to experience quite special truths, esoteric truths. They develop an impulse to separate themselves, on the basis of these truths, into sectarian groups.

The important thing is to make what is right the sole directive force in the Society, so that those deviating to one side or the other may always see again and again how those work who may call themselves the central representatives of the Movement, since they are its founders. Positive work for the substance of Anthroposophy, not coming forward with opposition against outgrowths which appeared—this was what Marie von Sivers and I considered the essential thing. Naturally, there were exceptional cases when opposition also became necessary.

The period up to my Paris cycle of lectures constitutes for me something in the form of completed evolutionary processes in the soul. These lectures were given during the Theosophical Congress of 1906. Individual participants in the Congress had expressed the wish to hear these lectures besides the program of the Congress. I had at that time in Paris made the personal acquaintance of Edouard Schuré, together with Marie von Sivers, who had already corresponded with him for a long time, and who had been engaged in translating his works. He was among my listeners. I had also the pleasure of having frequently in the audience Mereschkowski and Minsky and other Russian poets.

In this cycle of lectures I gave what I felt to be "mature" within me of the leading elements of spiritual knowledge pertaining to the nature of the human being.

This "feeling of the maturity" of elements of knowledge is essential in research in the spiritual world. In order to have this feeling it is necessary to have experienced a perception as it rises at first in the soul. At first it is felt as something non-luminous, as lacking sharpness in contour. It must be permitted to sink again into the depths of the soul to "mature." Consciousness has not yet gone far enough to grasp the spiritual content of the perception. The soul, in its spiritual depths, must remain together with this content in the spiritual world, undisturbed by consciousness.

In external natural science, an item of knowledge is not affirmed until all necessary experiments and observations have been completed, and until the requisite calculations are incontestable. In spiritual science are needed no less methodical conscientiousness and discipline in cognition. Only, one moves by somewhat different roads. Consciousness must be tested in its relation to the truth that is to be known. One must be able to "wait" in patience, endurance, and inner conscientiousness until the consciousness has undergone this testing. It must have grown strong enough in its capacity for ideation in a certain sphere to take over the perception in question into its conceptual capacity.

In the Paris cycle of lectures, I brought forward a perception which had required a long process of "maturing" in my mind. After I had explained how the members of man's being—physical body; etheric body, as mediator of the phenomena of life; and the "bearer of the ego"—are in general related to one another, I imparted the fact that the etheric body of man is feminine and the etheric body of woman is masculine. Thereby, within Anthroposophy, a light was cast upon one of the basic questions of existence which had been much discussed just at that time. It is necessary only to recall the book by the unfortunate Weininger, *Geschlecht und Charakter*[1] and the contemporary poetical works.

But the question was carried into the depths of man's being. As regards man's physical body, he is bound up with the forces of the cosmos quite otherwise than in his etheric body. Through man's physical body, he stands within the forces of the earth; through his etheric body, within the forces of the extra-terrestrial cosmos. The masculine and feminine elements were brought into relation with the mysteries of the cosmos.

This knowledge was among the most profoundly moving inner experiences of my soul; for I felt ever anew how a spiritual percep-

[1] *Sex and Character.*

tion must be approached with patient waiting, and how, when the "maturity of consciousness" has been experienced, one must lay hold by means of ideas in order to place the perception within the sphere of human knowledge.

XXXVIII

IN WHAT IS to follow, it will be difficult to separate the account of the course of my life from a history of the Anthroposophical Movement. Yet I should wish to introduce from the history of the Society only so much as is needed for the account of the course of my life. This question will have to be considered even with respect to mentioning the names of active members of the Society. I have come too close to the present time in the narration to avoid all too easy misunderstandings through the mentioning of names. In spite of complete good will, many a one who finds some other mentioned and not himself may experience a feeling of bitterness. I shall mention by name chiefly only those personalities who, apart from their activity in the Society, have a connection in the cultural life, and not those who have not brought such a connection with them into the Society.

In Berlin and Munich were to develop, in a sense, the two opposite poles of Anthroposophical activity. Persons came into connection with Anthroposophy, indeed, who found neither in the scientific world view nor in the traditional creeds that spiritual substance for which their souls had to seek. In Berlin a branch of the Society and an audience for the public lectures could be formed only out of circles made up of those persons who rejected also everything in the form of world views which had developed in contrast to the traditional creeds. For the adherents of such philosophies based upon rationalism, intellectualism, and so forth, considered what Anthroposophy had to give as something fantastic, superstitious, and the like. An audience and a membership arose which took in Anthroposophy without inclining in feeling or ideas to anything else than this. What had been given them from other sources did not satisfy them. Consideration had to be given to this temper of mind. As this was done, the number of members steadily increased, as well as the number to those attending the public lectures. An Anthroposophical life developed which was, in a sense, complete in itself and gave little attention to what else was taking form by way of endeavors to see into the spiritual world. Hopes rested upon the unfolding of Anthroposophical communications imparted to them. They expected to go further and further in knowledge of the spiritual world.

It was different in Munich, where an artistic element was effective from the beginning in the Anthroposophical work. A world view such as that of Anthroposophy could be taken up into this quite otherwise than into rationalism and intellectualism. The artistic image is more spiritual than the rationalistic concept. It is also alive, and does not kill the spiritual in the soul as does intellectualism. In Munich the leading personalities for the development of the membership and audience were those in whom artistic feeling was effective in the way indicated.

This condition resulted in the formation of a unified branch of the Society in Berlin from the beginning. The interests of those who sought Anthroposophy were of the same kind. In Munich the artistic sensibilities created certain individual needs in separate circles, and I lectured to those circles. A sort of center among these groups came gradually to be the one formed about Countess Pauline von Kalckreuth and Fräulein Sophie Stinde, the latter of whom died during the war. This circle also arranged for my public lectures in Munich. The ever-deepening understanding in this circle brought about a very fine response to what I had to say. Thus Anthroposophy unfolded within this circle in a way that can be designated objectively as very satisfying. Ludwig Deinhard, the older Theosophist, a friend of Hübbe-Schleiden, came very early as a very congenial member into this circle, and this was worth a great deal.

The center of another circle was Frau von Schewitsch. She was an interesting personality, and this is the reason, indeed, why she was just the person around whom also a circle was formed which was less concerned in going deeply into Anthroposophy than in becoming acquainted with it as one of the spiritual currents among those of the period.

Moreover, it was at this time that Frau von Schewitsch had published her book *Wie ich mein Selbst fand*.[1] It was a unique and emphatic confession of adherence to Theosophy. This also contributed to making it possible that this woman should become the interesting central figure in the circle here described.

To me, and also to many who formed part of this circle, Helene von Schewitsch was a notable piece of history. She was the woman for whom Ferdinand Lassalle came to an early end in a duel with a Rumanian. She became later a professional actress, and on a journey to America she became a friend of H. P. Blavatsky and Olcott. She was a woman of the world whose interests at the time when I gave lectures in her home appeared to be strongly spiritualized. The stirring experiences through which she had passed gave to her demeanor and to everything she did an extraordinary weight. I could look through her, I might say, upon the activity of Lassalle and his period; through her upon much that was characteristic in the life of H. P. Blavatsky. What she said bore a subjective coloring; was often arbitrarily shaped by fantasy; yet, after allowing for all this, it was possible to see the truth behind many veils, and one was confronted by the manifestation of an unusual personality.

Other circles in Munich took on a different form. I recall a person whom I met in several of these circles—a Catholic cleric, Müller, who stood apart from the narrow limits of the Church. He was a discriminating connoisseur of Jean Paul. He edited a really stimulating pe-

---

[1] *How I Found My Self.*

riodical, *Renaissance,* through which he defended a free Catholicism. He took from Anthroposophy as much as was interesting to him from his point of view, but remained always sceptical. He raised objections, but always in such an amiable and at the same time elemental manner that he often brought a delightful humor into the discussions that followed the lectures.

The descriptions I have given of Berlin and Munich as the opposite poles in Anthroposophical work do not imply anything as to the value of the one or the other; here divergencies among persons simply came to view which had to be taken into account in our work, each of them of equal worth in its way—at least, it is futile to judge them from the point of view of their relative values.

The character of the work in Munich led to the fact that the Theosophical Congress of 1907, which was to be arranged by the German Section, was held there. These Congresses, which had previously been held in London, Amsterdam, and Paris, included programs in which Theosophical problems were dealt with in lectures and discussions. They were planned on the model of the congresses of learned societies. The administrative problems of the Society also were discussed.

All of this was very much modified in Munich. In the great Concert Hall, where the conferences were to be held, we—the organizers—provided interior decorations which were to correspond artistically in form and color with the mood prevailing in the oral program. Artistic environment and spiritual activity in space were to constitute a harmonious unity. In this connection I attached the greatest possible value to the avoidance of abstract inartistic symbolism and to giving free expression to artistic feeling.

Into the program of the Congress was introduced an artistic presentation. Marie von Sivers had long before translated Schuré's reconstruction of the Eleusinian drama. I arranged it as to language for dramatic presentation. This play we introduced into the program. A connection with the ancient institution of the Mysteries—even though in ever so feeble a form—was thus afforded. But the impor-

tant thing was that the Congress now included an artistic element—
an artistic element indicating the intention of not leaving the spiritual life henceforth void of art within the Society. Marie von Sivers,
who had undertaken the rôle of Demeter, showed already clearly
in her presentation the nuances which drama was to reach in the
Society. Besides, we had arrived at a time when the art of declamation and recitation, developed by Marie von Sivers by proceeding
outward from the inner force of the Word, had reached the decisive
point from which further fruitful progress could be made in that
field.

A great portion of the old members of the Theosophical Society
from England, France, and especially Holland were inwardly dis-
pleased by the innovations offered them in the Munich Congress.
What it would have been well to understand, but what was clearly
grasped at that time by exceedingly few, was the fact that, in the
Anthroposophical stream, something of an entirely different inner
attitude was introduced from that of the Theosophical Society up
to that time. In this inner attitude lay the true reason why the Anthroposophical Society could no longer exist as a part of the Theosophical Society. Most persons, however, placed chief emphasis upon
the absurdities which in the course of time have grown up in the
Theosophical Society and which have led to endless wrangling.

EPILOGUE

By Marie Steiner

Here the life story abruptly ends. On March 30, 1925, Rudolf Steiner passed away.

His life, consecrated wholly to the sacrificial service of humanity, was requited with unspeakable hostility; his path of knowledge was transformed into a path of thorns. But he walked the whole way, and mastered it for all humanity. He broke through the limits of knowledge; they are no longer there. Before us lies this path of knowledge in the crystal clarity of thoughts of which this book itself affords evidence. He raised the human intellect up to the spirit, permeated and united it with the spiritual Being of the cosmos. In this he achieved the greatest human deed. The greatest divine deed he taught us to understand; the greatest human deed he achieved. How could he escape being hated with all the demonic power of which Hell is capable?

But he repaid with love the lack of understanding with which he was confronted.

> He died—a Sufferer, a Leader, an Achiever—
> In such a world as trod him under foot,
> Yet which to raise aloft his strength sufficed.
> He lifted men; they hurled themselves against him,
> They spewed forth hatred, blocked his forward way.
> His work they shattered even as he wrought it.

356

They raged with venom and with flame,
And now with joy defile his memory:—
"So he is dead who led you into freedom,
To light, to consciousness, to comprehension
Of what is Godlike in the human soul,
To your own ego, to the Christ.
Was this not criminal, this undertaking?
He did what once Prometheus expiated,
What gave to Socrates the poisoned cup—
The crime Barabbas wrought was not so vile—
A deed whose expiation is the cross:
He lived, himself, the future there before you.

"We demons cannot suffer such a thing.
We harry, hunt, pursue who dares such deeds,
With all those souls who give themselves to us,
With all those forces which obey our will.
For ours is the turning point of time
And ours this humanity which sickens,
Without its God, in weakness, vice, and error.
We never yield the booty we have won,
But tear to pieces him who dares such deeds."

He dared—and, daring, he endured his fate—
In love, long-suffering, and tolerance
Of weak, incapable humanity,
Which ever all his work in peril set,
Which ever misconstrued his uttered word,
Which misinterpreted his kind forbearance,
And in their littleness knew not themselves,
Because his greatness was beyond their compass.
'Twas thus he bore us—we were out of breath
In following his stride, his very flight
Which ravished us away. 'Twas our weakness
That was the hindrance ever to his flight,
The lead that weighted down his forward footsteps. . . .

Now he is free, an aid to Those on High
Who take whatever hath been wrung from Earth

As safeguard of Their goal. So now They greet
The son of man who his creative power
Unfolded thus to serve the Gods' high will;
Who, for the age of hardened intellect,
And for the time of dead machinery,
Stamped clear the Spirit, called the Spirit forth. . . .

They hindered him.

                    The Earth in shadow moves,
In cosmic space now see the shaping figures;
The Leader waits; the heavens part and open;
In joy and reverence stand the rangéd hosts.

But Earth is wrapped in gray enshrouding night.

Sonnenmächten Entsprossene,
Leuchtende, Wellen begnadende
Geistesmächte; zu Michaels Strahlenkleid
Seid ihr vorbestimmt vom Götterdenken.

Er, der Christusbote weist in euch
Menschentragenden, heil'gen Welten-Willen;
Ihr, die hellen Aetherwelten-Wesen
Trägt das Christuswort zum Menschen.

So erscheint der Christus Künder
Den erharrenden, durstenden Seelen;
Ihnen strahlet euer Leuchte-Wort
In der Geistesmenschen Weltenzeit.

Ihr, der Geist-Erkenntnis Schüler
Nehmet Michaels weises Winken;
Nehmt des Welten-Willens Liebe-Wort
In der Seelen Höhenziele wirksam auf.

Sprung from Powers in the Sun dwelling,
Radiant, to all worlds beneficent,
Spirit-Powers: to Michael's robe of rays
Foreordained are ye by Thought Divine.

He, the Christus Harbinger, shows in you
Man-upbearing, holy Will-of-Worlds;
Ye, the shining Cosmic-Ether-Beings,
Bear the Christus Word to man.

So appears the Christus Herald
To the longing, thirsting souls;
They behold your radiant Word-of-Light
In the cosmic age of Spirit-Man.

Ye, the pupils of the Spirit-Knowledge,
Take the beckoning wise of Michael;
Take the Word-of-Love of Cosmic Will
In your upward-striving souls effectively.

Note by the Translator:

In the light which Rudolf Steiner has cast upon the significance of sounds in language and upon the significance of the name of the Archangel appearing in this poem, that name should be pronounced in English as in German—so as to rhyme approximately with the name *Israel* as this is sung in sacred music.

Index of Contents by Chapters

sorbing problem: "To what extent is it possible to prove that in human thinking real spirit is the agent?"

Chapter III: At eighteen, *Technische Hochschule,* Vienna. Subjects: mathematics, natural history, chemistry. Extensive philosophical reading; audits philosophy courses in University. Through Karl Julius Schröer enters deeply into German literature, especially Goethe's poetry. Friendship with simple herb-gatherer, versed in spiritual aspect of nature. Since philosophy fails to arrive at spirit, begins to develop theory of knowledge: thought came to seem "reflection radiated into the physical human being of what the soul experiences in the spiritual world." Importance of mathematical thinking. Riddles of space, time. Selected courses supplemented by broad scientific reading. Supersensible knowledge not permitted to intervene in scientific study; hopes for ultimate reconciliation. In materialistic Darwinism, respected only evolution of physical forms. Conceives "inner man" as spiritual, dipping down into natural existence. Deeply impressed by physicist Reitlinger, but rejects theories of heat, light, color. Examines all theories of knowledge. Impressed by Schiller's conception of special state of consciousness in artistic experience. Felt he knew special state for cognizing the nature of things: when the human being has "thoughts that he experiences as thoughts themselves." In twenty-second year, knew that "spiritual vision thinks while it experiences spirit, and experiences while it sets to thinking the awakened spirituality in man."

Chapter IV: Rejected prevailing estimate of Wagnerian music, knowing that the world of tones is itself a reality. Cordial relations with many friends; he enters warmly into their lives; they not at all into his. Arguments with friend against Wagner; with another against materialism. Other friends. Becomes member, then librarian, finally president of German Reading Club. Obtained for Club numerous books as gifts from authors. Observations of political life in Austria.

Chapter V: Friendship with Schröer. His background, education, collection of German folk-plays, studies of dialects. Schröer's conception of ideas: creative forces; Rudolf Steiner's: "the idea appears on the spiritual object." Both held similar conceptions of folk-soul. Rudolf Steiner had to reconcile his "Objective Idealism" with findings of natural-scientific research. Confirmed through laboratory experimentation conception of light as supersensible entity. Rejected Newton's theory of light, color. Concentrated attention on human organism and soul activities; came upon "sensible-supersensible form," "between what the senses grasp and what the spirit perceives." Study of anatomy, physiology brings initial conception of threefold human being, organic and supersensible, published thirty years later. Deeply impressed by Goethe-Schiller conversation about Goethe's "archetypal plant." Convinced that Goethe's view of nature was spiritual. Thought of developing some branch of science in spiritual way. Tutoring for livelihood prevented this. Tutoring in many subjects prevented one-sidedness.

Chapter VI: At 23, became tutor in a family with four sons. Entrusted with complete responsibility for one extremely abnormal. Diagnosis of bodily-psychic condition and required education. Boy steadily improved to ultimate normal condition. Unique opportunity for learning nature of human being. Almost first opportunity for play. Studies Eduard von Hartmann; rejects pessimism and theory of inaccessible Beyond; respects ideas on evolution of moral consciousness.——Invited to edit Goethe's scientific writings. Considered prevailing scientific thinking suited only for the inorganic; Goethe founder of science of organics. Concise definition of true idea of evolution. Goethe anticipated everything justified in Darwinism, omitted everything unjustified. Contrast between prevailing ideas and Goethe's thinking required writing of *Theory of Knowledge Implicit in Goethe's World-Conception,* finished 1886.

Chapter VII: Friendship with son, two daughters of a father, recluse from the materialistic world. Close relation with father after his death. (See also Chapter XX.)—Through Schröer learns of youthful poetical genius, Marie Eugenie delle Grazie. Her pessimism alienates Schröer. Rudolf Steiner, admiring her genius, enjoys Saturday gatherings of her brilliant, distinguished friends; prevailing atmosphere, pessimistic, anti-Goethean. After hearing pessimistic epic, he circulates privately printed paper entitled *Nature and Our Ideals*—"original germ" of *Philosophy of Freedom.* Conversations with brilliant theologian on Christ and on reincarnation.—Meets young Austrian poets and Fercher von Steinwand. Observation of him contributes toward conception of reincarnation. How may persons be justifiably observed with this problem in mind? —First contact with theosophy through Sinnett's *Esoteric Buddhism*— repellent.

Chapter VIII: About 1888, absorbed in composing introduction, second volume, Goethe's scientific writings, but enjoying many friendships, and concerned about Austrian public life. Could withdraw wholly into inner world.—Hamerling's *Homunculus* published, symptom of darkening forces and declining spiritual life, since Goethe and the Idealists. These failed to pass through the gateway of Idealism into world of spirit; successors saw no reality in the idea; hence materialistic philosophy. Lectured on *Goethe As Father of a New Aesthetics*. Interpretation of art, in contrast with Hegel's. Saw in human personality, as a center, the union of true knowledge, the spiritual in art, and the moral will with the Primordial Being of the world,—a further step toward *The Philosophy of Freedom*. Description of personalities meeting at home of Protestant pastor, Alfred Formey, and of gatherings at home of actress Wilborn.— Edits briefly *Deutsche Wochenschrift*. Meets political leaders.—At twenty-seven, had clear perception of the soul and its relation to the spiritual world; filled with questions about the outer life.

Chapter IX: Visits Weimar, 1888, to survey Goethe writings he was invited to edit for Weimar edition. Interpretations confirmed by supplementary evidence. Goethe's characterization of human consciousness in relation to world. First acquaintance with leaders in Goethe-Schiller Archives and with visitors.—Conversation with Eduard von Hartmann, Berlin; shocked by his fixed idea of limitation of human cognition.— Visits art galleries, Berlin, Munich.—In Vienna, mingles with circle around fine mystical personality, Marie Lang. Becomes acquainted with remarkable writer, artist, Rosa Mayreder. *Philosophy of Freedom* gradually taking form.

Chapter X: Removal to Weimar; end of first chapter of life. Hence preparation of *Philosophy of Freedom*. Essence of work: In sense-free thinking man is within the spiritual essence of the world. Rejects theory of limitation of knowledge. Reality is found, not by breaking through external world in an outward direction, but by sinking into man's own being. He had declared in 1888: "As thinking takes possession of the Idea, it merges with the primordial foundation of the world." Secondly, book shows that, when acting upon moral intuitions grasped in sense-free thinking, man is free. "The human spirit, experiencing itself within, then meets the Spirit of the World, now no longer concealed from man behind the sense-world, but living and moving within the sense-world."

Chapter XI: At close of first life chapter, had to define attitude toward Mysticism. Not a true path to knowledge; leads only to inner realm of feeling, void of ideas. Mystic, denying accessibility of reality to thinking, supports Materialist. But experience, through spirit-illuminated ideas, having all the warmth of Mysticism, may be called "mystical" experience of ideas. Careful reflection led to decision that expression must be in the form of modern science.

Chapter XII: Protracted editing of Goethe due largely to difficulty in expression. But, while struggling to express Goethe truly, he had to advance in formulation of his own spiritual experience. Goethe's ideas not abstract; "pictures living in the manner of thoughts in the mind." But he had to express relation of these pictures to spiritual reality itself. No one, he felt, could comprehend Goethe without going beyond Goethe to experience of pure spirit. Through Goethe task he experienced difference between manifestation of spiritual world through grace and experiencing it through the soul's own transformation. Was warned constantly in spirit by Goethe not to advance rashly. Had to bring about an understanding of human consciousness with itself—in *Truth and Science* and in *Philosophy of Freedom.* Owed largely to Goethe task development of his "spiritual experience of knowledge."—In writing *Philosophy of Freedom,* subdued emotion, but kept inner experience alive in the thoughts, in order to give them "the mystical character of inner vision," but to make this "inner vision also the equivalent of the external sensible beholding of the world."—Felt that, in the fairy tale, Goethe glimpsed the world of spirit. Its origin in intercourse with Schiller.

Chapter XIII: Happy social life, but distressed by decadence in Austria. —First acquaintance with work of Nietzsche, through *Beyond Good and Evil.* Partly attracted, partly repelled.—Visits to Budapest and Transylvania. Impressions of Hungarians and emigrant Germans. Such journeys an education in knowledge of external world.—Depressed in Vienna by prevailing enthusiasm for superficial *Rembrandt As Educator.*—In long-continued tutoring, observed unfolding of many minds; noted differences between two sexes. Likewise valuable for his life was residing in family of his boy charges; acquaintance with Dr. Breuer, once associated with Freud; friendship with remarkable mother of his boy charges.—Destiny had so led him that, at thirty years, he was not bound to any external calling. Delimitation of his share in Weimar editing.

Chapter XIV: Again facing a task due to his own inner development.— Doctoral examination passed at University of Rostock. Comments on *Seven Books of Platonism* and author, Heinrich von Stein. His own different view of source of Platonism, primal revelation from spiritual world. Thoughts about relation of Plato and that of Goethe to world of ideas. Explanation published in 1891 of Goethe's archetypal plant. Enters Goethe-Schiller Archives as collaborator. Origin of Archives. Sketches of leading personalities connected with Archives; comments on dominant philological methods. Noted visitors. Relation of ducal family to Archives. Conversation with Herman Grimm on fantasy. Accidental death of librarian of Weimar library.

Chapter XV: Comments on two lectures given soon after removal to Weimar—on *Fantasy As the Creatress of Culture* and on the possibility of a Monism which could maintain a real knowledge of the spirit. Presented fantasy as the "gateway through which Beings of the spiritual world, working creatively in an indirect way through man influence the evolution of human cultures." Relation of dream life to fantasy. In such lectures he was trying to present spiritual knowledge in a form understandable to the age. His Monism in contrast with that of Haeckel. Contrast between Goethe and Haeckel. He becomes personally acquainted with Haeckel and sees his twofold personality. Personality of Heinrich von Treitschke and of Ludwig Laistner. Edits Jean Paul and selections from Schopenhauer.—Hans and Grete Olden circle. Impressive personality of Gabrielle Reuter.

Chapter XVI: Remarkable personality of Gabrielle Reuter.—Further description of Olden circle. Sketch of Otto Erich Hartleben.—Rudolf Steiner shares in many world views, especially in Weimar during beginning of 'nineties, while on final stages of *Philosophy of Freedom.* Could enter into lives and ideas of others, but no one into his. Had always lived in a world bordering on the sense-world, but had to "visit" the world of the senses. Such his relation to Haeckel and Nietzsche. Interpretation of Nietzsche. One who possesses a world of vision, such as the spiritual world must be, sees partial correctness in all standpoints, but must not be drawn too strongly to any. Yielding oneself in love to outer world and returning to spirit world teaches real being of outer world.

Chapter XVII: Establishment of Ethical Culture Society in Berlin—ethics divorced from spiritual reality. Indication of loss of confidence in possibility of knowledge above both nature and the moral-spiritual in man. Founders unconscious of this implication. Morality is thus made to appear a by-product of natural evolution. His futile efforts to interest

Herman Grimm and others.—Failure of Eduard von Hartmann to understand *Philosophy of Freedom;* contrast between his ideas and those of Rudolf Steiner. "I saw at the center of the soul's life its complete union with the spiritual world." Knew that man's ideas exist in the spiritual world; that he can experience moral impulses. Sense-world is a spiritual world, and can be so experienced through thinking.—This book gave to the world what had been demanded of the author by the first chapter of his life. "The further way could now be nothing else than a struggle to arrive at idea-forms for the spiritual world itself." Such a struggle occupied the decade between Rudolf Steiner's thirtieth and fortieth years.

Chapter XVIII: Profound study of Nietzsche. Analysis of personality and relation to materialistic age. Set this forth in 1895 in *Nietzsche, a Battler against His Age.* Relation with Frau Förster-Nietzsche; sets Nietzsche library in order; in Nietzsche's presence has a vision of his soul. Disagreement with Frau Förster-Nietzsche. Discovery of source of idea of "return of the same." Reincarnation shone dimly in Nietzsche's consciousness.—Published in 1897 *Goethe's World-Conception.*

Chapter XIX: Loneliness in relation even with close friends—for instance, friend of *Realschule* days, who considered him an abstract rationalist.— Limit of justifiable hypotheses. Views in mid-'nineties shown by quotation from *Magazine* of 1900.—Art life in Weimar: painters, the theater, musicians. Theories of color in painting. Gifted young painter, Otto Fröhlich. Good and bad influences of Weimar on artists. Need to avoid one-sided judgments even in art.

Chapter XX: Friendship with Eduard von der Hellen, Registrar of Archives, and his family. Sharing inwardly in his high-minded political aspirations gave insight into public life. Acquaintance with liberal politician, Heinrich Fränkl, brought indirectly acquaintance with recently widowed Frau Eunicke and family. Relation developed with husband in spiritual world identical with that developed in Vienna. (See Chapter VII.) These experiences, probably clearer because of no prior earthly relation, taught necessity and significance of scientific thinking when the will remains free of materialistic influences. Contributed toward final work on *Philosophy of Freedom.* This book and that on Nietzsche written in that home.—Comments on spiritism.—Personalities of August Fresenius, Franz Ferdinand Heitmüller, Joseph Rolletscheck, and Max Christlieb.

Chapter XXI: Useful experience of publishing articles in a paper issued by a bookstore.—Especially happy friendship with actor Neuffer, musician Stavenhagen, and families. Presented with bust of Hegel. Friendship with Danish writer Rudolf Schmidt; contrast with Georg Brandes. —Delightful evenings in circle around Conrad Ansorge, gifted musician, and von Crompton; circle wholly devoted to Nietzsche. Frequented also by Fresenius, Heitmüller, Fritz Koegel, Hartleben. Wrote *Goethe's World-Conception* while in close association with this circle. Like other writings, this also aims to present Goethe's world view, not details of information.—Reply to criticisms of his way of editing Goethe.

Chapter XXII: Experienced profound inner revolution, which began, apparently at beginning of thirty-sixth year. This became a decisive experience when he left Weimar after beginning of thirty-seventh year, in 1897. Description of effect both upon capacity for accurate and penetrating observation of sense-world and also resultant illumination of spiritual world. Previously, general ideas had been easily grasped, details with difficulty. This difficulty disappeared. He knew this change was occurring far later than in ordinary cases; the ordinary early change blurs outlines between physical and spiritual worlds, confusing the two. Sense-world now revealed its nature to sense-observation. Change brought also a far deeper comprehension of human beings. Explanation of the right experiencing and resolving of world riddles, and of the cosmic significance of human cognition. During last part of Weimar stay, wrote *Goethe's World Conception* and introduction to last volume of Kürschner edition of scientific writings. Three and a half years later, when writing *Conceptions of the World and of Life in the Nineteenth Century,* he had progressed further. In connection with this revolution came far deeper knowledge of significance of meditation, and realization of the three stages in cognition, the third being associated with knowledge of the inner spiritual man, free from organism, and also with an intimate communion with spiritual world. Through this highest stage of cognition, inner "spiritual man" is confirmed in his relation to world of spirit. Rudolf Steiner observed now a special relation among thinking, feeling, and willing. In his writings he was striving to make clear that the spirit is accessible to human perception. His experience led to utter rejection of prevailing theories of heat, light, color though not of certain physical aspects of modern theory of evolution. Clear definition of right attitude toward problem of cognition.—What had hitherto been conception had now become perception.

Chapter XXIII: Inner revolution ended second life-chapter. Thenceforth external indications of destiny no longer in line with inner strivings. Harmony of outer and inner had contributed to his clear conception of freedom and his ethical individualism. Latter idea now laid hold upon his whole being. Contrasting views prevailing in physical and physiological sciences compelled him to work toward perfecting his perceptions. Right thinking in physics, biology, and physiology shows that divine world cannot find access to human will from without. Moral impulses can arise only in thinking. Hence emphasis on free nature of thinking in *Philosophy of Freedom.* Meditation profoundly confirmed this idea; made clear the way in which thinking must be employed to solve world riddles: in such a way that one event is the solution of another. The Logos, Wisdom, the Word holds sway in the world. The Materialist misconceives matter, which is metamorphosed spirit. This idea was elaborated four years later in *Conceptions of the World and of Life in the Nineteenth Century,* in chapter *The World As Illusion.* Even in 1886, in *Theory of Knowledge,* the central question was the relation of man's mind to the Logos. He was now struggling to express what he knew in a way that could be understood.

Chapter XXIV: Seeking channel of communication, he acquired editorship of the *Magazine for Literature,* Berlin. Circulation insufficient for maintenance; hence took position with Free Literary Society requiring also activity in lecturing. His spiritual relation demanded immersion in life of this group, but no possible reciprocation. Spiritually necessary that he thus learn external world. Members of Society writers rather than persons. No possible understanding of his deepest aspirations.— Difficulties with co-editor of *Magazine.*—Instances of clear indication of reincarnation: Frank Wedekind, Paul Scheerbarth, and many others in the group. Meeting these persons was clearly karmic. Caution against unjustified observation of other persons.

Chapter XXV: Experience in staging plays for dramatic society associated with Literary Society. Introductory talks by Rudolf Steiner. His critiques in *Magazine;* his conception of the right kind of critiques. Quotations from *Magazine* articles to refute accusation of materialistic ideas at that time. Explanation of limited sense in which word *spirit* could be used. Efforts through *Magazine* to make clear that spiritual world is accessible to thinking. Quotation affirming capacity of true scientific thinking to give man a consciousness of freedom.

Chapter XXVI: Statements about Christianity referred then to existing creeds; hence seeming inconsistency with later interpretation. In this relation to Christianity, he passed through a crucial test between leaving Weimar and composition of *Christianity As Mystical Fact*—that is, before the turn of the century. He came into contact with Beings that he later called Ahrimanic. Did not fall in slightest degree under their influence. Succeeded in advancing only when he brought before his soul the evolution of Christianity. "The unfolding of my soul rested upon the fact that I had stood in spirit before the Mystery of Golgotha in most inward, most earnest solemnity of knowledge."

Chapter XXVII: Felt that turn of the century must bring new spiritual light to humanity. After Hegel, Goethe, no spiritual content taken up in thinking. Hegel the greatest thinker, but only a thinker; brought last dim rays of ancient spiritual light. Hence, inevitably, the opposite of Hegel—Max Stirner, representing all that man unfolds out of himself. To Hegel, the social objective comes into being out of life in association; to Stirner, from individual effort. These two extremes characterized nineteenth century. Rudolf Steiner's interest in Stirner colored by friendship with J. H. Mackay. Analysis of Mackay's social ideals. About 1898, author's inner world had to undergo severe test. Mastery of test is represented in *Mystics of the Renaissance* and in *Christianity As Mystical Fact.*—Takes up residence in home of Frau Eunicke; goes through ceremony of civil marriage with her.

Chapter XXVIII: Teaches in Berlin Workers' School—first, history and public speaking, then natural science. Mental attitude of workers. Necessary method of teaching. Invited to give many scientific lectures to unions; then to address 7,000 workers at Gutenberg Jubilee. Interference by leaders—opposed to freedom of thought—led him to discontinue this work soon after beginning Anthroposophical activity. Felt that later course of public events would have been different had there been more understanding of the workers.—Through *Magazine,* had to immerse himself in world of the bourgeoisie; through teaching, in that of the proletariat.

Chapter XXIX: Into knowledge acquired during last third of nineteenth century, new spiritual light on the evolution of humanity sought to enter; spiritual sleep prevented this.—Quotations from *Magazine* of March 1898 about art of speaking showing germ of art of speech, later developed in Anthroposophy.—Sketch of Ludwig Jacobowski, and association he founded, *Die Kommenden*. Another friend, Martha Asmus, sister of Paul Asmus.—He teaches history in free academy founded by Bruno Wille and Wilhelm Bölsche. Giordano Bruno Union, founded by persons interested in spiritual monistic philosophy. His interpretation of Scholasticism misunderstood. Later delivered before Union basic lecture initiating Anthroposophical work.—Explanation of rule of secrecy regarding ancient knowledge, and his reasons for ignoring this rule.

Chapter XXX: Decision to make known esoteric truth explains slightly esoteric article in *Magazine,* August 1899, on Goethe's fairy tale. Origin of tale. If experienced, it places one in outer court of the esoteric. Invited at that time by Countess and Count Brockdorff to speak on Nietzsche before circle meeting at their home. Observed spiritual interest in some of persons attending. Upon second invitation, spoke esoterically on fairy tale. Then invited to lecture regularly to Theosophists included in this circle. He made perfectly clear his independence in teaching. First season's lectures published in book form as *Mystics of the Renaissance.* At one of these lectures Marie von Sivers appeared. Before founding of German section, Theosophical Society, he delivered series of lectures before *Die Kommenden* under title *From Buddha to Christ.* Second season's lectures published as *Christianity As Mystical Fact.* This content not found anywhere in Theosophical Society. Only Theosophists would at that time have taken his teaching seriously. He and also Marie von Sivers attended London Theosophical Congress, 1902. Leaders whom he met. Visits to artistic and scientific collections.— In first issue of *Magazine,* 1899, published article on decadence in spiritual life and in true thinking. Gave up *Magazine* at end of September 1901. Felt it imperative that he impart truth about spiritual world.— Before beginning Theosophical work, had written *Conceptions of the World and of Life in the Nineteenth Century.* During writing of first edition, still held conception of evolution derived from Darwinian theory, though only as to physical forms. Before writing second edition, much expanded and entitled *Riddles of Philosophy,* had attained to imaginative perception in this field, and knew that man is the first of earthly beings, a cosmic being who eliminated all other earthly beings from himself. But had to limit second edition to what can be attained by thinking without spiritual perception. Learned to esteem Haeckel as courageous thinker, though without conception of spirit.

Chapter XXXI: Wrote chapter on literature for collective work on cultural achievements of the century. Dealt there with unfolding of fantasy; wrote on the basis of thinking without reference to experience of spiritual world. For another collective work, on influence of egoism in culture, wrote on philosophy, but really on individualism, not egoism, in philosophy; this also without reference to spiritual experience; again at the threshold of the spiritual world without entering. Task given him by spiritual world was to create for Anthroposophy foundations just as objective as those under science. Out of this knowledge he drew his experience of the spiritual, as presented in *Mystics of the Renaissance* and in *Christianity As Mystical Fact.* Calls attention to the way in which *Theosophy* is written, varying progressively from chapter to chapter. Anthroposophy was to be a continuation of science.—Such was his orientation when he and Marie von Sivers entered upon leadership of German Theosophical Society, in 1902. Characterization of Marie von Sivers. Her acquaintance with intimate friend of Blavatsky during London 1902 Congress.—Characterization of members of Theosophical Society. Worked from beginning with branches of Society, but also with public. Emphasis again on clear understanding as to his complete independence. Had Society not deteriorated, separation of Rudolf Steiner and his friends need never have occurred. Climax of decadence in announcement that Hindu boy would be vehicle for reappearance of the Christ.—He indicated clearly at London Congress that Sections in Society should be autonomous, and that German Section would be.

Chapter XXXII: Refutation of charge that World War created soul moods leading to expansion of Anthroposophical Society.—Difficulties to be overcome in Theosophical Society in developing essence of Anthroposophy: false conceptions of science and of method for harmonizing with it. For example, work of Dr. Hübbe-Schleiden. Explanation of only right conception of the atomistic. Justifiable and unjustifiable hypotheses.—Monthly magazine *Lucifer* founded; rapidly expands circulation; carried fundamental Anthroposophical writings. Description of inauguration of German Section, Theosophical Society. Invaluable work of Marie von Sivers.—*Gnosis* combined with *Lucifer;* pressure of work soon forced cessation of publication.—Explanation of relation between his work with advanced students and Blavatsky's inner circle, later called "esoteric school" of Mrs. Besant. Character of supersensible knowledge of Blavatsky and Mrs. Besant: neither a modern supersensible knowledge. Most Theosophists could not understand modern method of higher cognition.—While developing external work, together with Marie von Sivers, he was elaborating his findings in spiritual research.— Both attended London Congress, 1903.—Work developed in different ways in Berlin, Munich, Stuttgart, and other centers. To provide for publication, Marie von Sivers established *Philosophisch-Anthroposophischer Verlag* (publishing company).

Chapter XXXIII: Necessary retention of Theosophical terminology; gradually eliminated. During period 1901-'07 or '08, he stood under tremendous impression of being approached by facts and Beings of spiritual world. Out of general spiritual knowledge, developed that of special fields. Difficulty in presenting this knowledge. Very detailed explanation of method of writing such a book, for instance, as *Theosophy,* and its later revisions. Essential explanation of the way in which it must be read.

Chapter XXXIV: Theosophical Society misconceived art and lacked interest in it. Influence of true art upon spiritual knowledge. Gradual deterioration of the Word since development of consciousness soul.

Chapter XXXV: Anthroposophical activity began amid widespread discontent with prevailing cognitional endeavors and a craving to escape from restricted area to which man had condemned himself. All such efforts sadly doomed to failure by false presuppositions and lack of needed courage. Habits of thinking had to be overcome; inner senses had to be unfolded. He was happy at every evidence of a seeking for higher knowledge: for instance, in Max Scheler's questioning and commenting after a lecture. Such discussions valuable, requiring constant reexamination of his own mode of thinking.—Explanation of two productions resulting from his Anthroposophical work: books for general circulation and privately printed matter for members. Both wholly free from any deviation from truth.

Chapter XXXVI: Explanation of his accepting, together with Marie von Sivers, of authorization to institute, in historic succession, a symbolic ritualistic activity; the nature of the work in this form and its helpfulness to members—causing Anthroposophical truth to "speak directly to the vision, to the heart." Had to be discontinued at beginning of World War.—Another caution regarding privately printed matter.

Chapter XXXVII: Description of art element as developed in the Society, destined to become life-giving in the Anthroposophical Movement. Importance of his actually having seen great masterpieces of art: one way of beholding the course of human evolution. Reference to Cimabue, Giotto, Leonardo da Vinci, Raphael, Michelangelo. Curative influence of art against false sentimentality, which always tends to invade spiritual movements. Great importance of Marie von Sivers in this regard. Wrong tendencies in a spiritual movement best overcome by making what is right the central principle.—The spiritual law of awaiting "maturity" before revealing a new truth. Example in lecture at Paris Congress on human being, emphasizing truth that etheric body of man is feminine, that of woman masculine: a question then under intense discussion was thus related to the cosmos. Deeply moving experience for him.

Chapter XXXVIII: Rudolf Steiner planned to include in autobiography no elements from history of Anthroposophical Society except such as pertained also to course of his life.—Development of two opposite poles in work in Berlin and Munich respectively. Description of Groups in Munich. Meeting of Theosophical Congress in Munich, 1907. Art introduced for first time: decoration in harmony with themes discussed; presentation of Schuré play. Dissatisfaction of older Theosophists indicated that Anthroposophy would have to be developed apart from Theosophical Society.

Epilogue: Brief concluding words in prose, and poem in ode form, by Marie Steiner.